SEVENTEEN
SPORTS CARS
1919–1930
Landmarks in Automobile Design

CONTENTS

ACKNOWLEDGMENTS

For the entertaining drawings in this book we would like to thank the artist, John Blake, whilst we are indebted to the following photographers and owners of historic photographs for the other illustrations: Neill Bruce, Roger McDonald A.I.I.P., *Autocar*, T.A.S.O. Mathieson, T.D. Houlding, Thomas Richards, J. Butt, Ronald Barker, 20 Ghost Club Library, Anthony S. Heal, James Brymer and Indianapolis Motor Speedway. We must thank the owners or custodians of the cars which appear in the more recent photographs, of which the following are known to us: Allan and Angela Cherrett, Ian Woolstenholmes, John F. Blake, Serge Pozzoli, Dr John Mills, Hamish Moffatt, Dr Robin Barnard, Lytham St Annes Motor Museum, the Hon Patrick Lindsay, E.A. Stafford East, J.S. Hirons, Richard Odell, Bill Lakin-Smith, John Fasal, Ian Maxwell, John Norris, John Barwell, Anthony Craven, Chris Southall and Edward Riddle.

Mrs Laura Huxley and Chatto & Windus Ltd, together with Harper & Row Inc., were kind enough to let us quote from Aldous Huxley's novel *Those Barren Leaves*. The sources of other quotations and information are acknowledged in the text, but several people with specialist knowledge who are not mentioned in the text were most helpful in answering our questions. Amongst these we would particularly like to mention Dr Robin Barnard, Hamish Moffatt, Jim Whyman, Phil Ridout, Bill May, Bernard Harding, Roger Howard and Alisdaire Lockhart.

PREFACE

There are several arguments against writing a new book about Vintage cars, the main one being that it has all been said before. This is not really true, as not only is the subject almost inexhaustible, but new facts do keep coming to light as with any historical subject, whilst there are new conclusions to be drawn from facts already known. Another point is that many of the classic books on the subject are now out of print, and few of us are able to keep bound copies of the leading motor magazines in order to consult articles on Vintage cars which have appeared over the years.

It is a strange truth that some quite famous makes have been inexplicably neglected in print, whilst others have had almost too much attention paid to them. This book does not attempt to say a little about a great number of makes, instead it prefers to penetrate a little deeper into an examination of a selected few. Some of the shortest chapters are about the already well-documented makes, but it is hoped that something worthwhile emerges from them.

There is no particular rhyme or reason behind the choice of makes, except that they happened to appeal to the authors, who are much indebted to many friends in the Vintage Sports-Car Club who have given information about their cars which could not readily be found elsewhere.

"Could not be called Vintage in the wine sense".

INTRODUCTION

A Vintage wine is one which the experts agree is of outstanding quality, a wine of a particular district made in a good year and kept separate on account of its quality.

When the word Vintage was first used in connection with motor cars and outside the context of wine making, it was intended to imply that certain cars made during a particular period of time were of outstanding quality, and should be kept separate for that reason.

It is the first function of this book to examine a selection of these cars, and of others of the same period, with fifty years of hindsight, and to present them with all their faults and virtues so that the reader can decide whether the word was justly chosen or not. It must be remembered, however, that the word Vintage was first used in this context by a group of men in the mid-'thirties, barely five years after the end of the period, when they formed the Vintage Sports-Car Club. To them the word certainly did not apply indiscriminately to all cars of the period.

If experts are needed to decide which wines qualify for the Vintage accolade, then so it must be for motor cars, but there is a difficulty here which the wine-tasters cannot experience in the same degree. There are experts and experts. The engineer will look for one sort of quality, the experienced driver will look for another. The historian will look for the opinions of experts writing at the time when the cars were made; but there can be little doubt that contemporary opinions are suspect, because our yardstick for critical appraisal is now so much more clearly defined. And finally, alas, we have a new kind of expert who will judge these cars by their current market value.

There is a lot to be said for the idea that a successful motor car is a good motor car. Of course there were some good cars which were unsuccessful, but most were bad, and it is not the function of this book to seek out esoteric makes only to tell how bad they were. For those wanting to learn about them there are many erudite books available which will give all sorts of information, from the dates they were made to the engine capacities; everything anyone could wish to know except what sort of cars they were to own and use.

Since this book is a critical survey of the cars which have come to be known as Vintage, then it follows that very little will be found in it about cars of any other period. There is some discussion of cars which were made earlier, but directly affected the design or characteristics of the cars of our period; and there is also some discussion of cars which were made after the period but were the culmination of development during the period. By accepted standards there were many individual cars made before and after the period which were of outstanding quality and should be kept separate on that account. And by accepted standards there were many cars made during the period which could not be called vintage in the wine sense; it may even be felt after reading this book that the cars made today more nearly qualify for the accolade than those made in the nineteen twenties, but we can consider only the cars made in the defined period 1919 to 1930 which is, quite arbitrarily, the time-span of the Vintage Motor Car, and hence of this book.

This, then, is a book which is not so much about Vintage cars as about cars made in the Vintage decade (whether good or bad), an easy period to define historically, since it came between the end of the First World War, when few cars were manufactured but enormous advances were made in engineering knowledge and experience, and the beginning of the slump, when cost accounting and 'design by committee' were forced on motor manufacturers by economic conditions. This is an over-simplification of the reasons for the change that took place in 1931, but there is no doubt that the change, which was one of quality in the truest sense, did take place.

Having defined the objectives of this book, perhaps we can try to explain what it is that has made so many people throughout the world accept this very brief span of time as the true vintage, the zenith of quality.

In the early days of the motor car, even to 1914, there were very few cars made which could be compared directly with the cars of our generation. By the 'twenties nearly all of them had it in them to be the everyday, unassuming means of transport that they are today (get in, press a button and go there), and yet there was a fundamental difference in the attitude of the buying public, and hence in the approach to his subject of the designer, and therefore in the cars themselves.

There was a cartoon by Pont which was printed in *Punch* in the 1930s. It showed an old man with a long beard saying crossly: 'When I was a young man I wasn't perpetually rushing about in motor cars!'. Nor could he have been, because there *were* no motor cars when he was a young man.

That cartoon would be meaningless today, and cars are now as much a part of everyday life as the washing machine, the radio and the ball-point pen. Then they were still an exciting new development. Many people could afford them, so that there was a large enough market for a thriving industry, but with the classic exception of the Model T Ford in America, they were certainly not taken for granted. To go out and buy a motor car (even a Model T) was an adventure, leading to a freedom of movement which was literally unknown to any previous generation, and this sense of adventure permeated the whole industry. One result of this was a certain flamboyance among the more interesting cars of the period. They were so vastly different one from another, and whilst variety cannot honestly be equated with quality, it does at least help to make this a particularly interesting period.

There was one other thing which made the Vintage period quite different from the present day; an appreciation, however ill-informed, of hand-craftsmanship was still embedded in the mind of a potential buyer.

Today we look for performance, handling, reliability, comfort and 'finish' (which need only be skin deep to satisfy us). Hand-craftsmanship does not come into it. Of course, there are very few mechanical parts of a car of any period which were, in fact, hand-crafted, but, partly because of the limitations imposed by the machine tools available at the time, and partly because of a genuine desire to achieve a 'finish' satisfying to a craftsman, many of the machine-made parts of all the better cars of the Vintage (and earlier) periods were individually hand-finished. The knowledge that craftsmanship was appreciated undoubtedly influenced designers.

Does this craftsmanship enhance or increase the quality of a motor car? In many cases poor design or inadequate machining facilities forced the manufacturer into a great deal more hand-finishing than should have been necessary; but where the design was good, and the execution adequate, it would be difficult to argue that from an aesthetic point of view craftsmanship does not enhance quality. From a mechanical point of view, however, the ground is less firm. 'Handsome is as handsome does', and the modern motor car certainly does handsomely. But whether it was the influence of the idea of craftsmanship on the designer's thinking in the Vintage period, or whether it is the result of a deliberate policy of built-in obsolescence today, the fact remains that the better cars of the Vintage period were so constructed that they could last for very much longer if they were properly maintained. This attention to potential life is surely one aspect of quality. When we consider the less well-made cars of the period, we must not forget the different attitude to motoring. Since motoring was still an adventure, mechanical failures were accepted with more tolerance than they would be today, and there are some Vintage cars which were thoroughly badly designed or made but which are such fun to drive, and so accurately reflect the flamboyant personality of their designer that, like a magnificent wine which will not travel, they are worthy of the Vintage label.

One other, and perhaps the most important, result of this 'craftsmanship' is much less easily defined. It is the 'feel' of the car as it goes about its journey. Unless one has driven a really good example of a Vintage car, this is very difficult to explain. It could well be argued that the 'feel' of a well-balanced high-quality modern car is unexceptionable, yet in the handling of a really good Vintage car there is a feel of character, of crafts-manship, which is in a class of its own.

To find this in a Vintage car today is rare, and it would be quite wrong to suggest that they all had it when they were new, but to the initiated it is a joy which can only be described by the word quality.

Which is where we started.

Chapter 1
ALFA ROMEO

The Alfa Romeo models of the Vintage decade can be divided neatly into two, the earlier cars designed by Giuseppe Merosi and the later cars designed by Vittorio Jano.

Merosi was the original designer for Alfa (Societa Anonima Lombarda Fabbrica Automobili) when they commenced making cars in 1910 in a factory at Portello, outside Milan, formerly used for assembling small French Darracqs. Although a building surveyor by training, Merosi, who was born at Piacenza in 1872, soon became involved in the early manufacture of cycles, motor cycles and cars in Piacenza, first with Ing Bassi & Merosi, who made bicycles from 1893 to 1898, and then with Orio & Marchand, who made a few motor cycles and cars which Merosi designed. After a year in the Fiat racing car design department, Merosi moved to Milan, where three cars were built to his design by a firm called Lentz, and then from the autumn of 1906 until 1909 he was chief designer for Bianchi.

During the First World War the Alfa factory was taken over by the industrialist Nicola Romeo, car production ceased, and Merosi found himself working for a big combine to which Romeo kept adding further firms making all sorts of engineering products. From 1917 to 1918 Merosi was actually manager of a railway works in Naples belonging to Romeo.

Fortunately Romeo himself was an enthusiastic motorist, and improved versions of the pre-war side-valve Alfas began to be built once hostilities were over and some chassis laid down in 1915 had been disposed of. The improved cars were direct descendants of the original 24-hp model of 1910. The cars were now sold under the name of Alfa Romeo, and the improved model was known as the Tipo 20/30-hp ES Sport. A slight increase in the bore brought the capacity up to 4250 cc (102 × 130 mm) and the power of the four-cylinder engine was increased from 49 bhp at 2500 rpm to 67 bhp at 2600 rpm, largely thanks to cylinder-head improvements. The chassis length was reduced to that of some racing versions of the standard product that had been produced in 1911, 9 ft 6 in. In competition form the ES Sport was capable of 85 mph, but it was also fitted with formal closed bodywork.

It is said that the ES Sport specifications were suggested by Antonio Ascari, one of a talented team of competition drivers employed by Alfa Romeo, which also included the pre-war Alfa driver Giuseppe Campari, Ugo Sivocci and Enzo Ferrari, who all had successes in competition versions of the ES Sport. However, the first significant outright Alfa Romeo race victory was scored by Campari in the 1920 Circuit of Mugello race, in which he drove a special racing version of the pre-war 40/60-hp model, which had a four-cylinder engine of over 6 litres having pushrod ohv operated by two camshafts in the crankcase. Also in 1920 Ferrari came second in the Targa Florio race, behind a Nazzaro, driving a bolster tank ES Sport.

Merosi's first new postwar design was an attempt to build a big luxury side-valve car. This was the six-cylinder 6.3-litre G1, with twin cantilever rear springs. The chassis price was 55 000 lire compared with 37 000 lire for the ES Sport, and the G1 was not a success. Some 52 were built, compared with 95 of the pre-war type Series E20/30s sold in 1920, and 124 ES Sports in 1920–22.

Apart from some cars in the Alfa Romeo museum in Italy, Australia seems to be the only country in which examples of the very early Alfa Romeos have survived.

1921 saw the introduction of Merosi's most famous design, a six-cylinder pushrod ohv 3-litre, known as the type RL. This model, and four-cylinder derivatives of it, were the most successful Alfa Romeos in terms of numbers sold up to the outbreak of the Second World War, bearing in mind that motor cars were far from being the only Alfa Romeo engineering product in those days.

The 3-litre Alfa Romeo was, perhaps, to the Italians what the 3-litre Bentley was to the British, although the cars were really dissimilar and seldom met in competition. The Alfa Romeo was more comfortable than the Bentley, and in England cost about £200 less, thanks in part to a favourable rate of exchange. Although only about an inch and a half wider in track at 4 ft 9½ in, the touring Alfa Romeo had an 11 ft 3-in wheelbase to the 10 ft 10 in of the touring Bentley, whilst the Speed Model Bentley was shortened to 9 ft 9½ in whereas the equivalent sports Alfa Romeo's wheelbase was all of 10 ft 3 in. The '100-mph' 3-litre Bentley had a 9-ft wheelbase, yet the wheelbase of the starkest Targa Florio racing Alfa Romeos came out at 9 ft 3 in.

The touring RL Alfa Romeo was known at first as the RLN ('Normale'), and its 75 × 110-mm, 2916-cc, engine produced 56 bhp at 3200 rpm with a 5.2 to 1 compression ratio. From 1925, as the RLT ('Turismo'), the bore was increased to 76 mm to give a capacity of 2994 cc (identical to that of the 3-litre Bentley, as it happened), and the power went up to 61 bhp with a 5 to 1 compression ratio. In England the touring car was called the 21/70 hp.

A mystery about a complete (and presumably expensive) change in the cylinder-head design of the final RLT models was recently explained by Luigi Fusi who, besides being the leading Alfa Romeo historian, was also on the Alfa Romeo design staff in the Vintage period.

From the 1st to the 6th Series of the RL Normale and Sport, the exhaust manifold and piping for same were fitted on the right-hand side, that is under the driver's seat. The exhaust was moved to the left-hand side only on the 7th Series RL Turismo, in order to have the carburettor on the right-hand side so that, if necessary, it could be examined from the pavement.

Does one assume from this that a test driver from the factory was severely injured or even killed by a passing car when making a carburettor adjustment on a 6th series RLT? As Cav Fusi himself has remarked, it seems to show a certain pessimism with regard to the reliability of the single carburettor fitted to the RLT. Also, as the modification was never made to the sports versions of the RL model, does one assume that their twin carburettor layout was more reliable, or were the test drivers of the sports models more accustomed to taking risks than those assigned to the touring cars? The true answer will probably never be known.

The sports RL was first of all known as the RLS ('Sport') and had the 2994-cc capacity of the RLT, but two carburettors. It produced 71 bhp at 3500 rpm on a 5.52 to 1 compression ratio.

In its final form as the RLSS ('Super Sport') of 1925 to 1928, it produced 83 bhp at 3600 rpm on a 5.5 to 1 compression ratio. The weight was 32 cwt, and the sports models were known as 22/90s in England.

The six-cylinder Alfa Romeo engine design was much less advanced and more 'touring' than its four-cylinder Bentley counterpart, having pushrod ohv and two valves per cylinder to the overhead camshaft and four valves per cylinder of the Bentley. The 85 bhp of the RLSS engine compared quite favourably with the 85 bhp of the standard sports Bentley, but there was 10 bhp difference in favour of the Bentley between the touring versions of the two makes.

The detachable cast-iron Alfa cylinder head was completely flat, without recessed combustion chambers. All the inlet manifolding was internal, the two ports in the side of the head being joined by a Y-shaped pipe with the single carburettor at the bottom on the touring models, but the sports designs had twin Solex or Zenith carburettors at the end of two down pipes, and larger inlet and exhaust valves. There was hot-water induction heating.

The pushrods were substantial, and there was no automatic lubrication to the rockers; instead oil had to be squirted on to felt pads in the rocker pedestals by hand. Another quaint feature was the compression taps in the head, even on the last (1928) models. Tappet adjustment was carried out as on a side-valve engine, but the clearances were taken between the top of each pushrod and its rocker, another demonstration of how this engine combined the old and the new. Camshaft wear was not unknown as the valve gear was rather heavily loaded.

An advanced feature on the RLSS sports models (and on some, if not all, of the RLS models) was the use of dry sump lubrication, the oil being carried in a three-gallon tank in the scuttle. Bentley had used dry sump on the prototype 3-litre, but abandoned it on his production cars. The touring Alfas had wet sump lubrication.

The cast-iron RL block was bolted to the aluminium crankcase, which had inspection panels in the side like a marine engine, and carried the 50 mm crankshaft in four plain main bearings. The plugs were screwed into the side of the block, one per cylinder, fired by a Bosch magneto driven by an internal tooth chain. The H-section connecting rods had clamp bolts for the gudgeon pins, which were 20 mm on the RLSS and 18 mm on the RLT, whilst the RLSS had lighter pistons. An English engineer, well known for his work on Roesch Talbots, claimed when he overhauled an RLSS engine that it had the heaviest top end and lightest bottom end of any engine he had ever known.

The touring models had flat radiators, but the sports cars had handsome pointed radiators which were currently fashionable in both Germany and Italy in the early 'twenties. However, the Alfas were unusual in carrying two radiator badges, one on each side of the point. Coolant circulation was by centrifugal pump in tandem with the dynamo, and driven by helical gears at the front of the engine, as was the camshaft. The sports models had a 'hotter' camshaft than the tourers. Electrical refinements in-cluded a constant voltage control and a silent engagement coaxial Bosch starter.

The four-speed and reverse gearbox was bolted to the engine, with a central gear lever, and the worst feature from the sporting point of view was the low third gear and big gap between third and top. Boxes were available, however, with higher constant mesh pinions which raised the three lower gears relative to top, and this must have transformed the car. The multi-plate clutch was trouble-free.

The chassis was conventional, with semi-elliptic springs and friction shock absorbers, the fully floating rear axle being under-slung. On early cars, without fwb, the footbrake worked on the transmission, but after front-wheel brakes were introduced at the end of 1923, the handbrake worked on the transmission, the operation of all the wheel brakes being through the footbrake by means of non-stretchable steel ribbons. A short cable was attached to the operating arm of each front brake. This ran through the king-pin, and was pulled down to operate the brake via a small chain and sprocket. In 1926, brake drum diameter was increased from nearly $12\frac{1}{2}$ in to over $13\frac{1}{2}$ in, and certainly the later brakes were very effective indeed. The sixteen-gallon rear tank was pressurized.

The steering and handling characteristics were of a very high order, the cars being beautifully balanced. The engine was smooth, and the cars proved to be very reliable and long-wearing.

A few racing cars were made (five in 1923 and five in 1924), known as RL Targa Florio models after Sivocci's win in one in the 1923 Targa Florio race. Engine tuning in 1923 was by means of a slight rise on the compression ratio to 6 to 1, a different camshaft and lighter valve gear. A lighter chassis was used with a 9 ft 3-in wheelbase, but the track was increased by ½ in. The chassis was narrow at the rear with outrigged springs. 1923 cars had a radiator cowl, 1924 cars had a smaller version of the pointed radiator. Balance beams were used for brake compensation, instead of the differentials as on production cars, and this must have been a means of reducing weight, which was down to one ton on the racing cars. Some cars had the cylinder bore increased to 78 mm, 3151 cc, and this gave 95 bhp compared with the 88 bhp of the 2994 cc cars. Speeds were 90 mph and 97 mph respectively, compared with just over 80 mph for the sports cars.

New racing engines were produced for 1924 having seven main bearings instead of four. Some engines had 2994-cc blocks, but others had 80 × 120-mm dimensions, giving a capacity of 3620 cc. The 3-litre cars had a small increase in power to 90 bhp, but the bigger engines produced 125 bhp at 3800 rpm and the 3.6-litre cars were capable of 112 mph. The 1923 and 1924 cars had many successes in Italian events, and it is interesting that the current owner of an RL Targa Florio and a later Monza Alfa Romeo opines that the earlier car has better handling. Surprises are frequently happening in the world of vintage cars, and not long ago a mystery Alfa Romeo turned up in Peru of all places, having a seven-bearing Targa Florio engine in an RLSS chassis. The sports cars were also successful in competitions, their swan song being the 1927 Mille Miglia, when two RLSS cars proved to be the fastest in the race until they had to retire with transmission trouble, leaving victory to the smaller side-valve OMs.

1924 saw a turning-point in Alfa Romeo history, when the firm made a dramatic and successful entry into Grand Prix racing. The man behind this was Vittorio Jano, who left the Fiat racing department in September, 1923, to join Alfa Romeo, taking with him other members of the Fiat staff. Jano had been born in Turin in 1891, and had been with Fiat from 1911. Not only was he capable of designing and supervising the production of a racing car, but also he was capable of organizing and running a racing team. At Alfa Romeo he was able to prove this better

than he would have been able to do in a large organization such
as Fiat.

The design and construction of the new Grand Prix Alfa
Romeo, the P2, took Jano from October 1923, to May 1924.
Though owing much to Fiat inspiration, the P2 was not a slavish
copy of the Type 805 eight-cylinder GP Fiat, proved, perhaps
by the fact that it was always Jano's particular favourite, and
also that it succeeded where the Type 805 Fiat was eventually
to fail, on the day the P2 won its first Grande Epreuve, the French
GP at Lyons in 1924.

The P2 had a supercharged twin ohc 61 × 85-mm, 1987-cc,
straight-eight all roller-bearing engine, one of Merosi's unsuccessful 1923 six-cylinder P1 Grand Prix cars having been used
as a test-bed for the supercharging experiments. After 1924, Jano
took over from Merosi as the Alfa Romeo chief designer, and
Merosi went to Mathis, but later returned to his native Italy and
worked as chief designer on Isotta-Fraschini commercial vehicles
in the 'thirties.

The P2 engine was made up of two blocks of four cylinders
having welded-steel water jackets and a non-detachable head,
and there were ten main bearings. The engine was probably the
best part of the car, originally in 1924 it produced 134 bhp at
5200 rpm, but the power in its final 1930 form had gone up to
175 bhp at 5500 rpm, and the difficulty was in producing a
chassis to match it. The weight of the car was 14.9 cwt, and the
wheelbase was just over 8 ft 7 in.

The P2 was a race winner from the start on its initial appear-
ances in Italian races. However, on the difficult Lyons circuit it
was significant that of the three cars that started, the one driven
by Ascari did not have the long streamlined tail like those of
Campari and Wagner, but was cut off short and finished with a
spare wheel placed across the car, purely in the interests of improving the road holding. This was the fastest Alfa in the race,
until it retired with engine trouble and Campari went on to win.

All the cars had streamlined tails fitted for the Italian GP over
the fast Monza circuit, but the power was raised to 145 bhp at
5500 rpm by fitting two Memini carburettors instead of one, and
using a fuel known as 'Elcosina', composed of petrol with 44 per
cent ethyl alcohol and a small percentage of ether. To cope with
the extra fuel consumption – the race being 497 miles in length –

a 5½-gallon reserve fuel tank was placed in the scuttle, the oil tank being moved from that position to a new site under the passenger's seat.

This race was a walkover for the P2s as the opposition proved to be negligible, as was also the case in the first race of 1925, the Belgian GP, Ascari being the winning driver in both cases. It is interesting to note that all the P2s in the 1925 Belgian GP at Spa were Manx-tailed, with a spare wheel at the back. From 1925 onwards a mechanic was not normally carried in Grands Prix.

In the French GP at Montlhèry (in which the cars were withdrawn after a fatal accident to Ascari when he was in the lead) the P2s again had streamlined tails, but shorter and blunter than formerly, with three elongated holes in the point to allow the escape of air at high speed. Another easy win came at Monza in the Italian GP at the end of the season, Brilli-Peri being the winning driver.

Perhaps it should be pointed out that the 140-mph P2 was not exceptional in being hard to handle at high speeds, this being characteristic in virtually all the GP cars at the time. To quote from William Court's book *Power and Glory* (Macdonald, 1966), Pietro Bordino, the leading Fiat driver, is recorded as having said: 'The present cars are too fast even for the best of us' and André Boillot stated at Lyons in 1924, 'It was impossible to hold the cars on the straightaway'. Another expert with considerable racing experience, Jack Scales, commented that 'the great defect of modern racing cars is that their road adhesion is so low that they are dangerous'.

From 1926 to 1929 P2 Alfa Romeos were raced independent of the factory and power increased to 155 bhp, but three of the six cars originally built were greatly modified by the works for the 1930 season under Jano's supervision. An increase in the bore of the engine from 61 mm to 61.5 mm increased the capacity to 2006 cc and the supercharger drew from the carburettors instead of blowing through them, Mercedes fashion, as had been the previous practice. This 175-bhp engine was given a completely new chassis using components from the contemporary 1750-cc sports cars. No longer was the car crab-tracked, and the front and rear springs were now outside the chassis frame and nearer the wheels. On the original cars the rear springs had actually been

inside the chassis and had tapered towards the tail in line with it.
The rear track was increased by seven inches and the front by
three inches.

Ascari's discovery in 1924 that some extra weight was beneficial at the back was recognized by the fact that a spare wheel
was now carried fitted longitudinally in the streamlined tail. In
the years since 1925, independents like Campari driving their
privately owned P2s had fitted spare wheels to each side of the
tail to increase the weight. The fuel capacity of the rear tank on
the modified cars had to be reduced from 32 to 31 gallons, but
the ten-gallon oil tank was still under the passenger's seat. The
bull-nosed radiator was replaced by a 1750-like one, so that
from the front the car looked more like the standard Alfa Romeos
of the time. The dry weight, with the spare wheel, was increased
slightly from 14.9 cwt to 15.4 cwt. The most dramatic win by
this type of P2 was in the 1930 Targa Florio race, driven by Varzi
at record speed; yet the two cars entered were going to be withdrawn before the race as they were considered to be too fast and
too dangerous. Varzi only started on his own insistence, and
Campari was glad to drive a 1750 instead.

Before going on to discuss the production cars which Jano
designed for Alfa Romeo after his work on the original P2,
perhaps it is as well to discuss the cars they replaced, the smaller
four-cylinder designs of Merosi. The first of these was the RMN,
a four-cylinder three main-bearing version of the RLN, first
introduced in 1923 and producing 40 bhp at 3000 rpm from its
75×110-mm, 1944-cc engine. In 1924 there came the sports
RMS, with the same 9 ft 6-in chassis, but with a 76×110-mm,
1996-cc engine giving 44 bhp at 3200 rpm, having larger valves
than the RMN and a 6 to 1 instead of a 5.3 to 1 compression
ratio. Like the RLS the RMS had a pointed radiator, but only
one carburettor. The RMU ('Unificato') of 1925/6 was a sort of
combination of the two previous models, its 1996-cc engine producing 48 bhp at 3500 rpm, but in a longer chassis, with the
pointed radiator. In 1926, the last year in which Merosi designs
alone were produced, RMU production figures were 173, compared with 126 six-cylinder RLT chassis and only 12 RLSS
models.

Although mechanically differing from the P2, the Jano six-
cylinder production cars followed its philosophy, being light,

with short-stroke, high-revving, small-capacity, overhead-cam-shaft, multi-cylinder engines – a new concept at the time. The 'small six' was uncommon in the vintage years, although several manufacturers featured it in the 'thirties, often with not particularly happy results.

The first of the line was originally known as the NR (Nicola Romeo), later the 6C 1500, and it appeared at the Milan Motor Show in April 1926. It is instructive to compare it with Merosi's four-cylinder RMN of 1923. The shorter chassis NR had the same wheelbase as the RMN, 9 ft 6 in, with a slightly wider track, but the total chassis weight was two-thirds of that of the earlier car, and the engine of one-half litre less capacity produced 44 bhp at 4200 rpm compared to the 40 bhp at 3000 of the RMN.

The NR (known as the 15/60 in England, approximating to the RAC horsepower and maximum speed), had a 62 × 82-mm, 1487-cc, engine with a non-detachable cylinder head and a single overhead camshaft running in four bronze bearings. The compression ratio was 5.75 to 1. As on the P2, the camshaft drive was at the rear of the engine, consisting of a vertical shaft and bevel gears. A cross-shaft at the rear of the engine drove a gear-type oil pump on the right-hand side and the dynamo on the left-hand side. Coil ignition was fitted at a time when the magneto was almost universal on European cars, the drive for the distributor (which had an automatic advance supplemented by a hand control) was from the vertical camshaft drive. There were two valves per cylinder and valve clearance adjustment was extremely simple by means of a mushroom tappet base attached to the valve stem by splines, and a similar disc-like tappet head threaded on to the top of the stem. Pressure of the valve spring held the two serrated discs together, and adjustment was made by holding the tappet base and turning the tappet head by means of a special tool. A somewhat similar arrangement was used on vintage Stutz and Hispano-Suiza engines, the latter having the valve stems hollowed out with a fine internal thread. The P2 had employed more conventional fingers between valve and cam.

The external appearance of the NR engine was very neat, most of the inlet manifolding, for instance, being inside the block. The carburettor was a vertical Zenith, with a hot-air intake through the crankcase, gravity-fed by a nine-gallon tank in the scuttle.

A four-bladed aluminium cooling fan was driven off the end of the camshaft by means of a friction clutch, and acted partly as a damper. Water circulation was by pump.

The crankcase and one-and-a-half-gallon sump were aluminium, and the counterbalanced crankshaft, running in five plain main bearings, was machined and polished all over. The H-section two-bolt connecting rods were slightly offset, and the domed aluminium pistons had four rings.

.The gearbox was bolted to the engine, the gear lever and handbrake being central, and the clutch was a dry multiplate. There was a wide gap between third and top gears, the other three ratios being fairly close but rather low.

Chassis were in two lengths, 9 ft 6 in or 10 ft 2 in and, following Fiat and subsequently Bugatti racing practice, the front half-elliptic springs passed through the axle, this being of C-section with square eyes for the springs and brake controls inside the hollowed-out centre. The construction of the front axle was, in fact, the same as on the P2 cars. Another Grand Prix Fiat and P2 feature was in the location of the worm-and-wheel steering box, which was not attached rigidly to the crankcase or chassis member, there being a pivot bearing to the latter and a swivel to the former, with the object of minimizing vibration. The steering was notably excellent.

As on the P2, the propellor shaft was enclosed in a torque tube, the back axle being a welded-steel banjo. The brakes were rod-operated, the handbrake as well as the footbrake acting on all four wheels. Balance beams for the two front and two rear brakes were enclosed under the gearbox. The front brakes were operated via a rod through each hollow kingpin which was pushed up by a cam.

As might be expected, the $1\frac{1}{2}$-litre Alfa Romeo was an expensive car with a chassis price of £550 in England when an Austin 12 chassis cost £270. Nor was it a sports car, although with a maximum speed nearer to 70 than 60 mph, its cruising speed was probably 10 mph above the maximum speed of the average contemporary touring car of the same capacity.

The Alfa Romeos of the Jano era epitomized Italian skills in engineering. They were complete designs from the very start, there was no experimenting and redesigning of parts that proved to be insufficiently strong. In the case of the P2, it has been recorded that a complete drawing of the chassis was never made, but once in the metal, everything went together perfectly – and swiftly. A quick transition from the drawing to the finished product is all part of the art. Furthermore, development possibilities always seem to be part and parcel of the original design, whether it is a Vintage Alfa Romeo or a modern Weber carburettor. As an example, the basic 6C 1500 gearbox which first appeared on the NR model was used on the twin-cam 1500 and 1750 cars up to 1931, ratios being altered by changing the constant mesh gears which changed the 1st, 2nd and 3rd gear ratios relative to top gear, but left them the same relative to each other. Around 1931 there was a redesign of both the box and gear cluster, and this new box was used on both the 6C 1760 and 8C 2300 cars, even going on to be used in the 8C 2600 P3 Grand Prix cars. With the coming of the 2.9-litre- and 3.8-litre-engined P3 cars, this gearbox was redesigned again and was converted to three speeds in order to give it more strength to cope with the increased power, which had gone up from 44 bhp in the 6C 1500 to 330 bhp in the 3.8-litre P3 of 1935. Admittedly 330 bhp proved rather too much for it.

From the single-ohc 6C 1500 was developed the twin-ohc 6C 1500 Sport, with the same cylinder dimensions, but producing another 10 bhp, 54 bhp at 4500 rpm, using a 6 to 1 compression ratio. Bigger valves were fitted, at 90 degrees, in what was now a detachable head, and the shorter 9 ft 6-in chassis was used. A higher-ratio final drive was available, and the maximum speed was now 75–80 mph. The fan was no longer fitted and camshaft damping was by means of a small flywheel on the front end of each camshaft with a jockey wheel in between, though the latter was often removed. This car had the fuel tank at the rear and a slightly smaller radiator than the single-cam model and was introduced in 1928.

A Super Sport version of the above car was made available either with or without a supercharger, being raced successfully unblown in 1927 and blown in 1928. The unblown engine gave 60 bhp at 4800 rpm on a compression ratio increased to 6.75 to 1, and the blown engine 76 bhp at 4800 rpm, using approximately 5 lb of boost (half that of the P2!). The flat-top instead of domed pistons gave a 5.25 to 1 compression ratio. In order to accommodate the blower behind the radiator, the engine was moved back fifteen inches in the chassis. As the radiator was in the same position on the unblown cars, the Super Sport models had longer bonnets and scuttles than the NR and Sport versions.

Whereas 806 six-seater long-chassis NR models were built between 1927 and 1929, only 56 of the short-chassis four-seater cars saw the light of day. 171 Sport models were sold, but Super Sports were much rarer, the production figures being only ten blown cars and fifteen unblown.

Even rarer were some half a dozen blown Super Sports built specifically for racing which had fixed-head engines producing 84 bhp at 5000 rpm, capable of 95 mph, over 15 mph faster than the detachable-head blown models. The fixed-head cars had larger valves, and those raced in 1929 had sloping radiators. There are interesting stories of dummy nuts being welded to the heads for British races in order to make the scrutineers think these engines were standard ones with detachable heads.

In 1929 the 1750-cc Alfa Romeos came along, which have since rather eclipsed the 1500-cc models in fame, partly because they were in production longer, up to 1934. The new capacity of 1752 cc was obtained by altering the bore and stroke from 62 × 82 mm to 65 × 88 mm. In 1929, when the 3rd series 1750s took over from the 2nd series 1500s, crankshaft dimensions were the same as on the 1½-litre cars (46 mm for the mains, 40 mm for the big-ends), but these were increased to 48 mm and 42 mm respectively from the 4th series of 1930.

The 70-mph Turismo 1750 differed from its 1500 counterpart by having a detachable single overhead camshaft cylinder head on which the exhaust manifold was moved to the offside, hot-spotting with the inlet manifold, instead of being on the opposite side of the engine to the inlet as on the 1500. Bhp went up slightly from 44 on the 1500 to 46 at 4000 rpm, with a 5.5 to 1 compression ratio, and the 10 ft 2-in chassis was used. Instead of camshaft damping by flywheel or fan, the method on both the single- and twin-cam 1750 models (as on some of the 1500s) was by a series of spring-loaded brass slippers located behind the bronze bevel wheel on the camshaft. The later 1750s outside the Vintage era did not have any method of camshaft damping at all, and there seemed to be no disadvantage apart, perhaps, from a slight increase in engine noise.

The Vintage 1750 models ran much the same gamut as had

the 1500 series, the mildest twin-cam engines in the 10 ft 2-in chassis being the 1750 Sport (3rd series) and Gran Turismo (4th series). Both gave 55 bhp at 4400 rpm, and had a maximum speed of 75 to 80 mph, the difference being that the later 4th series engines had a twin-choke vertical Solex carburettor in place of a twin-choke Zenith, and the mixture was warmed by exhaust gases around the inlet manifold controlled by a dashboard lever instead of by a water jacketed inlet manifold.

The 6C 1750 Super Sport of 1929 had an uprated unblown or blown engine in a shorter 9-ft wheelbase chassis. The unblown engine had a compression ratio of 6.25 to 1 compared with the 5.75 to 1 of the Sport engine, and gave 64 bhp at 4500 rpm. With a blower pressure of 8.8 lb to the square inch and a 5 to 1 compression ratio, power went up to 85 bhp at 4500 rpm, nearly double that of the original 1½-litre engine. In England the single camshaft 1750 was called the 17/75 hp, the unblown twin-cam was the 17/85 hp and the blown twin-cam was the 17/95 hp.

The first 50 cars of the 3rd series had a blower like that on the 1½-litre cars operating at 1½ times engine speed, the gearing causing the rotor drive to go in the opposite direction to the engine crankshaft. On subsequent cars the intermediate gearing was dispensed with and the supercharger ran at engine speed, the pressure being maintained by making a bigger blower, the rotors being 50 per cent longer. The different direction of rotation meant the position of the double-choke Memini carburettor was altered from nearside to offside and the pipe from the blower to the inlet manifold was much less tortuously shaped. The name of the model was changed from 1930 onwards from Super Sport to Gran Sport. 52 blown 3rd series cars were produced in 1929 and 60 unblown. Turismo figures for 1929 were 327, and 268 for the Sport.

In 1930, 309 single-cam Turismo chassis were made, 372 twin-cam Gran Turismo and 67 Gran Sport. Later cars had a bigger clutch, and the Gran Sport cars had sloping radiators.

Various bodywork was fitted to the 1750 cars, perhaps the most famous being the all-metal Zagato two-seaters. Alfa Romeo also made bodies for their cars, and Italian specialist coachbuilders included, as well as Zagato, Touring, Castagna, Farina, and Brianza. In France there was Figoni, and in England James Young and Martin Walter. There is a romantic ring about the names of Italian coachbuilders, and it is sad for the non-Italian speaker to discover that the name Castagna simply means 'Brown', just as it is a disappointment to realize that the surname of the great Italian racing driver Luigi Fagioli has to be translated as 'Beans'.

The rarest and most powerful 1750 cars were the fixed cylinder head racing versions of which six Super Sport cars were produced in 1929 and six Gran Sport in 1930. The 1929 cars produced 95 bhp at 4800 rpm and the 1930 102 bhp at 5000 rpm and 105 mph. These engines were more special than the previous fixed-head 1½-litre racing engines as not only had the valve angle been increased from 90 to 100 degrees, but the bottom end was also modified and had 8 main bearings instead of the standard 5.

It is inevitable that comparisons are made between the cars of Alfa Romeo and its great Continental racing rival, Bugatti, and a generalization which would probably not please the enthusiasts for either marque is to say that the Jano-designed Alfa Romeo is an engineer's car and the Bugatti is a driver's car.

Although opinions on handling, like opinions on the comfort of seats, are often personal ones, it is a fact that the three-point mounting of the Alfa Romeo engine means that the chassis is flexible ahead of the steering box, and the steering box has to be mounted on a ball joint to take account of this. There is the suggestion, therefore, that an indefinite feeling between the drop-arm and the front wheels communicates itself to the driver of an Alfa Romeo in contrast to the direct feeling the Bugatti driver experiences due to his more rigidly mounted engine stiffening up the front of the chassis.

The more touring Jano Alfa Romeos suffered, as the Merosi 22/90 did, from too big a gap between 3rd and top gears and, to repeat an opinion of Cecil Clutton's, 'they were spoilt for English use by gear ratios which seem to have been plotted on the assumption that you were always either sweeping along a straight unobstructed highway at terminal velocity, or clawing your way up an Alp'. The sporting and blown versions had much closer ratios, and so there can be no criticisms of them on this score.

Even on the sporting Alfa Romeos, however, gear changing requires more skill than it does on a Bugatti, particularly in changing up from 1st to 2nd and down from top to 3rd. The explanation would seem to be that the Alfa Romeo gears are so exquisitely made that they have almost too many teeth on them, whereas the Bugatti teeth are coarser, like the gears on a mangle, and so they go into mesh more easily.

On the score of engine design and execution, the palm has to go to the Alfa Romeo, for not only does it avoid the Bugatti eccentricities, but the execution of such parts as the alloy castings, in particular, is superior. This is in no way to condemn Bugatti, whose engines are also a joy to behold, and it must be remembered that, despite their eccentricities, they worked.

The excellence of the design and construction of the Jano 1750 Alfa engine is illustrated by the experience of a well-known driver of racing Bugattis in the Vintage Sport-Car Club. For six months he drove a 1750 Alfa from which there came a mechanical noise which he put down to a faulty little-end bush. When the engine was stripped, it was found that the crankshaft was broken, yet it was so well supported that it had continued to function during six months of hard driving.

The marvellous noise that emanates from the multi-cylinder engines of both Alfa Romeos and Bugattis, gives the driver the impression that he is travelling considerably faster than is really the case. Thus road safety pundits would surely agree that resources spent on the preservation of such delightful engines are as beneficial to the community as those which go towards the cost of maintaining proliferating speed limits or the manufacture of unburstable door locks and safety bumpers.

Chapter 2
ALVIS

'A bad car and badly built' was the verdict of engineer Captain G.T. Smith-Clarke after he had examined a 10/30-hp Alvis in 1922 in the presence of T.G. John, who had founded the Alvis company three years before. John's reply was that Smith-Clarke had better join the firm and put it right. Smith-Clarke got the job, so perhaps there was an ulterior motive in the severity of his strictures as in later years he was to admit that the 10/30 hp had a very good performance, with a maximum speed of about 60 mph 'which was quite a lot in advance of contemporary cars in its class'.

The 10/30 hp had been designed by G.P.H. de Freville and had been inspired by the French D.F.P. which W.O. Bentley had raced so successfully before the war and with which de Freville had been connected. Having sold the drawings to John and invented the name 'Alvis',* de Freville had nothing more to do with the car, apart from driving one in one or two competitions

The 10/30 had a 65 × 110-mm, 1460-cc, fixed-head, side-valve engine of Edwardian appearance, but with aluminium pistons and pressure lubrication. It developed over 30 bhp at 3500 rpm and the car was put on the market in 1920. It proved quite successful in competitions, and a racing version driven by the works driver, Major C.M. Harvey, actually lay fourth behind the victorious Talbot-Darracq team in the 1921 Coupe des Voiturettes at Le Mans before retiring due to a stone being thrown up and cracking the sump.

In 1921 the sports 11/40 hp was introduced. This had the 10/30 engine, but with the bore increased to 68 mm, giving a capacity of 1598 cc and an output of 40 bhp. It also had a slightly

---

* 'Alvis' had been stamped on the alloy pistons produced by de Freville's firm Aluminium Pistons Ltd of Wandsworth during the First World War. It seems to imply lightness (A1' for aluminium) with strength ('vis') but was chiefly chosen as being easily pronounceable in any language.

shorter chassis than the 10/30 hp. In 1922 the 11/40 was renamed the 12/40.

In 1923 the first overhead-valve Alvis was produced and was named the 12/50. In the competition sense, as well as commercially, it can be described as the most successful British $1\frac{1}{2}$-litre sports car of the decade, and at the outset of its career in 1923 a racing version was the only British car to achieve an outright win in the classic series of J.C.C. 200-Miles races at Brooklands, then the blue riband of $1\frac{1}{2}$-litre racing in this country.

The 12/50 Alvis engine has inspired a monograph written by Michael Radford in 1970, and from his 'The Alvis 12/50 Engine' some interesting facts emerge, notably how direct a development the 12/50 engine was from the 'badly designed' 10/30 engine. For instance, from 1920 to 1932 (the last year the engine was catalogued, in the TL 12/60 Alvis), the three main bearing housings for the crankshaft had the same dimensions and longitudinal location and the critical dimensions affecting interchangeability of camshafts, camshaft bearings and timing gears were constants. Only the top half of the engine was entirely new, the cylinder block, cylinder head and, of course, rocker gear assembly for the pushrod-operated overhead valves. Both long-stroke and short-stroke versions of the engine were produced, each originally with a 68-mm bore, later increased to 69 mm for the long-stroke engines, and Michael Radford tells us that the dimensions of the 103- and 110-mm stroke shafts were virtually identical except for the crankshaft pin location which had a 3.5-mm variation in throw. The short-stroke engine had a capacity of 1496 cc on the sports models to bring them into the $1\frac{1}{2}$-litre class, whilst from 1926 the 69-mm bore 1645-cc long-stroke engine was fitted to the touring cars.

The majority of the new British car firms which sprang up after the First World War fitted proprietary engines to their cars, but from the start T.G. John was a very independent man and as much of his car as possible was made in his factory. Even a minor component like a Timken roller-bearing joint first fitted in 1925 to the front of the propellor shaft was made to Alvis design. In later years this bearing was described as 'quite impossible unless brand new'.

Other manufacturers, such as A.C. and Aston Martin, tended to build special engines for racing, but the majority of Alvis

successes were obtained with 'hotted-up' versions of the standard
12/50 engine. Undoubtedly it was a fine design, but it has two
shortcomings if it is consistently taken above its 4500-rpm rev
limit. In fact a standard 12/50 would not consistently pull 4000
rpm in top, except under very favourable conditions. For tuned
engines, however, the first obstacle to over-revving is the famous
'Achilles heel' of the 12/50 engine, the $\frac{1}{4}$-in little-end pinch bolt
fitted to the connecting rods of the majority of the engines. This
has been described by Michael May, a well-known pre-war
competition driver, as 'altogether an infernal device . . . (which)
would invariably break if the engine was taken over 4700 rpm'.

The second weakness if over-revving is indulged in is the
centre main bearing, referred to by the same Michael May as
'the worst point in the engine' due to 'rapid wear' causing low oil
pressure. At very high revs the whip from the crankshaft can cause
the centre main bearing cap to fail and break away, induced by
the fact that the offside stud hole is weakened by the centre
bearing oil drilling. The result can be a broken crankshaft.

On the racing Alvis engines steps were taken to deal with these
drawbacks. On the 1924 200-Mile Race engines, for instance,
stress was taken off the pinch bolts by doing away with the $\frac{3}{4}$-in
saw cut which featured on the standard rods. This meant the
gudgeon pin was less effectively clamped, but the resultant bore
wear was not a prime consideration in a racing engine. On these
engines the main bearing problem was alleviated by fitting steel
backing plates to strength the main bearing caps.

Stress was also relieved by lightening the connecting rods,
which were machined all over to bring the weight down from
28 oz to 20 oz.

In Michael Radford's opinion, sustained revs of over 4000
mean that the oil flows hot with the consequent risk of running
big-end bearings. Most of the racing engines were given a dry
sump, increasing the oil capacity from one gallon to four gallons,
thus bearing out the Radford theory. Radford reckons it is
unwise to run a standard engine at a sustained speed of 4000 rpm
and over, and says the safe maximum sustained speed is 3800 rpm
which he points out means 70 mph even with the low ratio 4.77
touring axle.

The side-valve cars employed fully floating rods without
clamp bolts, but these rods were very heavy, weighing 33 oz.

From February, 1928, the short-stroke engines also had fully floating rods without clamp bolts, and these rods were very light, being made of Duralumin, and weighing only 14 oz.

In standard form the 12/50 engine developed 46 bhp, and over 50 bhp was available with mild tuning. The 1924 200-mile Race engine was credited with 70 bhp, using modified valve timing. 5.3 to 1 was the standard compression ratio, going up to 6.2 to 1 for the short-stroke engines with big port heads, which had the inlet ports enlarged from 32 mm to 37 mm and the exhaust ports from 37 mm to 50 mm.

Chassis design was conventional with half-elliptic springs, and the back axle was fully floating. The big chassis change came in 1926 when the subframe which had held the engine was done away with and the front of the chassis was strengthened with the engine and separate gearbox being rubber-mounted on patented conical buffers – something of an innovation at the time. The cone clutch of the earlier models was replaced by a plate clutch with an enormously heavy cast-iron clutch body weighing all of 27 lb. 12/50 durability was to some extent gained at the expense of light weight, although the manufacturers knew all about the importance of lightness in competition cars and made a few clutch bodies in aluminium which only weighed 7½ lb. Front-wheel brakes were first fitted as an optional extra in 1924. Successful experiments were made in 1925 with Lockheed hydraulic brakes, but mechanical brakes were used on all the production cars. W.M. Dunn, the very talented Scottish designer at Alvis, had undertaken the Lockheed experiments whilst Captain Smith-Clarke, the chief engineer, was away ill, but Smith-Clarke scrapped these plans when he returned.

Traditionally the earlier Vintage sports cars are more pleasant to drive than the later ones. Their braking arrangements were inferior, but beaded-edge tyres and brakeless front axles usually produced excellent steering characteristics and handling. Later the cars were given balloon tyres and front brakes, the steering ratio was lowered to reduce effort on the part of the driver, and weight was increased by the fitting of more comfortable body-work. To counteract this more powerful engines were fitted. All this happened to the 12/50 Alvis, but the cars of the middle period epitomized by the beetleback two-seater with the big port engine were quite a good compromise, and 1927 turned out to

Von Taxis, a German from Stuttgart, driving a 1924 RL Targa Florio Alfa Romeo in the 1925 Circuit of Solitude race *Autocar*

1929 Alfa Romeo 6C 1750 Super Sport, twin o.h.c. engine with the early smaller supercharger

Bill and Ruth Urquhart-Dykes practising for the 1929 Double Twelve Hour race at Brooklands in a straight-8 f.w.d. Alvis *T.A.S.O. Mathieson*

This 1928 Carbodies saloon 12/50 Alvis started life as a 14.75 hp (hence the closed hub wheels), but the 6-cylinder engine was removed and a 12/50 unit substituted for a customer before it left the works *Roger McDonald A.I.I.P.*

be a most successful competition year for the sports 12/50s, with two long-distance race wins at Brooklands.

1927 was also the last year in which the works raced the 12/50 models, when the main successes were a first place in the scratch J.C.C. Four-Hour Sporting Car Race for cars up to 1½ litres, held at Brooklands over a course with artificial corners (Major C.M. Harvey, beetleback, at 63.2 mph in the rain): first place on handicap in the 230-mile Georges Boillot Cup Eliminating Race, Boulogne (Major C.M. Harvey, beetleback, at 61.83 mph); and first place on handicap in the Essex M.C. Six-Hour race at Brooklands, with artificial corners (S.C.H. Davis, duck's back, at 62 mph). Davis was second on scratch in this race to a 3-litre Sunbeam which averaged 64.3 mph, whilst a 3-litre Bentley was third after delays due to mechanical troubles. In 1928 a beetle-back with dry sump lubrication driven by Mr and Mrs Urquhart-Dykes took the 12-hour 1½-litre class record at Brooklands by averaging 81.83 mph to the 80.06 mph set up by the previous holder, a supercharged Lea-Francis, a few weeks before.

Despite the emphasis on competitions in the foregoing, it should not be forgotten that a large number of 12/50 models were produced in touring rather than sports form.

In the late summer of 1927 a six-cylinder Alvis was announced, known as the 14.75 because its RAC rating was 14¾ hp. The car used the 12/50 chassis and gearbox and was smoother though no faster than the 12/50. Engine construction was similar, although the added complication of a water pump was found necessary, and the exhaust and inlet manifolding were on the nearside of the engine, opposite to the arrangement on the 12/50. The stroke was 100 mm, but the bore was reduced to 63 mm, giving a capacity of 1870 cc.

'Crankshaft timing gears have always been one of the auto-mobile engineer's headaches' said Captain Smith-Clarke in a lecture to the Automobile Division of the Institute of Mechanical Engineers in 1948, and went on to say that the only satisfactory position for the camshaft and accessory drive was at the rear of the engine, as close as possible to the flywheel. On the 12/50, timing gears had been gear-driven and at the front of the engine, but on the 14.75 they were in the Smith-Clarke recommended position and driven by a duplex roller chain with an automatic tensioner.

In 1929 the bore of the 14.75 engine was increased to 67.5 mm, bringing the capacity up to 2148 cc, and in short-chassis sports and long-chassis touring form the cars became known as Silver Eagles. The short-chassis 16/95-hp Silver Eagle with three SU carburettors and close ratio gears was a genuinely fast car capable of 85 mph at any time and 90 mph under favourable conditions, and it formed the basis of the successful six-cylinder Alvises of the 'thirties, commencing with the Speed 20.

The six-cylinder cars sold well, and 12/50 production was discontinued from 1929, but the depression brought about the need for a cheaper model again, so the 12/50 was revived at the end of 1930, at that time in touring form only and known as the TJ. The 1645-cc engine was standardized, but now with coil ignition (the Silver Eagle had both coil and magneto), and amongst features borrowed from the Silver Eagle was a crank-shaft vibration damper which gave a worthwhile increase in smooth running, and wire wheels – reputed to be more likely to break their spokes under stress than the open-hub type on the earlier cars. Modified springs made the car lower and the fuel tank was at the rear, whilst the radiator had definite post-Vintage affinities, with a chromium-plated shell.

Alvis enterprise in design was first demonstrated in 1925 when, in pursuit of lightness and stability, they produced a sprint car with an all-Duralumin chassis, a Duralumin body of partially monocoque construction, and front-wheel drive. It weighed a mere 9½ cwt, was only 3 ft high and had a wheelbase of 8 ft. The engine was a racing pushrod 12/50 unit turned back-to-front in the frame which, when supercharged, was made to rev at 6000 rpm, when it produced 100 bhp.

On this car a de Dion-type front axle was used in conjunction with the front drive. Between 1918 and 1922, Ben F. Gregory of Kansas City, Missouri, had built about ten fwd racing and tour-ing cars, all using a de Dion-type front axle. In December 1924, the first Miller fwd racing car was announced in the USA, which also used a de Dion front axle. A front-wheel-drive Miller raced in the Indianapolis 500 in May 1925, and the fwd Alvis first appeared at Kop hill climb in March 1925. Gregory had used a transverse leaf spring in conjunction with the de Dion front axle, but both Miller and Alvis used quarter elliptics. The Alvis was ahead of Gregory's cars and Miller's first design in having inboard front brakes (operated by the handbrake only) to reduce unsprung weight, though these were adopted on all fwd Millers built after the prototype. Alvis and Miller transmission arrangements, however, were completely dissimilar, the the Miller gearbox being quite unusuable for anything but track racing in which no downward changing was required.

At this time none of these cars used constant-velocity universal joints to overcome snatch at large steering angles, and on this and all subsequent fwd models Alvis used pot-type universal joints which are recognized as being the next best thing to a true constant velocity joint.

Despite instability on a trailing throttle and troubles like wheel wobble in sand races and front tyres bursting at Brooklands, the prototype fwd Alvis, nicknamed *Tadpole*, was certainly fast round corners, and in 1925, when running unsupercharged, it was beaten only by a 2-litre Grand Prix Sunbeam at a wet Shelsley Walsh hill climb. It lapped Brooklands at over 104 mph when supercharged, and took standing-start class kilometre and mile records.

Two supercharged cars based on *Tadpole* but modified for long-distance racing were entered for the 1925 200-Mile Race incorporating artificial corners at Brooklands. They showed distinct promise, were the only cars to give any sort of challenge to the 'invincible' Talbot-Darracqs with their twin overhead-camshaft engines, and were finally let down by their brakes. One car retired, after the driver had held third place in his first big race, due to the transmission seizing after the heat from the front brakes had dried up the differential bearings. The other driver had over-revved his engine by using it as a brake and although still running at the end of the race he had lost half an hour at his pit changing a pushrod.

Still full of enterprise, Alvis threatened to put the rest of the British motor industry to shame by designing and building two Grand Prix cars to the current $1\frac{1}{2}$-litre formula in 1926, casting the blocks for the supercharged straight-eight engines in their own factory. This was in the early days of supercharging, and horizontal valves were fitted which kept the piston crowns well away from the plugs with the idea of preventing burnt pistons. The cars, of course, had front-wheel drive, again with de Dion axles.

The Alvis Grand Prix story is similar to that of Vauxhall, promising and even brilliant designs, but insufficient money, resources and therefore time, to give the cars proper development and preparation. The GP Alvises were not ready for the 1926 British Grand Prix at Brooklands, but ran in the 200-Mile Race. Here one car crashed when lying fourth behind the Talbot-Darracq team due to a slow car getting in the way, and just before half distance the other car retired with lack of oil pressure out on the circuit, subsequently traced to a faulty gauge.

For 1927 the cars were redesigned as true monopostos, with more conventional twin overhead-camshaft straight-eight engines, whilst ifs replaced the de Dion front axle utilizing transverse quarter-elliptic springs, four aside. One car practised for the British GP but did not start due to a piston breaking in practice. Two cars started in the 200-Mile Race, one of which led initially at the start only to retire at quarter distance with engine trouble. The other car carried on sounding most unhealthy, but held second place in the $1\frac{1}{2}$-litre class as the opposition was not very brilliant, only to retire at nearly three-quarter distance.

As T.G. John was quick to point out, it was always the engines and not the front-wheel drive mechanism which had given trouble, and in 1928 a production front-wheel-drive Alvis was put on sale to the general public. This had ifs as on the 1927 Grand Prix cars, but, a new departure, it also had independent suspension at the rear, each wheel being mounted on a forward-facing torque arm acting on a quarter-elliptic spring. A few components, such as the Duralumin connecting rods, in the 1482-cc (68 × 102-mm) engine were common to the 12/50 engine, but the new unit employed a single overhead camshaft driven by noisy timing gears. These were at the front of the engine, but as the flywheel was also at the front, they were still in Captain Smith-Clarke's approved position. As the engine was turned back-to-front in the chassis, this meant that the crankshaft turned anti-clockwise looked at from the front. The bell housing, gearbox casing and differential housing were all one casting, forward of the engine and bolted to it, and as the starting handle worked through the gearbox it acted in the normal clockwise direction. An Alvis-designed-and-made Roots-type supercharger was optional equipment, remarkable for the fact that at this time all other British manufacturers seemed to fit proprietary superchargers, the favourite being the vane-type Cozette. Even Sunbeams, in 1924, one of the pioneers of Roots supercharging on their Grand Prix racing cars, fitted Cozettes to their twin-cam 3-litre sports cars as optional equipment.

It was emphasized that fwd Alvises were not intended to be used for shopping, and in winter owners were expected to warm them up on touring plugs and then change to racing plugs. It was hoped that only knowledgeable enthusiasts would run them as they did not give of their best in inexpert hands.

Two unsupercharged cars were entered for Le Mans in June, 1928, and there were considerable alarums and excursions in practice. One car finished a circuit on three wheels as over-damping of the suspension of one rear wheel caused it to remain up in the air after the car came back on an even keel following some spirited cornering. On another occasion a car spun to a halt due to remaining on full lock after taking a sharp corner fast. This was because the outside springs had flattened to such an extent that they had tangled with a drag-link nut, a condition made all the more mystifying as there appeared to be nothing wrong with the car once it had come to a halt. Despite this, once the necessary modifications had been made, the cars proved to be both fast and reliable in the race, gaining 6th and 9th places, the faster car winning its class at 59.2 mph and only being beaten by two Bentleys, two Chryslers and a Stutz of roughly treble its capacity. Third in the $1\frac{1}{2}$-litre class behind the two Alvises was another fwd car, a 1481-cc Tracta, which averaged 53.3 mph. These French cars had sliding pillar ifs and their designer, Gregoire, who was driving an 1100-cc example in the race, spent a certain amount of time looking behind him in practise studying the behaviour of the front suspension of any Alvis which happened to be overhauling him. His race average was only 48.4 mph, but he was third in the competition for the Index of Performance and Biennial Cup, and all three Tractas in the race were finishers.

In August, 1928, a supercharged fwd Alvis, driven by Leon Cushman, came second in the Tourist Trophy 410-mile handicap race in Northern Ireland, 13 seconds behind the winning super-charged $1\frac{1}{2}$-litre Lea-Francis of Kaye Don. The five fwd Alvises prepared by the works for this race differed considerably from standard, and their engine modifications remained a secret in a most extraordinary way for over 40 years.

The first clue came in 1967 when an Australian Alvis enthusiast, Rob Gunnell, of New South Wales, purchased a fwd Alvis which had a spare block with it. This block was very unusual in that it had a fixed head, when a fixed-head 4-cylinder fwd Alvis engine was unheard of. Furthermore the block bore the engine number of 7582, which was the engine number of Cushman's 1928 TT car. This car is still in existence in England, but with a normal detachable head engine. Further, the fixed-head block bore an RAC stamp, which was evidence that it must have had a competition history, though its standard-size bores were almost unworn, showing that it had done a small mileage.

Rob Gunnell wrote to W. Urquhart-Dykes, one of the Alvis drivers in the TT, whose race had finished when his car overturned due to suddenly striking a damp patch on the circuit caused by a shower. Urquhart-Dykes wrote back to that to the best of his knowledge the cars had detachable-head engines, and added 'I still can hardly believe my eyes when I see (a photograph of) a 4-cylinder fwd engine with a non-detachable head'.

The writer of this chapter at the same time telephoned George Tattersall, the Alvis racing manager in 1928, who could not remember a fixed-head engine, whilst a letter to W.M. Dunn, the designer of the fwd Alvis brought the reply, 'I do not remember making a non-detachable head for the 4-cylinder, and nor does George Tattersall. . . . It may have been done, but certainly not in any number, or we would have had it in our minds'.

It was not until December 1974, that the secret (if it was a secret) was revealed in an article in *Motor Sport* by Hugh Torrens. From blueprints and notes which had been in the possession of the late John Cooper, at one time Sports Editor of *The Autocar*, and an apprentice at Alvis before the war, Hugh Torrens had found the specification for type FC fwd Alvis cars. The type letters FA and FB had described respectively the standard short- and long-chassis models in 1928, whilst their equivalents in 1929 were the FD and FE, with certain chassis modifications.

The FC specification referred only to the five or six cars (there was a spare car which was not entered for the race) specially prepared for the 1928 TT race, and whilst the chassis improvements were the result of lessons learned at Le Mans, some of which were later incorporated in the FD and FE cars, the engines were remarkable for having, in addition to fixed heads, rods with roller bearing big-ends and special crankshafts. These differed from the standard plain bearing cranks, whilst the stroke was longer by 1 mm, giving 68 × 103 mm (1496 cc) instead of the standard 68 × 102 mm (1482 cc). No secret was made of the capacity increase, as it was declared on the entry forms and was given in the TT programmes.

The blower pressure on the FC was increased from the standard 5 lb to 9.5 lb/in^2, whilst the compression ratio was 5.7 to 1 compared with the 5.1 to 1 of the standard blown cars. In fact, 5.7 to 1 was the compression ratio of the unblown standard cars. On a 50/50 petrol/benzole mixture, an FC engine was tested to produce 72 bhp at 4470 rpm and 70.75 bhp at 4430 rpm, using a larger main jet and choke tube than standard on its Solex carburettor.

An FC TT chassis with large headlamps faired into single-seater bodywork specially fitted for the occasion, took 500-mile, 6-hour and 1000-km 1½-litre class records at Brooklands in September 1928, at 91.77 mph, thus proving it had speed as well as reliability.

Also in that September, three weeks after the TT, Cushman's car was entered in the Georges Boillot Cup race at Boulogne, driven by C.M. Harvey, where it proved to be faster than the winning 1½-litre blown Alfa Romeo until it retired with a broken piston halfway through the race, after about 130 miles. On this occasion it was entered with the standard capacity 1482-cc engine.

How the fixed-head block of this car eventually found its way to Australia is a Vintage mystery. The block is the only remaining concrete evidence of the existence of an FC engine (although no FC crankshaft survives), but circumstantial evidence seems to show that all the 1928 TT cars almost certainly did have fixed-head engines.

The winning Lea-Francis was not exactly a catalogue model either, for Michael Sedgwick in his 'Profile' entitled *The Meadows Engined Lea-Francis* has revealed that it also was equipped with a special roller bearing crankshaft, as well as special pistons and rods, and only nine examples of its roller bearing crankshafts were ever made.

Although the 4-cylinder fwd cars as raced by the makers in sports car races were undoubtedly fast, the unblown engine of the production cars was not much more powerful than that of the 12/50 (compression ratio was 5.7 to 1 compared with 6.2 to 1 on the contemporary big port 12/50 engine which, incidentally, shared the same exhaust manifold). In view of the plug-changing ritual and excessive mechanical noise, the performance was not as exciting as might have been expected. The standard blown engine gave better acceleration and hill-climbing abilities, but little increase in maximum speed.

Drawbacks to the production cars were an ability to engage two gears at once and lock the transmission solid (though there is a modification to prevent this) and the undoubted inaccessibility of their engines compared with the 12/50. Like all Alvises they were sturdily constructed, but it now seems to be recognized that criticisms of excessive weight have been exaggerated. On the credit side were excellent brakes, superior cornering ability compared with conventional contemporary Alvises, and a very low, long-bonneted, aggressive appearance. They could even perform well in trials, one supercharged open four-seater gaining a 'gold' in the London–Exeter. They were cars which people either loved or hated, and perhaps Laurence Pomeroy's description of them was as apt as any – a qualified success. About 145 cars were made, a few with saloon bodywork.

The last front-wheel-drive model Alvis produced is one that readers of this book are unlikely to drive – the supercharged straight-eight with a twin-ohc 55 × 78.5, 1491-cc engine based on that of the 1927 Grand Prix car, with roller bearing mains and big ends. Unfortunately only ten of these cars were manufactured and sold between 1929 and 1931, and although they failed in the 1929 Le Mans and Double-Twelve Hour races, they successfully attacked long-distance records and performed well in the 1929 TT. They were notably successful in the 1930 TT where one finished just behind the victorious 1750 Alfa Romeos driven by the Italian aces Nuvolari, Campari and Varzi, these Alfas having special fixed-head racing engines. The Alvises came 1st, 2nd and 3rd in the 1½-litre class. At 18 cwt at the weigh-in, these cars were some ½ cwt lighter than the 1750 Alfa Romeos, and were the best fwd Alvises ever made. This race was run largely on wet roads.

The exciting specification of these cars, plus the raptures

expressed in writing about one example by an ex-owner, has made them legendary, for none apparently exist today in original form. What does exist is the body and chassis of one of the 1927 GP cars with an unused spare engine for the 1930 TT cars, but the two have still to be mated by their engineer-owner and the car made to run. Until that occurs, one more intriguing front-wheel-drive Alvis mystery has still to be unravelled.

Of the Vintage Alvis models, it is the 12/50 which is considered the classic. In *The Vintage Motor Car* (Batsford, 1954), Cecil Clutton and John Stanford said of the 12/50, 'We cannot but consider it one of the classic designs of the time, and it remains of all Vintage sports cars the one which needs the least apology'.

As if to emphasize this, it may not have escaped the reader's notice that our criticisms of the 12/50 have mainly been confined to the possible drawbacks if ever its engine is grossly over-revved.

Chapter 3
AMILCAR

Frenchmen adored sports cars. Light weight, a racy appearance, and no concession to comfort were essential features. Very narrow open two-seater bodies, often without doors and with the seats staggered, were normal. A pointed tail was naturally incorporated because Grand Prix cars had them. Sketchy cycle-type mudguards were fitted, and knock-on wheels were universal. Weather protection, if any, was primitive.

Thus wrote Francophile John Bolster in his book *French Vintage Cars* (Autosport and Batsford, 1964). Part of the recipe, also, were quarter-elliptic springs all round until the front ones were replaced by half-elliptics with the advent of front-wheel brakes, and generally a proprietary engine by obliging French firms like Chapuis-Dornier, Ruby or S.C.A.P.

The two most successful exponents of the art, Amilcar and Salmson, made their own engines, however, and very few components were bought out. They were also capable of making their own bodies, and the output of the two factories was about the same during the Vintage decade – approximately 15 000 cars. Amilcars were made under licence in Germany and Austria, and were assembled in Italy, but all Salmsons appear to have been exported to their agents in the main European countries. Both marques were manufactured in the environs of Paris, Salmson at Billancourt in the southwest and Amilcar at St Denis in the northeast.

The name 'Emile Akar' repeated quickly several times eventually becomes 'Amilcar', or something very like it, and this is said to be the origin of the name. Together with Joseph Lamy, Akar had put up money to help found the firm in 1920 and Akar became its President whilst Lamy was Sales Director. The engineering design staff, as well as Lamy himself, came from the Le Zèbre works in Paris, the Le Zèbre, or Zebra, car having first made its appearance as long ago as 1908 as a single cylinder.

John Bolster has described the 1913 four-cylinder side-valve Le Zèbre as the first really popular little car in France. Edmond Moyet was Amilcar's Chief Engineer, but the engine of the Amilcar seems to have been designed by the Le Zèbre Chief Engineer, Salomon, before he went off to Citroën to design what must have been the next most popular little French car following the Le Zèbre, the 5 CV Citroën of clover leaf body fame. Working with Moyet was André Morel, also from Le Zèbre, and he became the first Amilcar competitions driver.

The Amilcar engine had four cylinders and side valves. Capacity was 55 × 95 mm, 903 cc, compared with 55 × 105 mm for the Le Zèbre and 55 × 90 mm for the side-valve Citroën. The Citroën had a cast-iron block and separate aluminium crankcase, as did the Amilcar's rival the Salmson, but the Amilcar had a cast-iron block and integral crankcase. Incidentally, Salmson were parsimonious with their aluminium as their crankcases were made of very thin metal which some 50 years later is prone to cracking around the engine bearers. Power output of the Amilcar engine was given as 18 bhp, about the same as the bigger 1087-cc Salmson ohv four-pushrod unit.

The Le Zèbre had the engine, clutch and gearbox cast in one unit, and on the Amilcar, also, the engine oil was shared by the clutch and gearbox, the former component being multi-plate and the latter 3-speed, with a 4.28 to 1 top gear ratio compared with a 4 to 1 on the Salmson. Lubrication was by splash, oil being raised by the flywheel to a cup or reservoir, which then distributed it under gravity to the mains of the two bearing crankshaft and the big-end troughs.

The first Amilcar, known as the Type CC. was fitted with this engine. T.R Nicholson in his 'Profile' on the four-cylinder Amilcars tells us that the weight was 8½ cwt complete, but some cars were evidently sold 'incomplete' to get below the 350-kg (7-cwt) limit which allowed them to qualify for the very low cyclecar tax in France. The wheelbase was 7 ft 8 in and, unlike the 5 CV Citroën, the Amilcar did not have a differential. The back axle was in one piece, there being no separate half shafts, and early cars had a straight bevel final drive, later changed for a more silent spiral bevel. Quarter-elliptic springs were fitted all round, and usually skiff-type two-seater bodies.

Although not intended as a sports car, the Amilcar, with its maximum of about 50 mph, was faster than the Citroën and also was slightly more expensive. The sporting image came with Morel's victory in the 1922 Bol d'Or 24-hour race over a 12-km circuit at the Porte de Patin, where he beat the two four-pushrod Salmsons of larger capacity, and a third Salmson disguised as a Bignan, to win at 37.54 mph.

Three 903-cc cars were entered in 1922 for the 247-mile Grand Prix des Cyclecars at Le Mans, and here they did very well considering they were up against 1087-cc Salmsons with sophisticated dohc racing engines. Despite this opposition, the Amilcars of Fardeau and Morel came 3rd and 4th to the Salmsons, only 3 and 4 minutes, respectively, behind the winner, who averaged 61.26 mph. Another Salmson was 5th.

In 1922 the CC was supplemented by two further models, a more sporting version called the CS with a slightly larger 23-bhp engine of 985 cc (57 × 95 mm), and the C4 or Petit Sport with an engine still further enlarged to 1004 cc (58 × 95 mm) and a wheelbase lengthened by 2 inches to take larger bodies. The C4 had two pairs of shoes in each rear drum, one pair operated by the footbrake and the other by the handbrake.

A 1004-cc Amilcar, and therefore presumably a C4, was entered for the first Le Mans 24-hour race in 1923, and had to give best to the four-pushrod Salmsons, which were the fastest 1100-cc cars. The Boutmy/Mercadanti Amilcar finished 18th and averaged 39.7 mph to the 43.7 mph of the fastest Salmson in 12th place.

The works drivers, Morel and Mestivier, drove a similar Amilcar at Le Mans in 1924 and retired, whilst in 1925 the sole Amilcar entry again had Morel and Mestivier as drivers, but the latter was killed after a crash when his car unaccountably swerved off the straight. Amilcar did not contest Le Mans again in the 'twenties, where Salmson scored some notable successes.

In 1924 the CS was replaced by the most famous of the Vintage sports Amilcars, the Grand Sport, or CGS. These had a bigger-bore 1074-cc side-valve engine (60 × 95 mm), claimed to give 28 bhp at 3600 rpm. Except on early models, pressure lubrication was employed, the engine oil still being threshed around the clutch and gearbox once the engine was running. The oil pump was driven off the end of the camshaft, maintaining a pressure of 5 or 6 lb on the main crankshaft bearings and keeping the big-end troughs well filled. Rod-operated front-wheel brakes were adopted, the actuation being through the hollowed-out king-pins, with larger ribbed drums at the front than at the back, whilst half-elliptic springs now replaced the former quarter elliptics at the front. Very pretty bodies were fitted, with a long racing tail and staggered passenger's seat. It is interesting that this staggered seating was not normally a feature of the standard Salmsons, although it was used on the racing ones.

The higher power output of the CGS was unfortunately counterbalanced by additional weight, this having increased to $11\frac{1}{2}$ cwt, and the maximum speed was about 60 mph, performance not being helped by the fact that a 3-speed gearbox was still fitted, with ratios of 4.5, 7.25 and 12.8 to 1. The electrical system was by Ducellier with lamps by Cibié, Marchal or Blèriot, the original 6-volt system being replaced by a 12-volt in late 1926. Ignition was by magneto, and either steel or bronze helical timing gears were used. Carburation was by a single Solex.

The valve design was quite interesting, the end of each valve being threaded to take the tappet end, which gave the valve clearance adjustment and was secured by a lock nut. The cam follower, between each cam and its corresponding tappet end, was hinged to the crankcase wall and referred to in contemporary accounts as a rocker. This arrangement, besides being inconducive to friction, was possibly used as there was very little space for a conventional tappet and guide. In fact a contemporary owner wrote 'Valve adjustment is not particularly easy owing to the small space available in which operations can be conducted'.

The same owner wrote, 'The cooling system is adequate under the worst conditions and the engine runs better in winter with half the radiator blanked off'. There was no water pump and circulation was by thermo-siphon, but Amilcars generally have a reputation for running hot. The water passages were rather small, and if these silted up it was not unknown for most of the water to boil away. It was also possible to lose water out of the radiator overflow pipe through surging so that it was advisable to fit a baffle. Vernon Balls, a great Amilcar exponent at Brooklands, is said to have gone through innumerable blocks in the course of his racing career, and cracked heads were not unknown.

In late 1926 the CGSs model came out, the small 's' standing for 'surbaissée' or 'underslung'. This new model had a lowered chassis, redesigned steering, larger brake drums of the same size back and front, and a redesign of the gravity feed petrol tank and instrument board supports. A bigger sump was fitted, holding 9 pints to the 8-pint capacity of the CGS. The 'Petit Sport' capacity had been $5\frac{1}{2}$ pints. Incidentally, Castrol XXL was recommended, and at oil changes one pint had to be put through the gearbox filler, although the oil was common to both engine and gearbox.

As on the CGS, the propellor shaft was enclosed in a torque tube, there being a flexible coupling behind the gearbox, and the shaft was supported by four ball bearings.

On the CGS all brakes were rod-operated, but on the CGSs the linkage for the front brakes was via steel tapes as on the RL series of Alfa Romeo. Actually the Amilcar front brake operation was similar to that on the later Jano Alfa Romeos, which used rods all round as on the CGS. There seems no doubt at all that the Amilcar braking was exceptionally effective.

On the sports Amilcars the chassis finished in front of the rear axle and on the CGS and CGSs it was curved to follow the line of the tail or 'bottle-shaped'.

The CGSs engine was credited with 30 bhp at 4500 rpm and 70 mph, and it had a different camshaft to that on the CGS engine conducive to higher revs, but with less torque at lower revs. Later cars had 4-speed gearboxes and the passenger's seat was no longer staggered. On the long-tailed two-seaters the bodywork was steel or aluminium but never, apparently, fabric as on the rival Salmsons.

It seems to be generally agreed that the Amilcar had a superior chassis to the Salmson and better brakes (the Salmson used the Perrot system of front brake operation), but the Salmson scored in the engine department. Amilcar always went to the expense of fitting knock-on Rudge hubs, but Salmson defied John Bolster's dictum and secured their wheels with a key and centre-locking nut, only using Rudge hubs on their competition cars. Despite its touring car origins, nevertheless some sterling efforts were made to increase the performance of the Amilcar's humble side-valve engine. The works produced some Cozette super-charged engines fitted with water pumps to obviate the over-heating problems and roller bearings, giving 40 bhp, or more.

At Brooklands Vernon Balls had a car which was far from

standard, the chassis being shortened by 9½ inches, and the engine having a special crankshaft, still 2-bearing, but with huge circular webs, large balance weights and 40-mm journals in place of the 37-mm of the standard cranks. Special rods and high compression pistons were fitted, and a Cozette supercharger driven by spur gears from the front of the engine delivered mixture from a Solex carburettor at a pressure of 7 lb. It had a throttle-controlled oil feed with its own pump, and a water pump was connected to both the front and the rear of the block with twin pipes. In 1927 Balls won a Brooklands race with this car at an average speed of 88.88 mph, with a best lap at 95.78 mph.

Balls, who ran a motor business in Fulham, and subsequently in Holborn, London, was an Amilcar concessionaire, so too was another London firm called Boon & Porter of Castelnau, Barnes, one partner of which, R.C. (Bob) Porter, also used to race Amilcars at Brooklands.

Boon & Porter, as the main concessionaires until Vernon Balls reassumed the concession in 1928, fixed a cast-aluminium plate to the bulkhead of each Amilcar they sold and gave it their own number, these numbers running up to about 950. They also fitted a Pegasus flying horse radiator mascot to the cars they sold, modelled on an original Bob Porter picked up in a Paris accessory shop. Later the Pegasus was adopted by the Amilcar manufacturers, the 'Société Nouvelle pour l'Automobile' or S.N.P.A., and a reproduction stamped on various castings and components.

In England some Amilcars were sold with an 'Eldridge cowl' over the radiator. Ernest Eldridge himself was an Amilcar owner, as was Parry Thomas, and Eldridge utilized a CGS Amilcar chassis for his Eldridge Special racing car, fitted with a blown twin-cam Anzani engine. This cowl did nothing towards preventing the tendency to overheat.

Boon & Porter were responsible for a pushrod overhead valve conversion for the Amilcar engine, and Bob Porter entered a CGS fitted with one of these heads for the Essex Motor Club's Six Hours Race at Brooklands in 1927, but at the last minute the officials decided the modification did not come within the rules. Nevertheless Boon & Porter marketed a model known as the 'Manx', because it had the tail cut off and a spare wheel fitted at the back; it also could be fitted with the ohv head instead of the standard Ricardo side-valve head. Priced at £285 with the sv engine, the ohv version cost £35 to £40 more. Instead of having the carburettor and the exhaust on the nearside as on the sv engine, the ohv head had the exhaust on the nearside and the carburettor on the offside. The converted engine did not give higher speeds in the gears, but a better performance on hills due to a flat peak to the power curve, so that hills that would normally have called for a change to second could be climbed in top – an advantage with the 3-speed box that was still fitted when the modification was first introduced in 1926.

Speeds on the gears of the standard cars were quoted as 30 mph, 50 mph and 70 mph, but one tester remarked that it was pleasant to change into second at 15 mph and into top at about 35 mph. Nearly all testers seemed to have difficulty in actually recording 70 mph in top gear, which they put down to a stiff engine, or the weather conditions. All seemed to be agreed on the efficiency of the brakes, and roadholding and steering were praised. Petrol consumption was 35–40 mpg.

A model produced in 1924–26 was called the CGS3, as it was a three-seater with an extra chassis crossmember to allow for the third seat in the tail. The CGS4 of 1929, on the other hand, had a 4-speed gearbox, and 1929 was the last year in which the Grand Sports models were made.

It is interesting to compare the production figures of different models of Amilcar and Salmson, sports and touring, during the Vintage years, which show that just under 1500 sports twin-cam Salmsons were built compared with 4700 CGS/CGSs series Amilcars. In the Amilcar 'Profile', Tim Nicholson and Desmond Peacock tell us that 6000 CC, CS and C4 cars were built, and Chris Draper's figures for the 4-pushrod Salmsons in his book *The Salmson Story* (David & Charles, 1974) are 12 500, of which perhaps half had the cyclecar affinities of the CC, CS and C4 Amilcars, the others being heavier chassis with touring-type bodywork. Salmson only produced just over 1000 twin-cam touring cars, whereas Amilcar produced 2500 of their Type G touring cars and 3300 of their other touring types.

If we discount the 1500 twin-cylinder G.N. cyclecars built by Salmson in the first two or three years of the decade, we find Amilcar and Salmson production figures were roughly equal, but that the Salmson output of twin ohc-engined cars, on which their reputation came to be based, was actually comparatively small

MCO Amilcar Six with roller bearing engine in Serge Pozzoli's private collection in Normandy

Peter Hull borrows a 1927 Type CGSs Amilcar   *Neill Bruce*

1928 19/100, 3-litre Austro-Daimler

The 19/100 Austro-Daimler engine is a very clean design which has a great deal in common with the Mercedes Benz of the same period

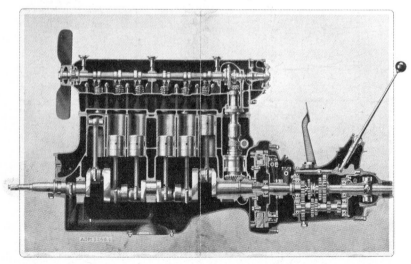

in the 'twenties, and it was their 4-pushrod cars which brought in the money, whilst the twin-cam cars earned the publicity in competitions, in which they usually beat the Amilcars.

The most popular touring Amilcar, the Type G, was in production from 1925 to 1927, and had a similar 1074-cc engine as the CGS but with a more 'touring' camshaft giving an output of 25 bhp and a 55-mph maximum speed. Wheelbase was 8 ft 6 in to the 7 ft 10 in of the CGS (the CGSs had an even slightly shorter wheelbase of 7 ft 7 in) and later models had full cantilever rear springing. The Type G developed into the Type L of 1927–28, which had a slightly enlarged 26-bhp pressure-lubricated engine of 60 × 105 mm, 1187 cc. Still with only 3 speeds and a final final drive ratio of 5 to 1, it also was a 55-mph motor car. The 'L' became the 'M' of 1929/30 with a 60 × 110-mm, 1244-cc motor of 28 bhp, which propelled it at 60 mph. The M2 of 1930/32 had a 4-speed gearbox. All these touring cars had differentials, and were often fitted with Weymann fabric bodies. A supercharged Type G won the Monte Carlo Rally in 1927.

Before the 'G' appeared, there had been a less popular, and larger, touring car, the Type E. This had a 10 CV 65 × 112-mm, 1458-cc, 40-bhp engine, a 9 ft 8-in wheelbase, cantilever rear springs and a 4-speed gearbox. It was produced in 1923/24, but the engine was enlarged in 1925 to 67 × 112 mm, 1578 cc. In 1926 the 'E' was replaced by the 'J' with an 11 CV 50 bhp engine of 73 × 112 mm, 1875 cc, later increased by 1930 to 75 × 112 mm, 1980 cc. These cars were credited with 60 to 70 mph.

The final Amilcar touring car design of the vintage decade was the most sophisticated and expensive, and at the time, when it was introduced in England in 1929 when the chassis price of the CGSs was a mere £195, the chassis price of the new model was £375. The new car was known as the C8, and it had a straight-eight engine of 62 × 77 mm, 1816 cc, said to develop 65 bhp, with five plain main bearings and a chain-driven single overhead camshaft. The 1st series prototype with the 1816-cc engine was found to be down on power, so the cylinder dimensions were increased to 63 × 80 mm, 1994 cc, in the 2nd series model known as the CS8, which in the 3rd series was given an increased stroke of 85 mm bringing the capacity to over 2 litres, i.e. 2116 cc. In the just post-Vintage period (1931), the capacity was increased again in the CS8 bis to 2330 cc (66 × 85 mm). The magneto was driven off a cross-shaft, the camshaft drove the water pump and fan, and a Dynastart was fitted projecting through the bottom of the radiator as on some Salmson models.

The new chassis was underslung, but still with cantilever rear springing as on the other touring models and semi-elliptic springs at the front. Weymann fabric saloon bodies were usually fitted to these good-looking cars, but the engines had a reputation for fragility, and despite the fact that the CS8 was pleasant to drive, production ceased in 1932. 75 mph was claimed and a 4-speed gearbox was standard. The wheelbase was 8 ft 7 in.

The most interesting Amilcar has been left until the last, the six-cylinder racing model. This was designer Moyet's reply to Emile Petit's four racing Salmsons, with dohc supercharged engines and desmodromic valves, which were invincible in the 1100-cc racing class from 1922 until 1925. The initial Amilcar Six, the Type CO, first appeared at Montlhèry in 1925, with Morel at the wheel. Cylinder dimensions were 55 × 77 mm, 1097 cc, and the twin overhead camshafts running in ball bearings were driven by a gear train at the rear of the engine. The cylinder head was non-detachable. There were seven roller main bearings and the big-ends were also roller bearing, the small-ends having a pinch bolt fixing as on the production cars. There was a single Solex carburettor, and this unsupercharged engine developed 75 bhp at 6500 rpm.

The chassis was very compact, with a wheelbase of only just over 7 ft and a weight of under 9 cwt. The frame differed from that of the current CGS, although quarter-elliptic springs were still used at the rear, and there was no differential. Front brake actuation through the king-pins was as on the production cars, but it is interesting that the standard brake rods and steel tapes were abandoned and all brake actuation was via cables.

By November, 1925, Desmond Peacock tells us, an Amilcar Roots-type blower had been fitted driven from the rear of the crankshaft, 83 bhp was claimed, and Montlhèry had been lapped at 118 mph, whilst by 1928 the engine was developing over 100 bhp at 6750 rpm. By this time some ten cars had been built, all raced by works drivers (Morel, Martin and Duray), none being identical, and differing from each other in chassis length and width, although all were nominally two-seaters.

The final development of the works racing cars was the Type

MCO, most examples, though not all, having single-seater bodies with the engine and transmission offset to the nearside and the carburettor moved to the opposite side of the supercharger. Engine dimensions were altered to 56×74 mm, 1094 cc. It is thought that only about three of the latter cars were made, one of which survives in France. An MCO was fitted with a block with a bigger bore of 58 mm, giving a capacity of 1174 cc, to bring it into the $1\frac{1}{2}$-litre class for record attempts over the kilometre, resulting in a time of 26.92 secs from a standing start. An MCO entered for the 1929 Indianapolis 500-Miles Race, which retired after 30 laps, appears to have had an engine with a 59×77-mm block giving a capacity of 1262 cc, the race being run under the $91\frac{1}{2}$-cubic-inch or $1\frac{1}{2}$-litre formula. The Amilcar qualified at 105.6 mph, this comparing favourably with the qualifying speed of Louis Chiron's $1\frac{1}{2}$-litre straight-eight GP Delage at 107.6 mph. However, the Delage did finish the race, in 7th place at 88.73 mph to the winning Miller's 97.58 mph.

The works Amilcars had many racing successes in the 'twenties, notably in the J.C.C. 200-Mile races at Brooklands in 1926, 1927 and 1928, and Amilcar Six successes continued into the 'thirties.

In 1926 it was decided to market a production version in limited quantities of the Amilcar Six, at the high selling price in England of £695. This car, known as the C6, had identical running gear to the works racing cars, but the chassis frame was wider and more robust, the engine was not so highly tuned and differed from the works engines in several respects, notably in having a detachable cylinder head and a plain bearing crankshaft, though with ball races at either end. The camshaft bearings were also plain white metal. Cylinder dimensions were 56×74 mm, 1094 cc, as on the MCO, but a smaller blower was fitted giving 10 lb pressure instead of 13 lb. Power output was originally quoted as 62 bhp at 5600 rpm.

There was no question of the engine and gearbox sharing the same oil on the Amilcar Sixes, in fact dry sump lubrication was adopted with a 12-litre (2 to $2\frac{1}{2}$ gallons effective capacity) oil tank situated at the front between the dumb irons. Some, though not all, of these tanks had cooling tubes. On the roller-bearing cars the oil tank had been beside the driver. Torque tube transmission was featured and a 4-speed gearbox, with reverse situated through the bottom gear position in the gate. A dry plate clutch was fitted.

Cam followers in the form of fingers were adopted, with caps on the valve stems. Shim adjustment could be used, although the thin shims tended to get hammered.

The C6 cars could be bought fully road equipped, although they did not seem to run with any success in the major sports car races of the 'twenties – no entries were made at Le Mans, until the 'thirties, and the two cars which ran in the 1929 Ulster TT driven by Vernon Balls and R.T. Horton both failed to finish.

All the Amilcar Sixes which came to England were of the C6 type and these were raced very successfully at Brooklands and in postwar events of the Vintage Sports-Car Club. The Brooklands cars underwent considerable development, to the extent that H.T.H. Clayton achieved his 120-mph badge on 16th October, 1937, by lapping at 121.47 mph in his ex-Major Gardner car, known as the Clayton-Amilcar.

Clayton raced two Amilcar Sixes at Brooklands, the Clayton-Amilcar with the chassis number 90016, registered as MPC 702, and 90009, registered as NPA 217. The latter car was fitted with special Amherst Villiers supercharger, and was previously raced by W. E. Humphreys. This car had longer springs fitted at the back to improve roadholding and a wide front axle, said to have been inspired by watching the behaviour of Frazer Nash cars cornering at the Fork turn in Brooklands Mountain Circuit races. Parts of these cars, including this axle, inevitably became interchanged and the engines were swapped, not only when Clayton raced them, but also after the war when they were owned by O.A.F. Finch and V.J. Hearn, 90009 is now owned by Bernard Harding, and its Villiers blown engine was actually fitted to the Clayton-Amilcar (now in the hands of J.B. Lyndhurst) when it achieved its 121.47-mph lap. The chassis of 90009 was chromium-plated by Humphreys.

A plain bearing car with a special single-seater body on an offset MCO chassis frame was developed by Henken Widengren (chassis no. 90030), and he took the Class G hour record at Montlhèry in it in 1933 at 115.32 mph. Later Paul Courtney raced it at Brooklands and Pat Green in early postwar V.S.C.C. events. When the body fell to pieces, Nigel Moores fitted two-seater bodywork. A similar body was fitted to two cars registered OXW 1 and OXW 2 and raced very successfully in V.S.C.C.

events by the Ecurie T.N.C. (Tozer, Narramore, Clutton), J.C.
Tozer winning the Vintage Seaman Trophy race in both 1954
and 1957. In 1974/5 Desmond Peacock raced a very well-turned-
out C6 built from spares, but did have some mechanical problems.

Michael May, a well-known competitor at Brooklands and
other venues before the war, produced some interesting memories
of the Amilcar Six in *Motor Sport* in 1948. Suspension, he said,
was virtually non-existent, the torque tube leaving the driver's
left thigh completely raw and bruised. Due to space limitations,
it was very difficult to fit an electric starter. When Vernon Balls
entered two Amilcar Sixes for himself and R.T. Horton to drive
in the 1929 TT (Balls led the race for a while until he crashed
and broke his collar bone), he had to recourse to 24 volts to make
the starters work, fitting small batteries under the seats.

May remembers that when A.S. Llewellyn was racing against
Basil Davenport's G.N. at Southport, his Amilcar threw No. 1
rod, which promptly jammed the steering. Fortunately the car
was going straight at the time, and there was plenty of room in
which to pull up.

Both in Britain and France there are still to be found devotees
of the Vintage French light sports cars epitomized by Amilcar
and Salmson, and catered for by the Amilcar and Salmson
Registers in England and Amicale Salmson in France. Others
still have happy memories of these cars. Each marque was very
successful, but Amilcar and Salmson tackled their design,
marketing and racing problems in a slightly different way. Probably the most suitable comment we can make today is 'Vive la
difference!'.

Type CC Amilcar

Chapter 4
AUSTRO-DAIMLER

One of the best, and most under-rated, of all sporting cars made in the Vintage period was the short-chassis ADM III or 19/100, Austro-Daimler. Historians will explain that the car was really a Porsche design, and whilst this is partly true the fact is that it became a much better car after Karl Rabe got at it than it ever would have been if Dr Porsche had stayed with Austro-Daimler through the 'twenties.

This needs a little explaining. Let us first consider Dr Porsche, and then the ADM III Austro-Daimler.

Dr Porsche receives, perhaps, too much adulation from the world of motoring. He was a man with a very fertile mind, an important and successful designer of engines and a keen sporting motorist, but he was not good at chassis design. Until he set up his own 'bureau' in 1930 he was not seen to produce a single car which had good handling, and that he did so after setting up his bureau was due not to his own efforts but to his intelligent choice of colleagues, notably Karl Rabe and many of the original Rumpler design team. He was, perhaps, a better co-ordinator than designer. Even then Porsche chassis designs were still influenced by his life-long obsession with a low polar moment of inertia, which means that the weight of the car is massed as much as possible about the centre point.

Porsche started life as an electrical engineer in Vienna, and his first invention to prove successful was the 'System Lohner-Porsche', the idea of electric motors in the wheel hubs powered by a petrol engine driving a generator. His first competition car, battery-driven with motors in the front hubs, was made in 1900 and since it had rear-wheel drum brakes as well as electrostatic braking available at the front wheels it could be said to have pioneered four-wheel brakes and front-wheel drive. The petrol-electric hub drive was used for heavy haulage in the First World War, and in his design for the 'Tiger' tank in World War II.

In 1905, at the age of 30, he joined Austro-Daimler and in 1906 became chief designer after Paul Daimler had returned to the German parent company. An interesting note here is that from 1905 to 1908 Austro-Daimler's main product was a car called the Maja. It is well known that the German Daimler Company's cars were known as Mercedes after their benefactor Mr Jellinek's elder daughter. It is less well known that the Maja was named after the younger Miss Jellinek.

In 1910 Porsche produced the famous 'Prince Henry' model, spurred by a moderately successful outing with the then current model in the 1909 Prince Henry trials. This 1910 car, with a very advanced 5.7-litre ohc four-cylinder engine developed from the Parseval airship engine which Porsche had designed earlier, was the first sports car in the present meaning of the term. With it Porsche won the 1910 Prince Henry trials, other Austro-Daimlers finishing in second and third places. The engine design was excellent, and served as the basis for successful aero engines produced by Austro-Daimler through the First World War.

During the war Porsche discovered, on his own shop floor, the man who was destined to become his right-hand man throughout his career, Karl Rabe. Directly after the war, car production was resumed at Austro-Daimler with a 4.4-litre ohc six, model 617, a pleasant and well-made quality car of no great interest except that with this car Porsche had already got close to the engine design which later became famous in the 'K' and 'S' series Mercedes – with engine and gearbox in unit, aluminium block/crankcase in one casting with dry liners, overhead camshaft and chassis-stiffening engine bearers.

This same layout was adopted for the ADM series, launched in 1923, from which the ADM III was developed, but in the meantime Porsche built a charming little sports racer of 1100 cc called the Sascha, after the colourful Count Sascha Kolowrat, who subsidized the making of this exciting little car at a time when the Austro-Daimler board were already becoming a little fed up with Dr Porsche's torrent of expensive ideas. The Sascha had a twin overhead camshaft four-cylinder engine, four wheel brakes and vestigial bodywork with a very high bonnet line. It was successful in competition, with 43 wins and 8 seconds from a total of 51 starts, but no examples appear to exist now, which is a pity. By the spring of 1923 the Austro-Daimler board finally lost

patience with Dr Porsche's continual changing of models and his
extravagant enthusiasm for racing, and he was given the sack
soon after their works driver, Fritz Kuhn, was killed testing a
2-litre car that Porsche was developing for the 1924 GP formula.

When Porsche left Austro-Daimler he went immediately to a
seat on the board of D.M.G., the German Daimler Company,
where, once again, he replaced Paul Daimler, who had now
moved on to the Horch Company. He left behind him at Austro-
Daimler, in the capable hands of Karl Rabe, the prototype
2½-litre ADM. The AD in standard form was a strong and reliable car, but by 1926 Rabe had developed the engine (which
was pure Porsche) and improved the chassis, notably with the
short-chassis version, to make the car which is the best-known
Vintage Austro-Daimler.

The short-chassis ADM III differs from the standard versions
in one important respect, it has semi-elliptic springs instead of
cantilevers, and this brings the whole car into balance. The long
chassis is virtually the same as the 1921 model 617, with a wheelbase of 3457 mm (136 in), whereas the short chassis at 2750 mm
(9 ft) is a real sports car.

The engine is a very clean design which has a great deal in
common with the Mercedes Benz of the same period, the main
difference being one of size. A 75 × 110-mm 3-litre six, the overhead camshaft is driven by a hefty vertical shaft at the rear of the
block, with spiral bevel gears at both ends and a skew gear take-
off in the middle for the magneto drive. Behind the drive gears
at the back of the cambox is the water pump, which draws water
from the block and pumps it through the head, with no other
passage between the head and block. This seems a very sound
idea; we wonder why the system is not used more often because
it ensures that cooling water flows everywhere. The fan is
mounted on the front of the camshaft, driven through a friction
clutch.

The cylinder head is conventional in design, with sparking
plugs on the inlet side together with two 36-mm Zenith triple-
diffuser side-draft carburettors. Porting is good, and there are
separate exhaust ports into a well-designed manifold. The block
is aluminium with liners held in by a lip at the top, and the
crankcase and mounting feet are in unit with the block, making
a rigid support for the 3-bearing crank. The rods are tubular,

and the whole bottom end is strong. One rather tiresome feature is that the head studs go right through the block to secure in the crankcase, an excellent way of doing it, but when a stud breaks halfway down its hole in the aluminium block there is an awful lot of electrolytically-corroded stud to get out. Lubrication, by plunger pump from an eccentric on the nose of the crank, gives plenty of pressure to the top and bottom end, and the spill from the camshaft feeds an oil bath to give plenty of lubrication to the magneto skew gears; a point which was often overlooked by designers who felt they had to have a skew drive. Bugatti was particularly thoughtless about this.

Transmission is through a single-plate clutch and ball-change gearbox to a torque tube and a well-braced rear axle. The steering gear is all a bit massive, with the drag link quite sharply angled to the fore-and-aft line. The front brakes are rather curious. The shoes are expanded by a wedge at the bottom. The wedge is attached to a spindle which passes up the centre of the king-pin. A short shaft passing through the outboard end of the axle, slightly offset from the centre line of the king-pin, has a lever at the outboard end which can depress the wedge spindle, and this shaft is turned by a lever at the inboard end and attached to the brake cable. Rather a complicated idea, but effective; the whole layout is so arranged that it is not affected by axle twist, and the system is well compensated.

The production version of the short-chassis cars had a distinctive body style. The driver sits very much inside the cockpit, the instrument panel and steering wheel are well back towards him, so that the door has to be hinged some way forward in the scuttle

Sascha Austro-Daimler — 1922 Targa Florio

side to allow him to get his legs in under the panel. The scuttle is shaped into two rounded cowls, the instrument panel following this shape, and the whole effect, from the driving position, is one of snug security which makes for a comfortable long-distance car.

It really is a delightful car to drive. The control is excellent, the gearbox sweet and with well-chosen ratios, the car feels taut and alive, and with three litres and 100 bhp it really is a very quick motor car, yet it has none of the rough, spartan feel of so many of the smaller high-performance cars of the period.

Karl Rabe was never satisfied with the handling, even though it was excellent by most standards, and in 1927 he introduced a completely new chassis design, the ADR, with the torque tube enormously enlarged to form a chassis backbone, to which was attached a large box-section fork at the front which passed either side of the engine to support the front suspension. The rear suspension had to be independent with this layout, and Rabe fitted swing axles with three leaf springs mounted across the car, one each side from the differential casing to the brake back plate, and one under the centre supporting the other two. The handling of this car is reputed to be even better than the ADM short chassis, and the two cars between them certainly won many competitions, chiefly hill climbs and sprints. Hans Stuck was the most successful driver of both models, and in 1930 he became European Hill Climb Champion in the racing class, ahead of a 2.3 Bugatti. Among many successes he broke the record at Shelsley Walsh with a time of 42.8 seconds, four full seconds quicker than Caracciola in the SSK Mercedes, a time which was unbeaten for three years. The engine of this car, remember, was virtually unchanged from Porsche's 1922 design. Remember, too, that Caracciola's Mercedes had an engine of almost identical design, but supercharged and twice as big, in a chassis which owed more to Dr Porsche than did the Austro-Daimler's.

Chapter 5
BENTLEY

The Bentley motor car was the motor car made by W.O. Bentley. He had help with the design from many other people, notably F.T. Burgess and Harry Varley, from Humber and Vauxhall respectively; he had a great gift for getting able men to help him to achieve his ambitions, but the car was W.O.'s and no one else's.

The Bentley car is truly the extension of one man's personality. It is also, perhaps, the most famous of all the Vintage cars, unquestionably the most famous of all British cars of that period, and one whose existence exactly spanned the period from its inception to its demise.

It is relevant, therefore, to study Bentley the man in order to understand the car. He was fascinated, as a child, by the great locomotive designs of the late nineteenth century, particularly those of the Great Northern Railway; the magnificent Stirling eight-foot Singles, and later the powerful Atlantic class. His apprenticeship at the locomotive works at Doncaster was in sharp contrast to his upbringing in a large, prosperous middle-class family in London, the youngest of nine.

His quietly aggressive, ambitious nature developed slowly. At the end of his apprenticeship, in his early twenties, he started to get interested in the internal combustion engine, had a number of successes in competition with motor cycles and then, with his brother, H.M., took on the agency for the French D.F.P. car in 1912, at the age of 24. He believed then, as he did throughout his

career, that competition success was the cheapest form of
advertising, and he set about achieving this in a determined
fashion. He had a rather uninspiring motor car to sell, but he
felt that the 2-litre model could be modified to go quickly enough
to achieve the competition successes he needed. In the pursuit of
this objective he did one extremely clever thing; he invented the
aluminium piston. Historians will no doubt prove that he did not
invent it at all (pointing, for example, to G.C. Cappa's Aquila
Italiana design of a few years earlier), and he certainly did not
invent the 12 per cent copper alloy which made such a piston a
practical proposition; that was developed at the D.F.P. foundry.
But credit must go to W.O. for using aluminium pistons to make
his D.F.P. go quicker than the opposition, and for pioneering the
use of aluminium pistons in the aero engines of World War I.

Encouraged by his pre-war successes, educated in internal
combustion engine design by his work with aero engines during
the war, desperately aware of the importance of reliability above
all else after getting to know many R.N.A.S. and R.F.C. pilots
who were killed during the war by engine failure over enemy
lines, he set out in 1919 to make a car to appeal to the rich
sporting motorist. His brother H.M. was still selling D.F.P.s,
which in the immediate postwar boom were selling like hot cakes,
and the money from this side of the partnership financed the
first year of development and construction of the new car. By the
time there were cars to sell, H.M. had sold the D.F.P. concession
and his sales organization was ready to market the Bentley.

The car which W.O. designed was very much in character
with the man himself, strong, reliable, aggressive in a refined
way, and as British as a bulldog. Nothing was left to chance, a
five-year guarantee was given with each car, and the customer
was unlikely to be disappointed.

The 3-litre Bentley, and particularly its successor the 4½-litre,
were in some degree out of character. W.O. did not like his cars
to be brutish or noisy, and if they were, it was the result of his
determination to advertise by success. The 6½, and most of all the
8-litre, were much more in character. These cars were designed
to carry luxurious coachwork, to be capable of very high cruising
speeds in great comfort and silence. The six-cylinder Bentleys
were the true W.O. Bentleys, and with the Speed Six, the 6½-litre
developed for competition, he came close to dispensing with

compromise, for in this he had the sort of car he had always wanted to make, and he had it bringing him the advertising value of competitions success. Certainly the six-cylinder Bentleys are large, heavy cars and they feel it at the wheel, but there are few, if any, other luxury cars of the late Vintage period which can honestly be said to be better cars than the 8-litres. In a curious way Bentley's obsession with competition success could have been his downfall; the marque had such a tremendous reputation for brute speed and power that many potential buyers of luxury Bentleys were frightened away to a less-sporting name like Rolls-Royce or Hispano-Suiza.

So much has already been written about the Bentley, the Bentley Boys, and all that, that it is perhaps unnecessary to go through it all in great detail.

The original design was virtually unchanged throughout the life of the make, the 6½-litre, 4½-litre and the 8-litre all having engines which were very similar in all their major points of design to the 3-litre. The 3-litre engine was a long-stroke four, a monobloc with integral cylinder head and well-separated bores, a water jacket which covered the top two-thirds of the cylinders being built-up round the block with aluminium plates. The cylinder head had 4 valves, inlet and exhaust valves at 30° to each other, operated by 3 cams for each cylinder, one each for the exhaust valve rockers and one inlet rocker, on the middle cam, pushing both inlet valves. The bore of 80 mm, with a stroke of 149 mm, gave the engine a cylinder head that was rather full of valves, and restricted the tuning potential, and it was not until the shorter stroke 4½, which had a bore of 100 mm, that the real tuning potential of the design was realized. From then on until the present day Bentley engines have been made to produce more and more power, as the enormous strength of the basic design is exploited.

The 4½ came later. In the heyday of the 3-litre, W.O. found that the huge success of the car had a curious and embarrassing side-effect. The Bentley had become the 'in' car, and people with money were buying them as town cars, and fitting them with wholly unsuitable saloon bodies. This was the cue for Bentley to make the car he had always wanted, the fast, discreet, quiet six-cylinder luxury car. The rather noisy camshaft drive of the four-cylinder cars was replaced by a curious device employ-

ing three connecting rods on eccentrics, and the engine was
rubber-mounted to reduce vibration. The prototype used the
bore of the 3-litre, the stroke being reduced to 140 mm, but this
proved to be slower than W.O. had hoped, and the production
car had a bore of 100 mm, giving 6597 cc.

The 3-litre, on beaded-edge high-pressure tyres, with the very
close-ratio 'A'-type gearbox, is a delightful sporting car, light and
responsive. A little noisy, perhaps, and it could be said that there
was really no need to have the gear ratios, particularly 2nd and
3rd, quite so close, but it is a difficult car to fault unless the
preference is for a smaller, more sophisticated design. The 3-litre
is not sophisticated from an engineer's point of view, it is as
honest and well-made a design as any of any period, and this is
its special charm.

The 3-litre, despite a series of misfortunes in competition, did
win twice at Le Mans (1924 and 1927), but W.O.'s intention to
advertise by competition successes had not worked out as well as
he had intended. The firm was in serious financial trouble by
1926, and W.O. had to approach one of his richest and most
sporting customers, Woolf Barnato, for money. Barnato coughed
up handsomely, and work started at once on a larger, beefier,
version of the 3-litre. The bore was increased to 100 mm, the
crankshaft strengthened and reduced in stroke to 140 mm, and
the weight of the complete car increased by some seven hundred
pounds. Undoubtedly a much faster car, the $4\frac{1}{2}$ had lost a lot of
the charm of the 3-litre, but it did prove a more successful car in
competition.

After two years of competition with the $4\frac{1}{2}$, W.O. felt that even
this design was not powerful enough to deal with the smaller but
more sophisticated machines with which it had to compete. His
first consideration in all his designs was reliability, and thus it
was against all his principles to increase the power output of a
given design if this could possibly be at the expense of reliability.
He was therefore thoroughly opposed to 'Tim' (later Sir Henry)
Birkin's plans to supercharge the $4\frac{1}{2}$-litre, Birkin, with the help
of Woolf Barnato who had become Chairman of Bentley Motors,
did persuade Bentley to produce the 50 supercharged cars
needed to get an entry for Le Mans, but W.O. was proved right.

The 'blower $4\frac{1}{2}$' was never the success that Birkin had hoped
it would be, for to perform satisfactorily it needed a sympathetic

driver and better than average maintenance and fitting, although the Amherts-Villiers supercharger itself was an exceedingly reliable instrument. Charles Amherst-Villiers also designed the special heavier crankshaft and connecting rods for the car, which produced 175 bhp at 3500 rpm compared with the 110 bhp at 3500 rpm of the unblown $4\frac{1}{2}$ Bentley. It cost £500 more than the standard unblown version.

So far as handling went, the extra weight of the supercharger at the front of the engine (where it gave approximately 8 lb boost) did make the car slightly nose heavy, though not disconcertingly so. Although a judiciously sited Bentley Drivers' Club or Vintage Sports-Car Club badge is permissible on a blower $4\frac{1}{2}$, a row of RAC, AA and Caravan Club badges in front of the radiator will invite overheating if the performance is to be used, despite the fact that a deeper radiator than that of the standard $4\frac{1}{2}$ is fitted. If full-throttle work is indulged in, the oil temperature, in particular, has to be watched.

Some driver skill is needed in operating the throttle, as if it is opened very suddenly, pops and bags from the engine will ensue. This is because the inlet manifold is about four feet long, and because it is so long a suddenly opened throttle causes a momentarily weak mixture. Thus if a quick change down is desired, it is best not to close the throttle completely when double declutching, but to keep the throttle open and allow the engine revs to increase of their own accord when the clutch is released and the gear lever put through neutral.

Also because of the long manifold, there is a fractional delay before the engine responds to the throttle both when it is opened and when it is closed, which may have provided good training for owners who were to be the future pilots of the early jet fighters.

The enthusiastic blower $4\frac{1}{2}$ driver, however, takes his car's mild vagaries in his stride, as he considers they are over-ridden by its advantages. A well-maintained and well-driven blower $4\frac{1}{2}$ is not by any means a blood-and-thunder car, with a screaming supercharger, bangings from the blow-off valves and oil all over the place. Instead, apart from the exhaust noise, it is a comparatively quiet car in normal use, giving a comfortable ride, yet with tremendous torque and a thrilling performance always on tap.

The tap, of course, is rather a large-bore one so that today the

blower 4½ Bentley is the delight of the oil sheikhs and the despair
of the conservationists. It is clear why W.O. did not like the car,
even though he volunteered to act as riding mechanic to Birkin
in one in the 1930 TT.

At the same time as the blower 4½ was being produced, W.O.
himself was pursuing his own logic, which told him that to make
a car go faster you must make it bigger. So he developed a racing
version of the 6½-litre luxury chassis. The first of these was an
immediate success, leading the line-ahead formation of four
Bentleys at the finish of the 1929 Le Mans, whereas the supercharged Birkin cars, though entered, were not ready in time for
the race.

The Speed Six, as the competition version of the 6½ was
known, weighs well over two tons, and has proved to be as
reliable and long-lasting as any competition car can be. The
8-litre, which first appeared at the 1930 Motor Show, was
brought to the public at a moment when Bentley Motors were
on the verge of liquidation, but it was a truly magnificent swan-
song. Based on the 6½, but improved in many ways, this is without
doubt the most underrated of all the Bentleys. This was the car
which satisfied all W.O.'s ambitions, and it was arguably the
best luxury car of its time, a far better car than the Phantom II,
and very much in the same category.

But Rolls-Royce survived, bought out Bentley Motors complete with W.O. himself, and took W.O. on to their staff, a sad
and disillusioned man; a virtual prisoner of Rolls-Royce Ltd.

A row of RAC, AA and Caravan Club badges in front of the radiator will invite
overheating

1930 Speed Six Bentley
engine
T.D. Houlding

A blower 4½ Bentley, complete with B.R.D.C., B.A.R.C., A.A. and R.A.C. badges,
plus some wire netting underneath, rolling out of the barrels at the Fork in a
Mountain race at Brooklands, *c.* 1935

Dashboard of a short chassis 'Brescia' Bugatti, T.13. The writing on the clock face
warns the driver to let the oil warm up for 10 minutes before driving at full speed
Neill Bruce

Mones Maury skidding in the 1922 French GP at Strasbourg in a Bugatti with the 'missing link' 3 main bearing T.30 engine exhausting out of the centre of the tail. Almost invisible is his riding mechanic, wearing a woolly hat

T.A.S.O. Mathieson

The most celebrated Type 35 engine, 2.3 litres supercharged   *T.D. Houlding*

Chapter 6
BUGATTI

'As an engineer Bugatti was inventive, ingenious and intuitive, but his formal engineering training was practically nil. He was self-taught, learning through intense powers of observation and a natural compatibility with mechanical objects. Above all he was an artist, and his cars disclose an aesthetic flair even more pronounced than his mechanical aptitude.'

This quotation, from Ronald Barker's 'Bugatti', sums up in the fewest words the remarkable quality that sets the Bugatti car apart from all others. How then do we set about a criticism of this most eccentric of all the really great Vintage cars? The problem is certainly not that there is nothing to criticize about the car; it is more that normal standards of criticism have to be modified for this one make if we are not seriously to underestimate it.

Bugattis are quite unnecessarily noisy. They are inclined to throw out a lot of oil; their clutches drag if they are not in perfect condition and alignment and even then can be upset if all four wheels are not on level ground. The lubrication system of the most-renowned models is unbelievably primitive; the flow of water through the radiator uses only half of the core, with the result that they overheat in traffic. Parts are seldom interchangeable without a lot of careful fitting; they have a reputation for unreliability which is perhaps undeserved, but stems from the absolute necessity for extraordinarily careful fitting. The combustion chamber, the heart of any design, leaves a lot to be desired and gives little opportunity for tuning.

On top of all this, the Bugatti is surrounded by a mystique that leaves all but the most devoted disciples floundering in a sea of meaningless type numbers.

First of all, then, let us examine the typical Bugatti and try to understand the reasons for its shortcomings and excuse these where we may. Then let us establish the other types of Bugatti in their chronological sequence, because the development is quite logical. Finally, we must go through the type numbers, because even if they are illogical they are the only labels we have.

All Bugattis had many features in common. They all had over-head camshafts and, with one exception in 1930, all Bugattis of the Vintage period had a single camshaft. All Bugattis from 1913 on had reversed quarter-elliptic rear springs. They all had four or eight cylinders – Bugatti never made a six. No Bugatti had a detachable cylinder head.

There were really two kinds of Bugatti engine, the ones that were rounded in appearance which normally had 4 valves per cylinder, and the ones that were square-cut in appearance which in single-cam form always had 3 valves per cylinder. The square-cut engines were first introduced in 1922, but it was not until 1924 that the typical Bugatti layout was evolved, and this layout remained virtually the same throughout the life of the firm.

Perhaps we may start at 1924, and work backwards and forwards from that point. In 1924 the classic Grand Prix Bugatti was introduced, and here we cannot avoid a type number, the 35. This was a 2-litre car (60 × 88 mm, 1991 cc), first raced at the French Grand Prix at Lyons, where the six cars entered had endless tyre trouble, and were in any case not fast enough for the opposition. Nonetheless, the car represented the peak of Bugatti's designs, and no other type had quite the same perfection of balance, either mechanically or aesthetically.

A description of this car can form a basis for them all. Starting with the chassis, the wheels were of the Bugatti cast-aluminium type for the first time. These wheels had two unusual features apart from their appearance; they were integral with the brake drums, so that the linings could be inspected when the wheels were changed, and they incorporated a clever split rim idea which trapped the bead of the beaded-edge tyres (710 × 90) so that in no circumstances could the tyre come off. The front axle was a very beautiful polished forging, made from a plain tube but so worked in the heat that when finished it was beautifully tapered and curved, with square holes through the forging for the semi-elliptic springs, which were located by wedges. Not a Bugatti invention – Fiat had certainly used this method of construction earlier – but a lovely thing to look at. The rear axle remained virtually unchanged throughout the history of the car.

The casing was vertically split, with axle trumpets extending to the hubs. Near the outboard end the reversed quarter-elliptic springs took the weight of the car through elongated eyes, location of the axle being arranged by two radius arms outside the chassis and a torque arm alongside the propellor shaft.

The axles are thus very well located, though the very stiff springs give a hard ride. The brakes on this and subsequent models were remarkably good. The old quote 'I make my cars to go, not to stop' must have been quoted out of context if Bugatti ever said it, but as with so much he designed the braking system must be in first class order if it is to work effectively. Fully compensated, geometrically excellent, the worst that can be said of the brakes is that if one cable breaks or if one of the clever pulleys above the king-pins should lift out of its socket, then total brake failure results. The original Bugatti shock absorbers were effectively a pre-loaded non-adjustable brake shoe in a small drum, though many owners, perhaps misguidedly, discarded them for Hartfords.

The chassis frame is of beautiful proportions and adequate strength, tapering gently from the centre to the ends and curving out to maximum width by the driver's seat. The engine, with four very rigid mounting feet, gives it a great deal of stiffness at the front. There are two curiously crude dropped cross-members to support the gearbox which are tubes split at the ends, the split half-tubes being flattened out to bolt to the top and bottom flanges of the chassis. No doubt this method of manufacture is effective enough but it is curiously unexpected on this car. Behind this are two angle iron cross members to support the seat and a fairly rigid tube between the rear shock absorbers. The front of the chassis, between the steering box and the axle, is thus very well stiffened, which contributes greatly to the road holding and steering precision. The rest of the chassis is left very much to its own devices.

The Bugatti gearbox is unusual in that the mainshaft and layshaft lie side-by-side. The constant-mesh gears are on the output shaft so that when double declutching only the gear cluster on the main shaft has to be speeded up or slowed down, which makes for a very sweet and quick gear change. The smaller constant mesh pinion is on the layshaft (19 to 27) so that the layshaft turns a lot faster than anything else. Unfortunately this

idea was not used on the later touring cars, which had a conventional layshaft driven from the input end, though it still lay
alongside the mainshaft. The gear lever and gate are mounted
on a cross-shaft at the right-hand side, the gate itself being very
small indeed. Gear changes can be made with one finger with
delightful precision.

Between the gearbox and the flywheel and clutch is a short
carden shaft with a wide flange at each end, not unlike an old-
fashioned cotton reel. The flange at the gearbox end transmits
the drive through a curious 'X' dog, the retaining bolts being
spring-loaded to allow for chassis distortion. Behind the gearbox
is an even more curious form of limited-movement universal
joint comprising a square block on the end of the output shaft
whose faces are cylindrically ground, which engages with a
brass-lined square 'box', open at the front end and attached to
the propellor shaft. This, Bugatti no doubt believed, had a
universal joint action, but it is geometrically unsound and only
works because of the very limited angularity it has to deal with.
This beautifully machined component epitomizes the whole
Bugatti philosophy 'if it looks right, it is right', and in this case
he was wrong.

The flywheel is a light cylinder, open at the rear end, of about
8-in diameter. Effectively, it is the clutch housing, and the
flywheel effect is minimal. The clutch within is multi-plate;
eight cast-iron discs and two rings are turned by six long bolts
which hold the clutch and plate to the front face of the flywheel.
Between these discs are nine steel plates with square holes in their
centres. These, when the cast-iron discs are squeezed up, turn the
square driven shaft, and the whole is designed to run in an oil/
paraffin mixture, which in fact leaks out fairly quickly. The
main disadvantage of this system is that the loading on the four
corners of the square shaft, and on the six driving bolts, is very
high and wear tends to be localized, making the clutch disin-
clined to free. Engagement is by two short pegs which pass
through the clutch and plate to press on the rear cast-iron ring.
They are made to press in by a form of over-centre device,
though when properly adjusted the device is not quite over
centre when it is exerting full pressure. Almost impossible to
describe on paper, erroneously described as 'centrifugal', this
system does result in a very light clutch pedal. When all is

property aligned and adjusted, and unworn, the clutch is very pleasant to use; when out of alignment or worn it can be very difficult indeed.

This brings us to the engine, which has two absolutely square-cut four-cylinder blocks of cast iron, surmounted by one square-cut aluminium cam box, sitting on an aluminium crankcase. The biggest and strongest part of the engine is the sump, with which are incorporated four wide engine mounting feet. The sump has a number of large oil cooling tubes through the length of the bottom of it (whose effectiveness is doubtful), but its main function is to give rigidity to the chassis and the rest of the engine. The rest of the engine can be pulled out of this sump, revealing a massive crankshaft carried on three double-row ball bearings and two split roller races. Each of these bearings runs on a short journal with which is incorporated either one large concentric disc and one massive crankpin (at each end), or two discs, one either side of the bearing, each carrying an equally massive crankpin (for the other three bearings). Thus there are eight discs and eight crankpins. The end of each crankpin is joined to its next-door neighbour by a substantial rectangular block of steel. The block of steel is drilled near each end to accept the two crankpins which are secured to the block by cotter pins, exactly as a bicycle pedal crank is secured to its cross-shaft. As with a bicycle pedal shaft the crankpin has a flat on it and the cotter pin has a tapered flat. The true alighment of the whole assembly is determined by the angle of this tapered flat. Since the centre main bearing is a ball race, the centre main journal is split with a conventional taper and key. There are thus eighteen individual component parts of the crankshaft, not counting the nuts. To take this assembly to pieces is difficult enough, because the cotters get very tight and must be freed with calculated brutality, but the job of re-assembly, if all the crankshaft is to finish up in perfect alignment (as it must – there is no tolerance with ball and roller bearings) takes a very great deal of time, patience and skill.

The main reason for this multi-piece shaft is to allow roller-bearing rods to be used, which do not have split big-ends. And the main reason for having ball and roller races throughout is because of Bugatti's lubrication system. The oil pump supplies oil under moderate pressure to a series of jets, each of them mounted in the side of the crankcase and directed into a narrow undercut in the face of each of the eight discs. This undercut is machined right round at about half the total diameter of the disc, on the side away from the crankpin. At the point where the undercut is behind the crankpin there is a small drilling through to the centre of the big-end bearing surface. The undercut acts as an excellent centrifugal filter, and collects any dirt or carbon in the oil, so that it needs fairly regular cleaning out if the oil hole to the big-end is not to get blocked.

This really is a most extraordinary way of dealing with a problem which Bugatti gave himself by refusing to accept the virtues of a pressure-fed crankshaft. We have to agree that it works, and when properly set up a very rigid crankshaft results, but what a complicated way to do it!

The eight-cylinder Bugatti crankshaft is not unlike two normal four-cylinder crankshafts at 90° to each other. The first 4 crank throws are in one plane, 1 up, 2 down, 3 up and 4 down, and the other four are the same, but in the horizontal plane. The firing order for each half is numerical, giving the unique (and curious) firing order 1.5.2.6.3.7.4.8. If the crankshaft was less rigid and well supported some fierce vibrations would have shown themselves, as they do in the earlier 3-bearing Bugatti eight.

The connecting rods are well proportioned, made of case-hardening steel and hardened in the big-end eye, where the rollers run directly in the rod, as they do on the crankpin, with no separate races. The pistons are flat-topped and conventional, the combustion space is cylindrical with the plug at one side, and the only interesting feature is the use of two inlet valves. They are of smaller area than one valve would have been, but the layout has two advantages; it allows for a larger exhaust valve and it gives good gas velocity at low speed, thereby improving the torque. Having said that, however, it must be admitted that the general design of the top half of the engine is uninspiring. To quote Pomeroy, 'There can have been few successful racing engines which have run with so little water in contact with so many hot spots'.

That the car was so successful was because of the excellent roadholding, because of the rigidity of the bottom half of the engine, and in spite of that part of the engine which is usually regarded as its heart. The power output was unremarkable but for its day the car handled so well and proved so reliable, that it was capable of winning races from cars with much more powerful engines.

The type 35 was developed from the 1½-litre four-cylinder car which Bugatti first put on the market in 1910. This four-cylinder car had developed by 1914 into a very successful all-rounder, capable of winning races in short-chassis form, or carrying comfortable family tourer coachwork in long-chassis form. It is typical of Bugatti type number confusion that no less than five type numbers cover this one model, the numbers referring only to differences of wheelbase – but more of that later. Let us call it the Brescia, which is what the car was known as after the 1-2-3-4 win in the Voiturette Grand Prix at Brescia in September, 1921. The victory was perhaps something of a hollow one, the only other cars to finish being the rather slow and heavy O.M.s, but it demonstrated the speed and reliability of the car – only four had been entered – in a very satisfactory way.

The chassis layout was similar to the T.35, though the front axle was conventional, and the rear springs were parallel, whereas on the 35 the rear springs tapered in towards the rear. The rear axle was located only by the springs, no radius arms being fitted, though axle torque was taken care of, as on the T.35, by means of a torque arm. The stiffening feet of the engine were part of the crankcase, not the sump. The engine layout was similar (but without the classic square-cut external lines) except for the crankshaft, rods (plain bearing), tappets and valve layout. The crankshaft in the case of the true Brescia was a two-piece design with three main bearings, the centre and rear mains having ball races and the front main a plain bearing. Cars before the Brescia race had a one-piece plain bearing crank with the exception of some pre-First World War cars, and the touring (long-chassis) versions continued with the plain bearing engine until 1923. Lubrication was on the lines of the T.35 with the added complication that the oil pump was mounted high on the front of the camshaft and had to be primed by hand with an oil-can before starting the engine.

The most interesting feature of the engine, not continued after this model, was the tappet arrangement. Faced with a central camshaft and two rows of valves either side of the centre line (4 valves to each cylinder), Bugatti devised a method of pushing the valves down without rockers. He made a banana-shaped tappet which pushed on the valve vertically but curved across towards the camshaft, effectively meeting the cam at 5 o'clock or 7 o'clock. The problem of guides for these tappets was neatly overcome by casting white metal round them *in situ*.

Bugatti was in many ways a conservative man, and like many other designers of the period he was distrustful of front-wheel brakes, which were not introduced for the Brescia until 1925, a year after the Type 35.

In 1922 Bugatti made what might be called the 'missing link', a car with an eight-cylinder, 60 × 88-mm square-cut engine but with the Brescia chassis and with the bottom half of the engine something of a compromise. The crankcase carried the engine mounting feet, and also carried the three ball races which were all that the eight-cylinder, two-piece, plain big-end crankshaft had to support it. The whole crankshaft, bearings and all, was threaded into the crankcase from the flywheel end. A plain sump was fitted to the bottom.

The three-bearing crankshaft was not really strong enough, especially with the vibration periods to which it was subject with the same crankpin layout and firing order as the Type 35. Several racing versions of this car were made, and some of them had primitive intermediate 'main bearings' in the form of bronze rings concentric with the disc webs between number 2 & 3 and number 5 & 6 crankpins. These rings came into contact with the crank webs only in the event of quite serious crankshaft distortion, but when they did the rubbing speed must have been phenomenal. That they had a job to do is evident from inspection of the hefty scores on the only example known to be still in existence. Lubrication was by the same jet system used in the Brescia and the T.35.

From the crankcase upwards the engine was more or less interchangeable, apart from smaller valves, with the Type 35 (although some racing versions did have bigger valves and two plugs per cylinder), and since this was the least exciting part of the 35 we may understand why this 'missing link' was not, by Bugatti standards, an inspiring car. One further comment in passing was that with this car Bugatti experimented for two years with hydraulic brakes, which were not a great success.

We have now returned in time to the Type 35, which formed the basis for all subsequent Bugattis of the Vintage period except for the fabulous 'Royale' and two other large-capacity cars.

The Type 35 originally had a 60 × 88, 2-litre engine to comply with the current Grand Prix formula. During its first year (1924) the car was in competition with well-organized teams from Sunbeam, Fiat and Alfa Romeo, all of them supercharged. These cars, and the unblown V12 Delages, were very much more powerful than the Bugattis, and it is a telling tribute to the extraordinarily controllability of the car that Friderich finished second by a fairly small margin from Segrave's Sunbeam on the rough and twisty San Sebastian Grand Prix course, though Bugatti had been hopelessly outclassed (and also dogged by tyre trouble) on the faster Lyons circuit earlier. This, however, was the last time Bugatti competed seriously in the 2-litre formula which petered out in 1925. During 1925 Bugatti gained the first of a series of wins in the Targa Florio, and demonstrated reliability rather than speed in other races, though 1½-litre versions of the car which were produced during the year had notable successes whether running as sports or racing cars. He also proved his claim that his racing cars were the same as the cars he offered for sale, and more and more Bugatti successes came from private entries. During 1926 Bugatti at last accepted that a supercharger would be a good idea and from then on his successes started to increase. The formula for 1926 called for 1½ litres, so the first supercharged cars were of 1½ litres, except for a team of 1100-cc supercharged cars which ran unopposed in the GP d'Alsace. 2-litre cars with superchargers appeared before the end of the season, which was Bugatti's most successful ever, with six Grand Prix wins and the Targa Florio, for which he had increased the capacity of the unblown car to 2.3 litres (60 × 100 mm). The blown 2.3 Bugatti, the most famous version of them all, was introduced in 1927.

In 1926, however, Bugatti had introduced two new engines for the car. The first was more of a throwback. The Type 35 was a very expensive car at £1250, so a cheap version was made using the crankshaft of the 1922 'missing link', running on three ball-race main bearings in what was otherwise a T.35 engine. The other new engine, a four-cylinder, was more of a step forward. The top half was similar to one half of the T.35, but slightly larger at 69 × 100 mm, giving 1486 cc. The bottom half consisted of a similar sump/crankcase design to the T.35 which

contained a strong 5-bearing crankshaft with circular webs, but
with no balls or rollers anywhere. The lubrication started off on
the usual spit-and-hope principle, but was later converted to a
proper pressure-fed crankshaft system. After eighteen months of
production in unblown form the later models of these 1½-litre
cars were supercharged.

During the same year he also introduced two new chassis
designs. They were not really so much new, as adaptations of the
1922 car's chassis, and they were similar to each other. One was
a touring chassis to carry the cheaper, 3-bearing version of the
2-litre T.35 engine, the other was a shorter chassis to carry the
new 5-bearing four-cylinder engine.

The longer chassis was also sold from 1927 with the 2.3-litre
blown T.35 engine. This was a very much more satisfactory car
than the plain bearing 2-litre version, and apart from a less
pleasant gearbox than the racing version, and inevitably a
heavier feel, it was, and still is, a very pleasant and exciting car
to drive.

A further permutation on the theme came out at the end of
1927 with an eight-cylinder version of the 69 × 100 four, giving
3 litres and a 9-bearing crankshaft in a longer chassis. A new
feature of this 9-bearing crankshaft was a far more logical crankpin and firing order layout, easily achieved because the shaft was
machined from a solid billet. The four centre crankpins were in
one plane, and the pairs at each end were at right angles to the
middle four, which gives a firing order of 1.6.2.5.8.3.7.4. The
shaft was joined by a taper in the middle, and the camshaft
vertical drive was taken off at this point, between the two
cylinder blocks. This arrangement makes for much smoother
running, and this car, and a more refined version which came
out in 1930 with 16 plugs and 3.3 litres, were the least noisy of
the range and the most docile.

One last complication was that in 1930 the four-cylinder
5-bearing tourer was given all the specifications of the 16-plug
3.3-litre car, so that it then had 8 plugs, a capacity of 1⅔ litres,
and a ball gear change.

To summarize, the Brescia chassis was used (with various
modifications) on all the touring cars, and all the racing cars
from 1924 used the T.35 chassis. The roller bearing crankshaft
was only used on T.35 cars and one touring car, the other touring

cars having either the Brescia engine, the 3-bearing 8, or derivatives of the 5-bearing 4.

We may now give these cars their numbers: –

'Brescias'	T.13	Short chassis, 2.0 metres
	T.23	Long chassis, 2.55 metres
	T.22	Rare, intermediate, 2.4 metres (same as T.35)
'Missing link'	T.30	Most racing versions had T.22 chassis. Others T.23 chassis or longer.
'T.35'	T.35	Unblown $60 \times 88 = 2$ litres
	T.39	Unblown $1\frac{1}{2}$ litre (normally 60×66)
	T.35T	Unblown $60 \times 100 = 2.3$ litres
	T.39A	Blown $60 \times 66 = 1\frac{1}{2}$ litres
	T.35C	Blown $60 \times 88 = 2$ litres
	T.35B	Blown $60 \times 100 = 2.3$ litres
	T.43	T.35B engine in T.38 chassis
	T.43A	As T.43 but different bodywork
'3-bearing crank'	T.35A	As T.35 except for crankshaft
	T.38	Same engine but touring chassis
'5-bearing crank and derivatives'	T.37	69×100, $1\frac{1}{2}$ litres, T.35 chassis body
	T.37A	As T.37, supercharged
	T.40	Same engine unblown, touring chassis
	T.40A	72×100 engine, $1\frac{2}{3}$ litres, 8 plugs
	T.44	Similar to T.40, but 8 cylinders, 9 main bearings, longer chassis
	T.49	As T.44 but 72×100, 3.3 litre, 16 plugs and 'refinements'.

This covers all the 'ordinary' Bugattis. There are three left, apart from one or two rare racing specials, like the 16-cylinder cars made in 1928. These are the T.41, T.46 and T.50.

The T.41 is, of course, the Royale. So much has been written about this eight-cylinder, 125×130-mm, 12 763-cc car that we may be excused from doing it all over again. M. Schlumph has two of them, Harrah in Nevada has two, the Ford Museum has one and Briggs Cunningham has one, so unless you are an old friend of one of these you are unlikely ever to drive one. However, the T.46 is effectively a scaled-down version of the T.41, and the T.50, apart from the innovation of twin overhead camshafts and

two plugs per cylinder, is apparently a direct development of the
T.46, though both were on sale together in the 'thirties.

A description now of the T.50. First, the gearbox is in the rear
axle. Second, the engine has no chassis-bracing mounting feet.
Third, the cylinder-block casting is extended downwards to
include the upper half of the nine plain main bearings, so that
one casting incorporates the cylinder head, the bores and the
crankcase. A big sort of open-top aluminium packing case
encloses the bottom half of the engine, aluminium side plates
keep the water in the block, and aluminium cam boxes surmount
the two rows of valves, set at 90°. Thus the engine appears to be
made largely of aluminium though, in fact, all its strength comes
from cast iron. This is an 86 × 107-mm 5-litre supercharged
eight, and a very powerful engine indeed. The cylinder head,
probably copied from the Miller design, became the pattern for
all Bugatti designs of the 'thirties, and was an improvement on
the three vertical-valve layout. It is surprising, therefore, that
the twin-cam development of the T.35B which was introduced
in 1931 as the T.51 is not significantly faster than the 35B in
current competition. Perhaps the blown 2.3 single-cam engine
gave out as much power as the chassis could reasonably cope
with, or perhaps the T.35Bs now in competition are better prepared or driven than the twin-cam T.51s.

The T.46 was very similar to the T.50. The engine had a
longer stroke (81 × 130 mm = 5.3 litres), single camshaft, and
was normally unblown. The blown version was known as the
T.46A. The main difference between the two cars is that the
T.46 was a relatively gentle, quiet and refined car – desperately
noisy by Rolls-Royce standards, but silent by Bugatti's. The
T.50 was intended to be the touring version of a racing car, and
is a much more raucous beast.

This dissertation on Bugatti is by no means complete, and it
covers only the cars made in the Vintage period, but from it one
or two conclusions may be drawn. Because Bugatti was inventive,
unrestricted by hidebound engineering dogma, untrained, a
perfectionist and an artist, he made a range of unique cars. Their
biggest virtue is the feel of precision which even the most insensi-
tive motorist cannot fail to appreciate. To maintain this feel the
car must be very carefully looked after, and this involves the
most painstaking workmanship.

The range of machine tools available to Bugatti, and even perhaps his knowledge of machine tool usage, was limited. There is evidence throughout the car that he made do with methods of manufacture which would have been unacceptable elsewhere. He got away with these methods (square shafts instead of splined shafts for example) only because whatever he did, he did to such fine tolerances and with such careful fitting.

A reputation for unreliability which is perhaps undeserved

Chapter 7
DELAGE

Very little has been written about Louis Delage or his cars, and this account of the man and his work starts at the beginning because his story cannot really start logically with the Vintage period, but must work its way right through.

Louis Delage was one of the greatest of all the great names of the Vintage period. He was a brilliant constructor of motor cars, a ruthlessly efficient businessman, but he also had an endearingly eccentric nature which showed up early in his career, and eventually brought about his downfall.

Born in Cognac in modest circumstances, educated as an engineer, he started work with the very early racing-car constructors, Turgan-Foy, whose two-cylinder Filtz engine had the most curious crankshaft arrangement: two vertical crankshafts geared at the top to a third vertical shaft transferred the drive at its base, through a pair of bevels, to the back of the motor car. But this was around 1899. He then spent several years with Peugeot, left them in 1905, having found financial backers and having taken Peugeot's chief designer, Legros, with him, to start up on his own. From the beginning he was successful. His first appearance in racing was in the 1906 Coupe des Voiturettes, which was a five-day reliability run (200 kilometres a day) and a race on the sixth day. He entered two cars, one crashed on the fifth day, and the other came second in the race, propelled by a 9-hp de Dion engine.

His entry of three cars in 1907 was less successful, but for the 1908 GP des Voiturettes he had originally intended to fit his cars with a new engine design by a young engineer called Nemorin Causan. There was trouble with the development of this engine, so Delage ordered three special de Dion engines to be prepared for his cars. Near the time for the race the Causan engine was becoming more reliable and, on the insistence of Guyot, one of Delage's drivers who was the Delage agent at Orléans, this engine was fitted to Guyot's car. Guyot won the race easily, and the Marquis de Dion approached Louis Delage with a deal. If Delage allowed de Dion to claim that Guyot's car had a de Dion engine, Delage could have his three special engines free, and a discount of 5 per cent on the engines for his production cars. Without hesitation, Delage ditched poor Causan and accepted de Dion's deal.

By 1910 Delage was making production cars with his own engines, a 2-litre four-cylinder and a 2½-litre six (66 × 130 mm), but for the 1911 Couple de l'Auto race he made a special four-cylinder, 3-litre of 80 × 149 mm, a popular size used later by, for example, Bentley. This was a very advanced, low-built car with five forward gears, horizontally opposed push-rod-operated valves in what an architect would call a clerestory head, and very good handling. One of these cars is still in regular use in England, and it really is a very pleasant, effortless touring car, capable of cruising all day on the motorway (or anywhere else if it is legal) at 70 mph and a leisurely 1800 rpm. The gear positions take a little getting used to, but the steering, the overall balance of the car and the performance would do credit to a car many years younger.

Bablot's Delage won the 1911 Coupe de l'Auto race, with Thomas and Guyot third and fourth to Boillot's Peugeot. Delage rested on his laurels in 1912, and got on with the business of selling motor cars and making money, but in 1913 he entered a team for the French Grand Prix, which he did not win, with a 6.2-litre car very similar to the 1911 design. It was at the end of this race that the financier Alphonse Clement came up to Louis Delage, who had previously asked him for financial help, and said that on the strength of the day's successes he was prepared to put money into Delage's company. The next week Legros brought a long shopping list of machinery needed in the factory, which they could now afford. Delage told him to forget the shopping list. He had already spent the money on a great Château which he had coveted for some time.

Delage could afford to be conceited, extravagant, even arrogant. He was a self-made man, not at all good-looking, with only one eye that worked, the other giving him an appalling squint. But he was a brilliant engineer and a very astute business-man, and he had no doubt about his ability to pay off the

Château and buy the machine tools Legros wanted.

Two of the 1913 Grand Prix cars went to America in 1914, managed by W.F. Bradley, and there René Thomas won the Indianapolis 500. One of these cars is still in America, in great shape and excellent voice. A splendid car.

Meantime, Delage had developed a much more elaborate engine for the 1914 Grand Prix at Lyon. This was a very elegant twin-cam 4½-litre (94 × 160 mm) design with 4 valves per cylinder at 90°, each valve with a separate port, operated in pairs by a desmodromic apparatus for closing the valves as well as opening them. A fully counterbalanced crankshaft with five large-diameter ball or roller bearings were carried in a split crankcase; 4-bolt tubular rods carried short aluminium pistons, the gudgeon pins located by a through-pin in the piston, not the little-end. Because of the desmodromic arrangement the cam-shafts were quite a long way apart, and the vertical drive shaft from a reduction gear at the front of the crankcase transmitted the camshaft drive to a cross-shaft via bevel gears, all enclosed in beautifully shaped aluminium housings. This engine really was an engineering *tour-de-force*, developed by Michelat, then Delage's chief designer. The chassis had four wheel brakes, Perrot at the front, a 5-speed gearbox mounted some way behind the cone clutch on separate, integral chassis cross-members, and at the back of the gearbox was a transmission brake. Suspension was semi-elliptic all round, the chassis was fairly shallow but nicely shaped and well braced; it had a great deal in common with the postwar designs, which are a joy to handle. The rear axle was light and simple, two trumpets attached to a vertically-split, drum-shaped differential housing, the whole axle braced by a tie-rod underneath. The brakes were exceptionally large for the period, the rear drums larger than the front, some 16 in and 14 in respectively.

This car, of which an example is now undergoing restoration in Australia, was not a success in the 1914 Grand Prix. It is tempting to suggest it could have been a match for the Mercedes if there had been more time to develop the engine, but there is no evidence to support this idea. Barney Oldfield raced the car, now in Australia, in the USA in 1915 and 1916, and although he finished fifth in the Indianapolis 500 in 1916, he never won an important race with it and it was said that its mechanical

The touring bodied version of the two 1922 5-litre pushrod Delage hill climb Specials seen at the start of Mont Ventoux hill climb in 1924

1928 DIS Delage with boat tail Kelsch bodywork. The original North East oval switch panel on this car, as on many others, has been replaced by a more satisfactory one, in this case a C.A.V.   *Neill Bruce*

Single-seater Model T racer with a 16-valve, single o.h.c. head by the Speedway Engineering Co. of Indianapolis. This car is domiciled in England, and used to be raced on Southport sands *Roger McDonald A.I.I.P.*

Beauty and the Beast, but which is which must be decided by the reader — a 1925 Anzani Frazer Nash berthed alongside a 1930 Phantom II Rolls Royce
Thomas Richards

problems cancelled out its speed whilst it was in his hands.

The Delage factory, started at Levallois, took on additional and much larger premises at Courbevoie in 1910. During the First World War this factory was fully occupied with war work, and as soon as the war was over car production started again.

The first postwar models were 4½-litre six-cylinder side-valves, the very 'clean' lines characteristic of all postwar Delage engines were already apparent, and four-wheel braking, two carburettors and electric starting were standard. This car bred a cheaper, four-cylinder 3-litre version in 1920 which did not have four-wheel brakes as standard (they were an optional extra), but this was soon superseded by the 2120-cc side-valve 'DE', which did have front-wheel brakes and was close in type to the later pushrod 'DI' series.

In 1922 Delage's mind was back on the idea of advertizing by competition. Prudently, he felt that the time was not yet ripe for the expense of a racing team, so he constructed a pair of hill-climb and sprint specials, one in racing form, the other in touring car trim. With these two cars he hoped to gain publicity by breaking records at the many hill-climb and sprint events throughout Europe. Both cars had engines based on the 'CO' 4½-litre six, but they had pushrod-operated overhead valves and were bored out to 85 mm, giving 5 litres. The racing car had a similar chassis to the 2-litre production car, but with a 9-ft wheelbase, some 9 in shorter than the 2-litre chassis, and more than 2 ft shorter than the current six-cylinder production car.

It might be thought that with such a large, tall (150-mm stroke) engine in such a short chassis the handling would be twitchy, but in fact this car, which is still very much a runner, handles extremely well. It is, perhaps, a little top-heavy under fierce cornering, and lifts the inside rear wheel fairly readily, but it is totally predictable and has never given its driver a moment's anxiety. A very fast car by any standards, it held a comfortable 113 mph over a twenty-mile stretch of autoroute near Lyon in 1974, and has been timed in speed trials at 120 mph in the 1920s and the 1960s.

Delage entered this car, which was known as *La Torpille* because of its torpedo-like shape, in every hill climb and sprint event which it could be taken to during the three years 1922 to 1924, and during that time it gained valuable publicity, breaking a total of 32 course records.

In 1923 a lot was happening at Courbevoie. The overhead-valve 14/40 'DI' model (75 × 120 mm) was introduced, as was an overhead-valve version of the six-cylinder car, known as the CO_2 and, on the competitions side, two V12-cylinder cars were made.

One was effectively a big version of *La Torpille*, with an engine which had most of the features of the earlier six, but with twelve separate cylinders of 90-mm bore, giving $10\frac{1}{2}$ litres. This car broke the Land Speed Record at 143.31 mph in 1924, only to have the record taken away shortly afterwards by Eldridge's *Mephistopheles*, and did well in a few relatively straight hill-climb attempts. Later it had a successful career at Brooklands, particularly in the hands of John Cobb, and it was revived by Cecil Clutton for V.S.C.C. racing after the war.

The other V12 was a much more exciting design. A Grand Prix 2-litre, it was designed and built by Plancton, then the Delage chief designer, in only four months. The reason for choosing twelve cylinders for only 2 litres (the GP formula from 1922 to 1925) has been well explained by Pomeroy. Compare a twelve-cylinder engine with a four-cylinder engine of the same capacity, with the same bore/stroke ratio, at the same piston speed and the same B.M.E.P. figure. The twelve-cylinder engine has a 44 per cent increase in piston area and a 45 per cent increase in revolutions per minute under these conditions which, according to the PLAN (B.M.E.P. × stroke × piston area × revs) equation gives nearly 45 per cent more bhp. The logic is inescapable. The complexity of such an engine, however, is also inescapable, and the Delage design cut no corners anywhere; it was probably the most complicated engine ever made for a motor car (except for the V16 B.R.M.?), especially when, redesigned by Lory, it was supercharged in 1925. It then had a timing train of twenty-one pinions to drive the four camshafts, two magnetos, two water pumps, two superchargers and the oil pump; roller bearings supported the camshafts between each cam; the crank-shaft was one-piece, machined from the solid, yet all main- and big-end bearings were rollers, entailing very careful assembly of the split big-ends and main-bearing caps. The only plain bearings in the whole engine were in the oil pump.

Delage's works were substantial, covering some twelve acres;

he employed 2000 workers and had some 1500 machine tools, many of which were designed and built by Delage. Output of cars was over 3000 a year, but the cost to the firm of the racing department must have been very considerable indeed.

To complete the racing story of the company, they were fully committed to Grand Prix racing by 1924. The first appearance of the 2-litre V12 was in 1923, but with a completely untried engine it was no surprise that it only lasted a few laps of the French Grand Prix at Tours. For 1924 they were well prepared, and Lory had made a number of alterations and improvements to the Plancton design. Although superchargers had been tried on the cars before the European Grand Prix at Lyon, they ran unblown in that race, finishing 2nd, 3rd, and 6th in a race dominated by supercharged cars. For 1925 they were supercharged, and this raised the power output from 130 to 190 bhp at 7000 rpm (3675 ft/min piston speed, close to the limit). The rewards in 1925 were 1st and 2nd and fastest lap in the French GP at Montlhèry and a 1-2-3 victory in the Spanish GP.

The 1925 season had seen the end of the 2-litre formula. For 1926 the famous 1½-litre straight eight was produced, to Lory's design. This was again a very complex unit, full of ball and roller bearings and in an improved, lower chassis. The 1½-litre GP Delage has rightly been regarded as one of the classic racing cars of all time. In 1926 it had teething troubles, not least of which was a tendency to roast the driver, but by 1927 it had become by far the most advanced and successful racing car of its time, reliable, and developing 113 bhp per litre, which was later increased to the remarkable figure of 130 bhp per litre. In the 1960s, at any rate, it could be dogmatically stated that this engine had the best gas-flow characteristics of any engine of any period, and it was in every respect a winner.

The 1½-litre GP Delage represented the zenith of all that Louis Delage had worked for. It was the culmination of his racing car designs from the 1911 Coupe de l'Auto onwards; each fresh design, though generally produced by a different designer, was still a close relative to its predecessor. The 1914 GP and the 1927 GP cars had a surprising number of detail similarities and there is no doubt that, whoever was the designer, each was a child of Louis Delage's mind. The 1927 car was very 'modern' by Vintage standards; with relatively little torque at low revs the five gears

were all needed; but the handling was exceptionally good, the
very low centre of gravity and the excellent balance which is a
feature of most Delages contributing to this.

One other racing Delage should be mentioned; the successor
to *La Torpille*. This is a curious story. The original 1922 car had
been so successful, and had become so well known by the general
public by 1924 that even now, when this car goes back to France,
old men from all walks of life come up to it and say 'Ah! *La
Torpille!* I remember seeing this car at so-and-so in 1924.' The
publicity value of this one car was enormous, and by the end of
1924 Delage was faced with a dilemma. The car was unlikely to
be fast enough to go on getting fastest time at every meeting in
1925, but to make a new car would mean starting all over again
with the public; it would mean introducing a new 'star' to them.
Improvements were needed in many parts of the design, and it
seemed impractical to 'hot-up' the old car, so they came up with
a crafty compromise. They made a completely new car with a
much more powerful, twin-cam, Lory-designed 6-litre engine,
bigger brakes, and other alterations, but they disguised it to look
almost exactly like the 1922 car. They then claimed that it was
in fact 'La Torpille', the original car. Forty years later René
Thomas, Delage's racing manager, wrote emphatically in a
letter 'Donc de là est née La Torpille, c'était son nom. Elle n'a
été que d'un *seul* examplaire' (his italics). So he even fooled
himself. The bluff was called when the two cars were bought in
1928 by Captain Alastair Miller and brought to England, where
they raced at Brooklands side by side, the 6-litre car being called
'Delage I' and the 5-litre car 'Delage II', which is chronologic-
ally confusing. In fact the 6-litre car was unable to continue the
5-litre car's winning streak; it was faster but less well-balanced
and met with only intermittent success, and hardly competed at
all after 1925.

'Revenons à nos moutons', in the delightful French phrase, we
come back to the more ordinary motors of the period. The pushrod 2-litre became the mainstay of the firm's production until
1927, while the 4½-litre six continued in production probably
until 1926 when the 3-litre six, which was a direct development
of the 2-litre, superseded it.

Throughout the period, however, Delage had on sale his great
luxury car, the 'GL' or Grande Luxe' This, and its short-chassis

sporting version known as the GS, are rare birds. No expense was spared to make this the ultimate in luxury cars. The first two or three cars had 7-litre engines, but from 1924 the capacity was 6 litres (95 × 140 mm) with an overhead camshaft, 12 ft 10 in wheelbase, and every possible sophistication. To give a few examples of the sort of details which were incorporated in the car, the fan, which was gear-driven from the front of the camshaft vertical drive, carried an adjustable clutch which was controlled by a small lever on the dash panel, and the dash panel itself, incorporating instrument bosses, pockets and other details, was a very handsome and complex casting. The propellor shaft was carried in a large torque tube, and the ball joint at the front end of the torque tube needed lubrication. This joint was carried in a huge cast-aluminium cruciform chassis-bracing cross-member, and later models had a cast-in oil tank in this cross-member which kept the torque tube joint lubricated for life. The GL handles like a much smaller car than it is (two examples, at least, have survived), and were it not for the fact that all the best people bought Hispano-Suiza cars at the time, there is little doubt that the 40/50 Delage would have been more of a success than it was.

Teething troubles, not the least of which was a tendency to roast the driver

The 14/40, or the DI series, is perhaps the best known of the Vintage Delages. It can be described together with the DM series which came out in 1926 and effectively superseded it, since the six-cylinder DM is a 3-litre development of the DI.

The DI came in three varieties. The plain DI was in production from 1923 to 1927, had a 10 ft 6-in wheelbase, a wide radiator and a 30-mm Zenith carburettor, and was a gentle unexciting means of reliable transport. The other two models, the DIS and DISS, were much more interesting to the drivers of Vintage cars today. Both had a narrower radiator, a 35-mm Zenith and a 9 ft 9-in chassis. There was very little difference between them, the only obvious differences were in the switch panel (DIS oval, DISS round), the magneto position (DIS nearside, DISS offside) and the starter motor/dynamo, which was chain-driven on the DIS and directly driven off the nose of the crankshaft on the DISS. Less obvious was the fact that the DIS and DISS had larger valves and a more efficient camshaft than the DI, and in 1926 the DISS had a closer-ratio gearbox. All models had five-main-bearing crankshafts giving 3200 rpm and four-speed gearboxes. The DISS, which was in no sense more sporting than the DIS, was only made in 1925 and 1926. The DIS was in production in 1924 and 1925, took a Sabbatical in 1926, and reappeared as the Series 6 in 1927 with coil ignition and the addition of a water pump, all the other models having had thermo-syphon cooling. It also had the close-ratio gearbox.

The 2-litre engine could not give the car true sports-car performance, but the DIS/DISS is a very good all-rounder, a reliable car with excellent handling and a rare feeling of tautness and responsiveness. Every part of it is well designed and well made. A thoroughly unpretentious, honest car which has proved, in recent years, to be able to hold its own with such unlikely competitors as 3-litre Bentleys and Frazer Nashes in long-distance high-speed road rallies.

The 3-litre, on the other hand, is a much more sporting car in short-chassis (10 ft 7 in) form, when it was known as the DMS. The DMS, with a light body, is a wonderfully smooth car with superb balance, a remarkably flexible engine, very underrated by historians, and one of the best sporting tourers of the period.

By 1928 the 40/50 and the 14/40 had been withdrawn and a cheaper 2½-litre model had been introduced. Known as the DR, its only claim to fame is that it hid a side-valve Ricardo cylinder head under a bogus valve cover so that it was nearly indistinguishable from the DM engine.

Late in 1929 came the D8 straight eight-cylinder model. This car has, perhaps, been over-rated. The standard of workmanship on the engine is not as good as it had been on the earlier cars, the handling is not as good, and the car feels as big as it is, which a big car should not. It is a powerful car of 4050 cc, again a direct development of the six-cylinder car, and many D8s were provided with very handsome, long-bonneted coachwork. The more powerful versions of this car, notably the D8SS100 with 'divorced' valve gear, came after the end of the Vintage period, and the car itself really belongs to the post-Vintage era.

By 1930 Louis Delage himself was in something of a decline. Fame went to his head, his magnificent racing cars had cost him dearly, and in the middle 'thirties he had decided to make more of his life than just producing motors cars. He took elocution lessons, and gave lengthy speeches, he took too much interest in women, which cost him his marriage and a great deal of money, and he gave huge parties.

By 1935 Delage had gone into liquidation, and he died in 1947, very poor, but sustained in his later years by an almost mystical religiousness.

Chapter 8
MODEL T FORD

In production from 1908 to 1927, and they made more than 15 million of them, 2 million in 1923 alone. The Flivver, Tin Lizzie or just plain Ford was more than just part of the American scene; to a few million people who grew up with it, the 'T' practically *was* the American scene. The greatest peak in the range of motor manufacturing history, immortalized by poets and writers of two generations, yet the Model T was really a very bad car by the standards of this book. However, it was so widely distributed, so many are still in use, and they held the affections of so many owners, that a thorough explanation of the car and its curious features is warranted.

Henry Ford was a stubborn and determined man. His dream was to make motoring commonplace, and by 1906 he was a long way towards the goal of a soundly made, cheap car which could be driven with the absolute minimum of mechanical understanding and very little maintenance. The Model N was in production for two years, by which time Ford had persuaded his backers that the design he had developed from the N was able to fulfill his dream.

The basic design was very simple; a flexible chassis frame of straight 3-in, 8-gauge channel, to which axles were attached by transverse semi-elliptic springs and 'A' bracket radius rods. The chassis measured only 23 in at its widest, the track (after 1916) was 56 in to line up with cart tracks, and with a single front spring 'U' bolt, the suspension was 3-point mounted. Into this, again 3-point mounted, the engine and gearbox unit was slung by simple pressed-steel mounting straps.

The engine was a four-cylinder side-valve of $3\frac{1}{4}$ in × 4 in, nearly 3 litres. The best feature of the whole car was the main engine casting. The crankcase, cylinders, water jacket and manifolds were cast as one unit, and this very farsighted design gave the whole engine a rigidity which few other designs of the period could approach. The crankshaft was supported in this monobloc by three main bearings, and the one virtue of this spidery component was that, like many parts of the car, it was made of very high-quality steel. Lubrication was by splash, dribble and mist from a very shallow and inadequate sump. A Ford owner had Number One Bearing constantly in mind. This big-end bearing was the one that always melted out because the oil would recede just when it was most needed, when the car was climbing hills. It was like a weak heart; when the knocking started, gently at first, the car had to be stopped and allowed to cool off.

Mounted on the end of this spidery crankshaft and completely overhung from it was a heavy, multi-purpose assembly, the fly-wheel magneto and the epicyclic gearbox. The gearbox casing had three pedals sticking out of it. From left to right, the functions of the first pedal were low gear (when pushed), neutral (when halfway, and held there when the handbrake was on or partly on) and high gear (when released). If the first pedal was held in mid-position, pressing the second pedal would make the car go backwards, and at any time would slow it down. The third pedal was a transmission brake. It was that first pedal which must have sold more Model Ts than any other feature of the car. The human leg is incapable of letting in a clutch with anything like the forthright abandon that used to send the old Ford on its way. Pull down on the throttle lever, just under the steering wheel, and shove hard with the left foot, and the car would lunge forward with a roar. After a few seconds of this tumult, release the pedal and the car would catapult directly into high gear – there were only two. There can be no simpler way of setting off short of automatic drive.

The driving of the Ford was simple; starting the engine was not. To produce a spark at the points of the special taper-threaded plugs when the engine was cold was an art which had to be acquired. There were four basic components in the very primitive ignition system; low-tension current was generated by 16 permanent magnets on the flywheel facing 16 field coils on a stationary plate attached to the back of the engine; the low-tension current passed through a 'timer', a form of distributor mounted on the front of the engine, awkwardly placed for cleaning, which was driven by the camshaft. The current then went back to the dash and a trembler coil for each cylinder, the

vibrator of which needed frequent adjustment; finally high-
tension current passed from these coils to the plugs. The timer
was the most troublesome component. Simple in construction, it
needed to be kept dry and clean, and it also needed lubrication
because electric contact was made through the medium of a
roller. These two requirements were in conflict, and each Ford
owner developed his own theories. Some people, when things
went wrong, clenched their teeth and gave the timer a smart
crack with a spanner. Others opened it up and blew on it. Some
were continually oiling it, others were convinced it should run
dry as a bone, and were continually taking it off and wiping it.

The epicyclic gearbox was in unit with the engine, and ran in
the same oil. Cold starting was thus made even more difficult,
and it was a common practice to jack up one back wheel so that
the transmission was free to turn with the engine.

Once under way, the Model T was so flexible that before the
car was a year old steps had to be taken to check the alarming
disintegration. The car swayed and rattled, the steering was
more of an invitation to the car to go where the driver wanted
than a command, and for all its 3 litres and 20 horse power the
performance was disappointing. Perhaps this was just as well,
because the rear-wheel brakes, applied by the handbrake, were
hopelessly inadequate and the foot brake (or brakes, if the reverse
gear pedal was included) could have the alarming effect of
causing one wheel to spin backwards while the other rolled
gently on.

The Model T was not a Vintage car, but it had a most
endearing character.

Perhaps because of its inadequacies in standard form, the
Model T instigated the beginnings of the 'bolt-on goody' trade
so popular today, particularly in the manufacture of those parts
which aimed to turn the Model T into a racing or sports car. To
this end an Indianapolis firm called Morton & Brett made
speedster bodies, Hassler made modified running gear and Rajo
and Laurel-Roof built 'Peugeot-type' ohv heads.

The most famous of the modifiers, however, was the Chevrolet
Bros Manufacturing Company of 410 West Tenth Street,
Indianapolis, who made the famous 8-valve pushrod Frontenac
head, designed by C.W. van Ranst.

In the first instance the head was designed for dirt-track cars,

and Griffith Borgeson tells an amusing story of the first road test
of the prototype head. As no racing car was available the head
was tested out on the nearest Model T to hand, an ordinary
two-door sedan belonging to 'Skinny' Clemons, later well known
as a racing driver and builder of the Clemons racing engine.

Louis Chevrolet drove the car with van Ranst as passenger,
neither of them having driven an ordinary Model T for years.
Soon they were roaring along at what felt like at least 100 mph
when the paved road they were on suddenly turned into a dirt
road. Before they knew what had happened, the car was upside
down, skating on its roof, whilst the occupants were hurled
together on top of each other and were desperately trying to kick
open the doors in case the car caught fire. Finally it came to a
halt and Chevrolet and van Ranst stumbled out and gazed at the
still-spinning wooden wheels and the roof that had been ground
down all the way through its wooden slats.

'It's fast enough for a race car,' said Louis.

The Frontenac head caught on almost immediately and was
bought not only by racing drivers but by the general public, so
that before long sixty per day were being turned out and over
10 000 were manufactured altogether.

Frontenac Ford, or Fronty-Ford, racing cars featured in big-
time racing at Indianapolis. In 1922 the two cars entered had
half-elliptic front springs replacing the single transverse spring
and single ohc 16-valve heads. Knock-on wire wheels were fitted,
but there was the normal Ford epicyclic 2-speed transmission,
axle, etc., although special steels were used in the axle shafts.
The cars were reliable but the slowest in the race, the fastest
finishing 38 laps behind the winner.

Things were different in 1923, when a single Fronty-Ford was
driven by L.L. (Slim) Corum and came 5th at 82.58 mph to the
90.95 mph of the winning Miller, beating all the Mercedes and
Bugatti works entries in the process. The car was called a Barber-
Warnock as it was sponsored by the Ford dealers in Indianapolis
of that name. Contemporary reports say this car had a pushrod
8-valve head, but Ford transverse springs were used in an 8 ft 2-in
wheelbase chassis (8 ft 4 in was standard), with knock-on wire
wheels. Alterations from standard included full-pressure lubrication, twin Zenith carburettors and a Scintilla magneto, but the
Ford transmission was still used with a 3.25 to 1 rear axle ratio

replacing the normal 3.63 to 1. Pistons, rods and crankshaft were Fronty, each rod weighing 15 oz. Tyres were not changed throughout the race, and the car received the biggest cheer of the day from the innumerable Model T owners present as it crossed the line.

A team of three Barber-Warnocks was entered for the Indianapolis '500' in 1924, one driven by Alfred Moss, father of Stirling, who apparently was an importer of Frontenac speed equipment in England. The cars were single-seaters, as Corum's had been the year before, and Henry Ford himself was photographed sitting in one of them before the race. Although the two fastest cars of Moss and Bill Hunt qualified at over 85 mph, speeds were up this year by nearly 10 mph, and none of the Fords completed the distance, although the fastest was flagged off with only 10 laps to go, and all were running at the end. Both 16- and 8-valve heads were used, and it is interesting to note that a 16-valve car had a 7.5 to 1 compression ratio to give 80 bhp and an 8-valve had a 6.75 to 1 compression ratio to give 60 bhp at 3700 rpm. The 16-valve Fronty head incorporated a chain-driven overhead camshaft. 75 per cent of the components of a Barber-Warnock were said to be standard Ford.

Even front-wheel-drive cars were made from Model T components. In 1925 the Massachusetts Institute of Technology built a two-seater fwd car as a study exercise. This consisted of a T-Ford engine with a Frontenac pushrod ohv conversion, reversed in the frame and driving forwards through the usual 2-speed gearbox, and a very short prop-shaft to a De Dion axle using the Ford differential with fabric universals in its drive shafts. Front suspension was by cantilever, also using Ford springs, and the radiator was from a First World War Ansaldo aero engine, complete with a hole in it for the propellor drive. In 1955 its then owner, Arthur Eldridge, brought it to England and continued on a Continental tour with his wife.

For Indianapolis in 1926 the Chevrolet brothers built a 16-valve De Dion axle fwd single-seater Fronty-Ford racer, but had to sleeve the engine and fit a short throw crank (bore and stroke 2.875 in × 3.5 in) to bring the engine within the 91-in (1½-litre) limit for the race. The car was known as the Hamlin Special, and it had a Roots supercharger driven off the crankshaft at the rear of the reversed engine. The compression ratio was 6.75 to 1, and to use the words of Griff Borgeson in his book *The Golden Age of the American Racing Car* – 'peak revs were 6000 to the delirious inspiration of all Model T owners'. Unfortunately the car ran a connecting rod bearing on the 22nd lap, but raced successfully in smaller events at least up to 1932. Borgeson added 'about 70 per cent of the car's components were right out of the local Ford dealer's parts bin'. He also said that there were technical connections with the forthcoming Ruxton fwd production car.

In 1930 a rear-wheel-drive 16-valve Fronty-Ford prepared by Arthur Chevrolet and driven by Chet Miller averaged 96 mph at Indianapolis, excluding a long 41-minute stop to change a broken front spring, the replacement being borrowed off a parked Model T belonging to an unsuspecting spectator. The spring was allegedly returned to the car after the race without the owner realizing that part of his car had been competing in the big race that day.

In Europe, only the Montiers, father and son, who were Ford agents in the rue Pierre Charron, Paris, seem to have seriously raced 2780-cc single-seater Model T-based specials, which they called Montiers or Montier-Fords. In 1927 they had a second place on the sands of La Baule and on the Torvilliers Circuit, near Troyes, sandwiched between two Bugattis, but two cars entered in the Coupe de la Commission Sportive at Montlhery, a fuel consumption race, retired. These cars had ohv engines, and one suspects the Montiers probably made use of Frontenac parts.

Chapter 9
FRAZER NASH

The first thing that strikes the driver when he tries out a Frazer Nash is the very unusual handling. The second thing may well be that the driver will strike something with the Frazier Nash if he is not forewarned. Engage the first gear dog-clutch with a characteristic 'clunk' and let in the crude but effective clutch, negotiate the 'U' change into second (a more conventional gear lever movement was available from 1927 with the 4-speed arrangement) and push the car into a corner. With such high-geared steering no more than a firm pressure on the steering wheel will do this, and a definite movement of the wheel has dramatic effects. As soon as the car is into the corner the tail starts to slide out and the steering must be allowed to centralize, or opposite lock applied. This is the first surprise. There is a temptation at this stage to ease off on the accelerator, but this must be avoided. On a trailing throttle the steering goes heavy and the front wheels may slide, but with a neutral or open throttle comes the second surprise – how controllable it all is. The front wheels are always where the driver wants them to be, no matter what is happening at the back, and an awful lot can happen at the back before you actually hit anything. This is, perhaps, the biggest surprise of all, that the car seems almost incapable of going round a corner without sliding about, and yet it can be put into a corner much too fast, or the corner can tighten up in a horrid and unexpected way, without the car getting out of control or bumping into things. The Frazer Nash is every inch a 'fun' car.

When Captain Archie Frazer-Nash left G.N. in 1922 and started up on his own with the financial backing of an ammunitions disposal millionaire, his first cars were little more than G.N.s with Rudge-Whitworth wheels and hubs. It was not until 1924 that the true Frazer Nash was first made. It is difficult to separate the Frazer Nash from the G.N., since one was a direct

94

development of the other, yet the two cars have quite different characters.

Certainly they have a great deal in common. The chain transmission layout is almost identical, but not quite. The chapter in this book which describes the G.N. explains in some detail the transmission from the simple, single-plate clutch to the plain back axle shaft. The Frazer Nash has a very similar arrangement, but the system was improved, which is to be expected since the Frazer Nash was not a car for the cheap end of the popular market, but rather a relatively cheap sporting car for the man who took his motor sport seriously. Except for the earliest models, the clutch is attached to the flywheel by a positive method; flexible steel strips bolted firmly to the flywheel and clutch give some universal-joint action, but effectively remove the source of noise and wear which was a problem with the G.N., where the clutch had four bushed holes round the driving plate which engaged with four pegs sticking out of the rear face of the flywheel. When the bushes wear the clutch runs out of balance and rattles.

The front end of the propellor shaft is located by a self-centring ball bearing in the flywheel nut, in contrast to the G.N., which had a spigot on the flywheel nut which engaged with a bronze bush in the end of the propellor shaft. Chassis distortion was largely ignored with the G.N., but the Frazer Nash does have a fabric universal at the rear end of the propellor shaft. The chassis is very flexible, and this joint is necessary even though the crown wheel and pinion (spiral bevel on the Frazer Nash, straight-cut on the G.N.) are located to the chassis and ought not to move in relation to the engine.

These and other subtle differences do a lot to improve the feel of the transmission. The chassis is much the same as the G.N.'s, the main differences lying in the stronger attachments for the axles, shock absorbers, and greatly improved steering linkage. The front axle is stronger and wider and the springs are heavier, though all four springs remain quarter-elliptic. Location of the front end is achieved by two double brackets on the front axle, each having a locating pin above and below the axle. The top pin is fastened through the eye of the spring, the spring thus acting as a radius arm, and the bottom pin holds the front end of a shock-absorber arm whose radius of movement corresponds with the effective radius of the movement of the spring. At the back, the main spring leaf has no eye, and merely rubs on a fibre block shaped to lie on the top of the back-axle bearing housing. This housing is firmly attached to a pair of radius arm side plates which, at their forward end, hold a block of metal carrying a screw-shanked ball joint (on the earlier cars) or a screw-shanked silentbloc bush, either of which attaches to the chassis. By adjusting the length of the screwed shank, the chain tension can be altered.

Adjusting the tension of the four chains on a Frazer Nash is a fine exercise in compromise. The mathematically-inclined owner will start with the assumption that all chains with the same number of links have the same length, and he will then do complicated sums to decide which four pairs of sprockets will give him reasonably spaced ratios and still keep the axle parallel to the countershaft and the chains in roughly the same tension. The pragmatic owner will discard the first assumption, because he knows that an old chain is longer, for the same number of links, than a new chain, that an old, worn chain with just the right tension is less likely to break than a new chain which is too slack (or too tight), and that, being a pragmatist, he has a box of old, new and middle-aged chains at the back of his garage. The pragmatist, however, is likely to be less tidy and methodical than the mathematician, and the chances are that he will find that the nicely-worn bit of chain that he has found which gives him just the right tension for top gear is about eight links too short. He then adds eight links from another bit of chain without realizing that it is virtually unworn, and takes the car out for a test drive, which is when he finds the car leaps along like a kangaroo. It is extraordinary how two bits of dissimilar chain joined together to make one chain length can have such a devastating effect, when the actual difference in pitch length of each link cannot be more than a few thousandths of an inch. The pragmatic owner, however, has one big advantage over the mathematical owner – he is totally unworried by theory and can fit whatever ratios he likes.

Frazer Nashes never had engines of their own manufacture. In the Vintage period they nearly all had the British Anzani $1\frac{1}{2}$-litre side-valve. About 170 of these cars were made, and a further 13 cars were made before 1931 with the more sophisticated 4ED Meadows, which was to be the mainstay of the post-

Kim II had pushrod o.h.v. with exhaust valve springs outboard of the rockers.
Neill Bruce

The only way to get some sleep in a 1922 G.N. is to be overcome by the fumes . . .
J. Butt

The 2-litre Lagonda engine, showing the carburettor attached to the block, necessitated by the unusual method of valve operation from two high set camshafts

The 1923 11.9 hp Lagonda which was driven from London to the Cape in 1953 by Hamish Moffatt, photographed in a recent V.S.C.C. Welsh Trial still wearing its Sahara badge on the radiator   *Neill Bruce*

Vintage production. It is remarkable that some two or three dozen of the original 13 Vintage Meadows-engined Frazer Nashes still exist.

The Anzani side-valve is a remarkably effective engine. Well made, very light, perhaps a little fragile when made to produce its maximum power, it meant different things to several different manufacturers. At one end of the scale was the A.C., which used a detuned Anzani with a large flywheel to give great reliability but rather modest performance. In between were such manufacturers of fairly sporting cars as Horstman, Crouch, Marendaz and Lea-Francis (though the latter firm only produced about fifty Anzani-engined cars in 1926, at a time when they were unable to get delivery of enough Meadows engines to meet their requirements). Frazer-Nash, however, got the maximum performance from Anzani engines, rating his different models according to the power output of the engine. The Fast Tourer claimed 38 bhp at 3700, the Super Sports 47 bhp at 4000, the Boulogne 54 bhp at 4500 and the Supercharged Boulogne 85 bhp at 4000 rpm. The Anzani Company's own catalogue claimed to be able to supply a supercharged engine giving over 100 bhp, and the performance of the very fast Eldridge Specials at Brooklands, which had supercharged Anzani engines, makes this figure nearly believable.

By 1925 the British Anzani company were in financial trouble, but Frazer-Nash, by a succession of complicated deals, kept the engine in production until H.J. Aldington took over the Frazer Nash Company in 1929 and gradually changed from the Anzani engine to the 4ED Meadows, a pushrod engine with a lot more tuning potential. With the passing of the Anzani engine the Frazer Nash lost some of its charm. The heavier Meadows has less low-speed torque, and its weight alters the handling characteristics of the car a little. The Meadows car may be more of a sports car, but it is a little less versatile.

It seems almost unbelievable that such a very primitive, essentially Edwardian light car design should have survived into the late 'thirties virtually unchanged. There are two reasons why it did; the first is that although it was a thoroughly uneconomic production venture, people kept appearing on the board of directors who were so enthusiastic that they were prepared to sink money in it; the second is that in spite of its primitive design, or perhaps because of it, the car is remarkably light, well balanced and effective by any standards. Only a very small band of happy fun-lovers bought the car; even the diligent Frazer Nash historian, David Thirlby, cannot find evidence of more than 348 cars, 181 of them made in the Vintage period; but those who did buy them got their money's worth. It is a tribute to the design of the car that its heyday is as much now, fifty years later, as it was in the 'twenties and 'thirties. Frazer Nash owners have called themselves the Chain Gang since the 'thirties, and the Chain Gang are as successful now, in competition with other cars of the period, as they have been at any other time in the car's history. A more enthusiastic and competitive gang of one-make devotees would be hard to find anywhere.

They have to be enthusiastic and devoted. It does not take a new owner long to discover some at least of the many design failings. These are likely to demonstrate themselves dramatically, like the Clutch Accident, when there is a loud bang, and the scuttle suddenly becomes peppered with holes; the Radius Arm Accident, when the screwed shank on the chain adjuster breaks and the back end of the car catapults into the air; the Two-Gears-At-Once Accident, which often results in a two-part back axle. All these little foibles and many more come to be accepted or overcome by minor modifications and adjustments, because the car is so simply constructed that the enthusiastic amateur can take it all to pieces and put it together again with very little trouble. Indeed, he will almost certainly have to at frequent intervals. The curious handling of the car can be attributed partly to the solid back axle and partly to the steering geometry. With true Ackerman steering the projected lines from the front wheel centres meet at a common centre on a line projected from the centre of the rear axle. Whilst this principle may be modified with advantage, on the Frazer Nash these lines converge roughly in line with the rear engine mounting, which is overdoing it.

It all makes for a lot of fun, if you have that sort of masochistic personality.

Chapter 10
G.N.

The G.N. was a successful, everyday cyclecar. Thousands were made and sold in England and France. Just how many thousands is a matter for historians to dispute.

It is important to bear this fact in mind, because subsequent generations have a very distorted idea of the place held by the G.N. in motoring history. They think of it as the parent of the Frazer Nash, and as the basis of innumerable 'Specials', many of which were and still are very successful competition cars. They forget that the car was designed and made for ordinary people who had almost certainly never owned a car before, who wanted to use it for ordinary transport, and who probably had little or no mechanical knowledge.

The G.N. was a successful cyclecar largely by default. The other cyclecars available at the time were even more crude and unreliable, and by the time G.N. Ltd went bankrupt the day of the cyclecar, which was mercifully a brief one, was over.

The car was first designed and made in 1910 by two friends in their early twenties, Ron Godfrey and Archie Frazer Nash. Early, pre-war models were excessively crude, with belt drive, wooden chassis, and wire-and-bobbin steering, but by the time it was in full-scale production after the war the layout of the chassis was of classic simplicity. The engine was a 90° V-twin of 1087 cc, made by G.N. themselves. The crankshaft consisted of a 10-in length of fairly mild-steel round bar, $1\frac{3}{8}$ in in diameter, with a taper, key and thread at each end. This ran in bronze bearings in the rear half of the crankcase, and was fitted with a flywheel at one end and a counterbalanced crank web at the other. Offset in the web was fitted the crankpin, a $3\frac{1}{2}$ in piece of $\frac{7}{8}$ in round bar secured to the web with a taper and nut. In the front half of the crankcase, concentric with the crankshaft, was a shaft geared to drive the short camshaft with just two cams on it; this shaft was rotated through the medium of an ugly great piece of $\frac{1}{2}$ in × 1 in flat steel, slotted at the end to engage with the end of the crankpin, steel-to-steel. On the crankpin ran a forked connecting rod with a full-width bronze bush through the fork, the other rod running on the outside of this bush. Lubrication was by total loss drip feed, with an optimistic dipper on the bottom of the forked rod in case any oil got left lying around in the bottom of the crankcase.

This detailed description is made to give the reader an example of the extraordinary simplicity of the whole design. The two cylinders had side exhaust valves, with the inlet valves overhead, opposing the exhaust valves in small finned chambers off the cylinders. Induction was through a small Capac carburettor into an exhaust-heated sort of tobacco tin halfway between the cylinders. The curved manifold joining this to the inlet ports is reputed to have been made out of a pair of bicycle handlebars, though this story should perhaps be taken with a pinch of salt; it would have been rather an unusual bicycle. The sparks were taken care of by one Fellows magneto with a normal, symmetrical armature; since the sparks were needed at intervals of 135° and 225° of armature rotation the ignition of both cylinders was unlikely until the engine was going quite fast. 'Flux timing' a 90° twin with one magneto is a fine exercise in compromise; such an engine cannot start or tick over on two cylinders.

The transmission of the G.N. was the stroke of simple genius that set it apart from its fellows and assured it, and its successor the Frazer Nash, lasting fame. From the engine the drive was taken through a very simple but surprisingly effective single-plate clutch engaged by a huge spring round the propellor shaft. The propellor shaft had no universal joint and ended as a pinion shaft in the nose-piece of a plain bevel box whose cross-shaft, attached to the chassis with self-centring bearings, lay some 18 inches ahead of the rear axle. On the near-side of the cross-shaft were two sprockets, free to rotate on the shaft but connected by a $\frac{3}{4}$-in pitch chain with fixed sprockets on the rear axle. Between the cross-shaft sprockets, keyed to the shaft but free to move along it, was a double dog, shaped like a deep-grooved cotton reel, with a 3-dog dog clutch at each end, the groove locating the end of the bell-crank selector which was connected by the simplest possible means to the gear lever, so that one or other of the sprockets could be driven by it. This side of the cross-shaft

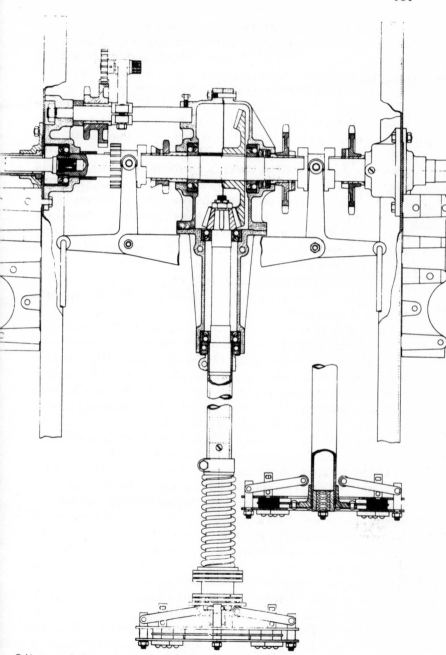

G.N. transmission — the stroke of simple genius which set it apart from its fellows
(Neill Bruce)

produced second and third gears. A similar arrangement on the offside gave first and reverse, the sliding dog in this case having a pinion on the outboard side of the selector groove and a three-jaw dog, like the 2nd and 3rd double dog, on the inboard side. This dog engaged the first gear sprocket, and the pinion engaged with another, larger, pinion on a short shaft to the rear of the main cross-shaft. This larger pinion carried a small sprocket for the reverse gear chain, so that there were four chains in all. The axle itself was a plain piece of $1\frac{1}{2}$-in round steel, keyed for the sprockets, and tapered at the ends for the hubs, which was held to the chassis by simple radius arms with cup and cone bearings on which pressed the ends of two quarter-elliptic springs.

This really was a brilliant piece of design, which allowed the novice to make noiseless gear changes and the enthusiast to alter the gear ratios with very little trouble. The unsprung weight was very low and maintenance and repair, though messy, was very easy. No other part of the car rates such praise and the method of attaching the wheels, and the steering arrangement, left a good deal to be desired.

One very odd feature of the car was the method of starting it, which was by a handle which could be engaged with the off-side end of the bevel box cross-shaft. One complete turn of this handle, geared up by the crown wheel and pinion, turned the engine over 3.2 times. It was hard work, and knuckles often met the road unless the foot technique was mastered, which involved jumping on the handles. The foot technique often resulted in a broken leg, but at least the knuckles stayed intact. From 1922 the handle was in the more normal position at the front of the car.

The wheel attachment was notable for the fact that the wheels were detachable. This was considered a great boon at the time, when punctures were frequent, but the method by which detachability was achieved left a good deal to be desired and there must have been moments in every G.N. owner's life, as he searched the undergrowth for a missing wheel, or worse, extricated himself from the remains of his three-wheeled car in a ditch, when he wished the wheels had been less readily detachable. To avoid the expense of splined hubs, the G.N. had a plain hub with a plain wheel centre on it, relative movement being prevented by a 7-dog 'dog clutch' at the inboard end (or 8-dog on French G.N.s, and 3-dog on late English G.N.s). The hub was threaded with a very fine right-hand thread at the outboard end, and on this screwed a simple hub cap butted against the wheel centre to hold it into its mating set of dogs.

Inevitably there was always some movement at the dogs, so that the wheel centre was continually fretting at the hub cap, trying to undo it. To avoid this, a series of slots were milled along the threaded portion of the hub, rendering the fine threads even less effective, and a spring plunger in the hub cap engaged with one of these slots. With the continual fretting, either the plunger became dislodged from its slot, or the hub cap, with its poor purchase on its fine thread, would jump a thread or two, and in time the fretting would complete its work and the wheel would fall off.

It is not too difficult to overcome this problem by making a hub cap which is clamped firmly to the threaded portion of the hub by pinch bolts, which can be prevented from unscrewing by a steel tongue held into the slot by one of the pinch bolts, but G.N. never did this themselves, and fretting still wears away the butted faces. Frazer Nash himself never liked this idea, and it was the first thing he altered when he started making cars on his own.

The steering gear is desperately crude, most of the steering joints being of the clevis-and-pin variety which, apart from the king-pins, have to be sloppy if they are to work, and the gearing, through a pair of unequal-size bevel pinions, is quite unnecessarily high. From full lock to full lock is less than half a turn of the steering wheel, and the technique is to hold the wheel quite loosely, applying pressure rather than movement when a change of direction seems advisable. In moments of crisis full opposite lock is only too readily at hand, but with no shock absorbers, a narrow track and rather inadequate lock, the standard G.N. is not a car to play bears with too enthusiastically.

However, because the car was so simple and light, it was clear from the start that in modified form it had great sporting potential. Godfrey and Frazer Nash were both enthusiastic sporting motorists, and a number of 'works racers' were made; Godfrey's *Bluebottle* was a pre-war chassis with wood frame and belt final drive, Frazer Nash's *Kim* had a pre-war wood frame but chain final drive, and his *Kim II* and *Mowgli* were similar in design to the normal postwar G.N. These last two, in particular, were very successful cars, particularly in sprints and hill climbs. There is little doubt that Frazer Nash's preoccupation with racing contributed to the downfall of G.N. Ltd, but it was also the reason for the birth of the Frazer Nash car.

On the road the excellent power-to-weight ratio, even with the standard car, gives an exhilarating punchiness to the car. Each bang can be felt doing its bit. The roadholding is not in the same class as the Frazer Nash, and the absurdly high-geared steering is no help, but the car probably handles a lot better than any other cyclecar and better than most light cars. Given a few modifications – wider front axle, shock absorbers, flattened springs, better hubs and wheels and more power – it can be transformed into a very exciting and remarkably controllable 'Special'. Since G.N.s were very cheap in the 'twenties and 'thirties, it is not surprising that most 'Specials' of the period were G.N.-based. The most famous of them all is Basil Davenport's *Spider* which broke the record at Shelsley Walsh in 1926, 1927 and 1928 in the face of opposition from cars costing ten or twenty times as much. *Spider* is still going strong, and Basil Davenport has now celebrated 50 years of Shelsley-storming with this splendid device. Two other famous G.N. Specials of the period were *Gnat* and *Wasp*, and all three insects are still in good shape.

If we have been critical of the G.N., it has been levelled at design faults which were dictated largely by a low selling price. It set out to be a cheap and spartan little car and as such, with a few reservations, we think it succeeded very well indeed.

At least the knuckles stayed intact

Chapter 11
LAGONDA

During the Vintage period Lagonda produced but three basic models, one of which is now generally regarded as a classic.

The founder of the firm must have been an interesting character, of which not a great deal is known, and as he died in 1920 he did not greatly influence the Vintage designs, although one feels they would have had his approval. His name was Wilbur Gunn, an American, who served his engineering apprenticeship at the Singer Sheepshearing Co Inc of Springfield, Ohio, a firm which was owned by his family. Just before the turn of the century he came and settled in England, where he bought a large house in Staines, some 18 miles west of London, and began to take an interest in local affairs. He was a large, generous and good-humoured man, always immaculately dressed, and with a good singing voice. Opera was one of his passions.

At first he apparently used his engineering abilities as a hobby, and built a steam launch to settle a bet on its speed capabilities with an American friend. He then built, in his greenhouse, a motor cycle with an air-cooled engine and by 1900 had begun to market motor cycles, giving them the name of Lagonda after the creek where he played as a child by the Great Lakes.

The first Lagonda car was a three-wheeler, with a V-twin-cylinder engine, in which the passenger sat between the front wheels. The driver steered by handlebars and sat above and behind the passenger with the single-driven wheel behind him. This tri-car appeared at the end of 1904, by which time Gunn had been joined by an engineer called A.H. Cranmer.

Gunn drove the tri-car in competitions, winning a gold medal in the Auto-Cycle Club's London–Edinburgh Trial of 1905, and then in 1907 a medium-sized side-valve four-cylinder four-wheeled Lagonda car appeared, followed by a big 30-hp six-cylinder.

Strangely enough nearly all the production of these cars went to Russia, and, driving a four-cylinder 16/20-hp model, Gunn won a gold medal in the 1910 Moscow–St Petersburg Reliability Trial. He was accompanied by Lagonda engineer G.H. (Bert) Hammond.

Gunn was an independent man, rather like T.G. John of Alvis in this respect, and, apart from the carburettor, all the parts for the tri-cars were made at Staines, even the nuts and bolts.

The first Vintage Lagonda was Edwardian in concept and dated back to 1913. At the end of that year Lagonda changed to a single-model policy and brought out an inexpensive £150 light car, known as the 11.1 hp, with a 67 × 77.8-mm, 1098-cc engine. The outstanding feature of the car was that the body panels were riveted direct on to the angle-iron chassis so that the body and chassis were of unit construction, though for reasons of economy rather than rigidity.

Production was continued after the war, the car still having a distinctive bullnose radiator and rounded tail, but gradually it was developed into a luxury light car, a flat radiator replaced the more conspicuous bullnose and the body and chassis became separate.

By 1921 the model was known as the 11.9 hp, for the engine dimensions had been increased to 69 × 95 mm, 1420 cc, and the wheelbase went up from 7 ft 9 in to 9 ft. The engine had overhead inlet and side exhaust valves operated by a camshaft on the near-side, and the rockers were unusual in that they operated in the fore-and-aft line of the engine instead of across it as is the usual practice. A rather deep cover enclosed the valve gear on the later postwar cars, but David Scott-Moncrieff has remarked on the curious effect of the unenclosed rockers when the engine was running on a pre-war car. These were rather long and as No. 1 cylinder's pushrod was behind No. 2 cylinder and No. 2's pushrod was in front of No. 1, the appearance of a succession of exposed beam engines was given.

Although the trough and dipper system was used to lubricate the big-ends, a rotary pump fed the two main bearings, the over-head valve gear and the timing chain. A second enclosed silent chain drove the fan and dynamo, the magneto being set trans-versely and driven by skew gears off the dynamo shaft between that component and the combined chain case and oil filler. Cooling was by thermo siphon. The transmission was via a cone clutch to a unit three-speed gearbox, then by enclosed shaft with a fabric joint to a worm drive back axle. Springing was by a transverse leaf spring at the front and quarter elliptics at the back.

The price was at its highest in 1920/21 at £495, at which time rear-wheel brakes only were featured, but there was also the fly-off racing-type handbrake which had been pioneered on the 11.1 hp Lagonda before the war. The car was light, 12 cwt in two-seater form, and so had quite a good performance with notable fuel economy, over 40 mpg being frequently attained.

Two works cars were built for Brooklands racing and were mainly driven by Major W.H. Oates. The first car, a single-seater, appeared in 1921 with a 70.5 × 95-mm, 1483-cc engine, gaining several places in Brooklands handicaps and putting in a fastest lap at 86.62 mph. In October Oates took five Light Car Class records with this car, covering the flying-start mile at 86.91 mph and taking the hour record at 79.17 mph despite a 2½-minute stop to change a wheel. Five days later Kensington Moir in an Aston Martin took all but the mile record from the Lagonda, covering 86.21 miles in the hour.

Two Lagondas with Oates and Bert Hammond as drivers took part in the 1921 200-Mile Race at Brooklands, finishing 13th and 10th respectively.

In 1922 Oates had another successful season with a car with the engine enlarged to 69 × 100 mm, 1496 cc, and in this form his fastest lap was at 88.62 mph, faster than a side-valve Aston Martin. After running well, this car, a two-seater, retired in the 1922 200-Mile Race.

In contrast, the top speed of a standard 1924 11.9-hp Lagonda was quoted as 53 mph, with 32 mph in second and 16 mph in bottom. By 1925 the price of a two-seater had gone down to £275, with £370 for a saloon.

Oates did very well in trials with these small Lagondas, achieving several successes in events like the London–Edinburgh and Scottish Six Days with a saloon, and an epic trip overland from London to the Cape was carried out in 1953 in a 30-year-old 11.9 Lagonda driven by a member of the Vintage Sports-Car Club.

In 1925 the model became known as the '12/24', by which time a plate clutch was fitted, the valve gear was enclosed, and gear ratios were 4.7, 8.8 and 16.5 to 1, with a bevel-drive rear axle. Rubery front-wheel brakes, for which the axle was specially modified, could be fitted at an extra cost of £20.

By 1926 the 12/24 had been replaced by a completely different car, a medium-sized luxury touring model known as the 14/60, which was to form the basis of the famous 2-litre Lagonda sports car in 1927. The 14/60 chassis cost £200 more than that of the 12/24, and a saloon cost £720, with £570 for the tourer. The car was roomy and comfortable, fitted with wire wheels and Rudge hubs, and its outstanding feature was its engine, the brainchild of the car's designer, Arthur Davidson, late of Calthorpe.

This was a four-cylinder 72 × 120-mm, 1954-cc unit with a very long stroke in relation to the bore, which made the RAC rating only 12.8 hp, and the annual tax £13. This was only £1 more than the tax for the average 1½-litre car with a similar bore and a stroke of under 100 mm in the days when the RAC rating took only the size of the cylinder bore into account.

Davidson decided to make his new engine an advanced one by adopting hemispherical cylinder heads with the valves at 90° to each other and operated by twin camshafts. He designed the upper half of the engine so that the camshafts were high, but not overhead, thus the cylinder head could be removed without disturbing the timing, and at the same time he decided against the use of pushrods, which would mean extra reciprocating weight in the operation of the valve gear. His way round the problem was an unusual one, as he placed the camshafts so high in the block that they could operate the valves by means of long angled rockers. In this way it would seem that he was getting the best of both worlds, avoiding some of the snags of both pushrod and twin overhead camshaft engines. He had not made a complete breakthrough, however, because with both twin overhead camshafts and with twin camshafts high in the block operating short, light pushrods, as on the Riley, there is room in the head for good porting, with the carburettor attached to one side of the head and the exhaust manifold attached to the other. In Davidson's design the head had to be shallow, and the configuration meant that there was not room for the normal transverse inlet and exhaust passages in the head, so the Zenith carburettor and exhaust manifold were below the head and attached to each side of the block. For the gases to connect with them it was necessary to have three exhaust and two inlet ports in the head connecting

vertically with corresponding holes in the block in the same way
that the water transfer holes connected. Thus the very tortuous
inlet and exhaust passages went a long way towards nullifying
the advantages of the excellent hemispherical combustion spaces.

At the front of the engine there was a chest containing two
chains connecting seven sprockets for the camshafts, and dynamo,
oil and water pump drives. The magneto was spirally driven off
the offside, or exhaust, camshaft. This expensive and well-made
engine also featured a five-bearing crankshaft and would run
smoothly up to 4200 rpm with good fuel economy which
approached 30 mpg and a speed of over 60 mph.

The 10-ft wheelbase chassis was equally well made, the four-
speed gearbox being separate from the engine, and the single-
plate clutch incorporating a clutch stop. Suspension was by half
elliptics and there were grouped chassis lubrication nipples. The
brakes were large and effective, the compensator involving
chains and sprockets, and the steering was pleasant.

The 2-litre speed-model Lagonda differed from the 14/60 in
having different valve timing, the compression ratio raised to
6.8 to 1, the engine moved back in the frame and a higher back-
axle ratio with different oil-filling arrangements. A good close-
ratio gearbox gave 50 mph in second gear, 70 mph in third and
80 mph in top, although a good long straight was necessary to
obtain these figures as the car was heavy for a 2-litre sports
model – the handsome open tourer, which was fabric-covered
and on 3-litre Bentley lines, weighing something like a ton and a
half. This was heavier than the equivalent Speed Model 3-litre
Bentley. In 1928 the 2-litre Lagonda tourer cost £675 to the
£650 of the equivalent 14/60, the situation being reversed in
saloon form where the 14/60 cost £785 and the 2-litre £750.

Although the 2-litre Lagonda understandably did not appear
in the lists of prize winners at Shelsley Walsh or at events where
acceleration was at a premium, it obviously had a potential in
long-distance races on fast courses such as Le Mans and those
held at Brooklands.

Some tentative racing was undertaken in 1927, Frank King
driving a saloon in the Six Hours race at Brooklands in May, but
retiring with a broken piston after 157 miles, having averaged a
respectable 57.6 mph. At the Whitsun meeting King drove an
open black 2-litre Lagonda entered by the Lagonda engineer A.H.

Cranmer, who had joined Wilbur Gunn at Staines back in 1904. King lapped the outer circuit at 81.37 mph, but was unplaced.

A 2-litre Lagonda owned by Bob Nicholl and prepared by his famous firm Fox & Nicholl was raced in 1928 at Brooklands by Howard Wolfe and Arthur Fox, the latter putting in a lap at 88.94 mph according to W. Boddy's famous history *The Story of Brooklands*.

Wolfe was still racing a 2-litre Lagonda entered by Arthur Fox in 1929, by which time he was lapping at over 90 mph.

To return to 1928, the works appointed H. Kensington-Moir as their racing manager and teams of Lagondas were entered for major long-distance events, many of the drivers, like Moir himself, having raced with Bentleys. In the Six Hours race all the cars retired, at Le Mans two of them crashed, that driven by Samuelson and King retiring, but the other car driven by d'Erlanger and Hawkes struggled on to finish eleventh at 56.4 mph, and came second in its class to an Itala which averaged 58.5 mph. The third Lagonda, driven by Gallop and Hays retired before midnight. These cars all had dual carburettor engines. In the TT the cars retired again, although E.R. Hall lay fourth at two-thirds distance before a big-end went. In October W.M. Couper, of the Lagonda staff, broke the Class E 200-kilo and 200-mile records with a works 2-litre at Brooklands at between 79 and 80 mph.

In 1929 Fox & Nicholl bought a team of 2-litre Lagondas and raced them under an arrangement whereby the works were responsible for the supply of spares, overhauls and repairs to keep the cars raceworthy, and the season started well when Mike Couper finished ninth in the Double Twelve and won his class. Only one car was entered for Le Mans, driven by Brian Lewis and Tim Rose-Richards, and this retired after four hours with a head-gasket leak which caused a small fire. Low placings were obtained in the TT and at Phoenix Park, but throughout the season there were fifteen finishes out of nineteen starts. Nevertheless the arrangement between Fox & Nicholl and Lagondas was discontinued at the end of the year and Fox & Nicholl went over to Talbots.

In late 1929 a new version of the 2-litre Lagonda appeared, a low-chassis model to replace the previous high-chassis cars. Cycle-type mudguards were fitted, and a few supercharged

versions were sold incorporating a Cozette blower mounted
vertically at the front of the engine drawing mixture from a single
SU carburettor on the offside. On these cars an A.C. pump
replaced the Autovac.

So far as handling is concerned, it is certainly arguable
whether a low-chassis 2-litre Lagonda offers any improvement
over the high-chassis, and many people prefer the older car. In
general the earlier Vintage cars did handle better than the later
ones. It is also arguable as to whether the low-chassis cars were
better-looking than the high-chassis ones – a matter of personal
taste.

As with other hand-built cars, the specification of Lagondas
varied according to the customer's choice, but most low-chassis
2-litres had twin-carburettor engines. The addition of the supercharger increased acceleration and top speed at the expense of
higher fuel consumption, this going down to 18 mpg. The additional torque at low revs was one of the charms of the supercharged car, but it suffered like the supercharged $4\frac{1}{2}$-litre Bentley
in that the cooling system was not up to coping with sustained
high speeds, which resulted in boiling unless the cylinder-head
water passages were modified. If we compare the 1954-cc open
four-seater supercharged 2-litre Lagonda with two cars in a
similar category, the 2276-cc Talbot 75 six-cylinder and the
2468-cc 18/80 M.G. six-cylinder, we find that all have similar
acceleration figures in contemporary road tests, but the Lagonda
was fastest over a timed flying $\frac{1}{4}$ mile when it achieved 88.23 mph
to the 81.82 mph of the Talbot and the 79.64 mph of the M.G.,
which only had a 3-speed gearbox. The Lagonda really was
unusually heavy (and the low-chassis cars were generally a bit
heavier than their high-chassis predecessors). The supercharged
Lagonda road-tested weighed 29 cwt to the $25\frac{3}{4}$ cwt of the Talbot
and the mere $22\frac{3}{4}$ cwt of the M.G. Despite this its fuel consumption of 18 mpg compared favourably with the 17—18 mpg of the
Talbot and the 18–20 mpg of the M.G. Incidentally, the sporting
3-litre Bentleys had weighed about 25 to 26 cwt in 1922–24 and
$28\frac{1}{2}$ cwt in 1925–28.

In braking tests the blown Lagonda's figures were identical to
the Talbot's, 27 ft from 30 mph, whereas for the M.G. the distance was extended to 31 ft, despite its lighter weight. Annual tax
on the Lagonda was £13 to the £18 of the other two cars, and its

price was £775 where £735 was asked for the Talbot and only £525 for the M.G., which was based on the Morris Isis costing £435 in saloon form.

The Talbot and M.G. mentioned above had six-cylinder engines, and in 1927 Lagonda, also, had entered the six-cylinder market with their 16/65 model. This had a similar chassis to the 14/60, except that it was longer by 9 in, giving a 10 ft 9-in wheel-base. At a time when rival firms were often fitting proprietory engines from manufacturers like Meadows, Lagonda produced their own engine with pushrod overhead valves and a chain-driven camshaft. A very fine engine it was too, with a seven-bearing crankshaft where the contemporary six-cylinder Mead-ows engine had a five-bearing crankshaft. The Lagonda engine had a capacity of 2692 cc with a bore and stroke of 69 × 120. By 1929 the bore had been increased to 72 mm, giving a capacity of 2931 cc, and this model was known as the 3-litre. A stronger gearbox than that on the 2-litre was fitted.

The speed model 3-litre was raced, and one of the cars, much drilled for lightness, was entered by Fox & Nicholl in the 1929 Brooklands Six Hours race. It won its class, whilst Lagondas won the team prize in this race in which six 2-litres were also entered.

The 3-litre was probably the most underrated of all Lagonda models, and anyone who has ever owned or driven one seems to speak well of it. Not a large number was produced as they were very expensive. In 1930 the 'Special Tourer' cost £1000. Whilst not so fast as a blown 2-litre (82.95 mph over the flying quarter mile compared with 88.23 mph for the smaller blown car), at the same time it had better acceleration, and the fuel consumption of 20 mpg was also superior. Being over one-hundredweight heavier at 30¼ cwt braking was inferior, 34 ft being taken to come to a stop from 30 mph. It was undoubtedly a very satisfying car to drive, and the last 'real' big Lagonda (i.e. with an engine made by Lagonda in contrast to the Crossley and Meadows-engined models of the early 'thirties) until the coming of the V12 Lagonda.

All the Vintage Lagondas were made at Staines, where Wilbur Gunn had produced the first Lagonda motor cycle, and of the three models produced it is the 2-litre which is considered the classic.

An early 40/50 hp Napier seen in its natural habitat   *Ronald Barker*

1911 Silver Ghost engine   *Neill Bruce*

A 1912 Silver Ghost Rolls-Royce photographed in N. Africa by Percy Northey. '... during the first two hours we averaged 6½ mph and got stuck in two sand drifts.'

A 1922 20 hp Rolls-Royce, one of the earliest still in existence, originally supplied to the H.H. Maharaja of Udaipur.

Chapter 12
NAPIER

Napier was one of the great names in motoring in the years prior to the First World War, so it was a fair guess that their first post-war design would be of some importance. This proved to be the case.

In the pre-war days the Napier name was inexorably mixed with that of S.F. Edge, who gained Britain's first great international racing victory driving a Napier in the 1902 Gordon Bennett race, and who relentlessly publicized Montague Napier's six-cylinder engine, which powered the world's first commercially successful six-cylinder car. In those days Napier held a place in the British motor industry equal to that later held by Rolls-Royce.

Edge and Napier parted in 1912, so there was no Edge-inspired publicity to boost the new 40/50 Napier which was introduced to the public in 1919. During the war Napier had been engaged in the design and manufacture of aeroplane engines, and this was the field in which Montague Napier felt the future of his company lay. He looked upon the car as a sort of interim measure prior to the complete concentration by his firm on aero engine manufacture.

Towards the end of the war the famous Napier Lion twelve-cylinder aero engine had been designed by A.J. Rowledge, and it was Rowledge who was the designer responsible for what turned out to be the only Vintage Napier car to be produced.

Intended as a rival to the 40/50-hp side-valve Rolls-Royce, the new Napier immediately scored over the Rolls-Royce by virtue of its engine, which was a thoroughly new conception, an overhead camshaft six-cylinder which was also one of the pioneers in light-alloy construction. Whereas Rolls-Royce had a six-cylinder side-valve engine of 114 × 121 mm (7410 cc), the Napier engine was smaller, with a bore and stroke of 102 × 127 mm, 6177 cc. In this it conformed with the practice of the time in luxury-car design, for the Lanchester 40 was of almost identical capacity, whilst the Hispano-Suiza and Isotta Fraschini had capacities of 6½ and 6 litres respectively. All these luxury models had overhead camshaft engines, the Hispano-Suiza's, like the Napier's, predominating in light alloy.

Immense efforts were made on the Napier to make the operation of the valve gear as noiseless as possible and, to quote the instruction book, 'the new Napier swinging tappet system of valve actuation, which multiplies the motion of the cam and so allows the use of a small cam, with gentle slopes' was featured. There were two vertical valves per cylinder in an alloy detachable head which had screwed-in valve seats, the central camshaft operating the valves on each side of it by striking each rocking lever between its fulcrum and the valve. There was negative valve overlap, the exhaust valve closing 2° after top dead centre, with the inlet valve not opening until some 3½° later. The Hispano-Suiza had no valve overlap (although not negative overlap), in its case the inlet valve opened and the exhaust closed a full 8° after tdc. Only the modest revs at which the Napier engine operated prevented the late opening being the cause of noise. Valve clearances were very narrow, 0.002 in for the inlet and 0.003 in for the exhaust, adjusted by set screws in the tappet ends, locked by clamp bolts. Thus the upper end of each valve stem was threaded, not for clearance adjustment as on the Hispano-Suiza, but to contain a lock nut holding the upper valve spring carrier, which also formed a cap over the valve guide to restrict oil entering the combustion chamber, for the valve gear was very thoroughly lubricated.

The camshaft ran in seven bearings, and an extra cam on it operated an air pump mounted on top of the alloy valve cover to pressurize the petrol tank, a handpump being used to build up initial pressure so that the engine could be started. The camshaft was driven from the front of the engine by worm-and-wheel gears, and an adjustable spring-loaded disc rubbed against the forward end of the bronze wormwheel to act as a camshaft damper. The valve operation was completely silent, something difficult to achieve with an overhead camshaft design in 1919.

There were two sparking plugs per cylinder, set horizontally opposite to each other in bronze inserts in the head, with twin ignition by C.A.V. coil and magneto. There was a single water-

jacketed Napier-SU carburettor with an inclined dashpot, and
Ronald Barker tells us that it was left to Napier to develop the
metal dashpot piston that superseded the old leather bellows that
had featured on the SU constant-vacuum carburettor since 1903.
On the Napier an auxiliary carburettor, built into the main
instrument, was used for starting and slow running, and it drew
air from beneath the valve cover which retained heat long after
the engine had been stopped. The inlet manifold was cast in the
head on the offside, with a six-branch exhaust attached to the
head on the nearside above the plugs.

The alloy block had light-steel cylinder liners shrunk into it,
and the alloy pistons had lightening holes in their long skirts and
cast-in steel expansion control rings, so the pistons expanded at
the same rate as the cylinders. The two-bolt connecting rods
were tubular on the early cars, H-section on the later ones. The
7-bearing crankshaft had neither counterweights nor a vibration
damper.

The engine, which was very handsome in appearance, was
designed to have plenty of torque at low revs, and the instruction
book advised starting in second gear under normal circumstances. Thus there was some consternation when it was found
on the prototype that the engine ran very rough when under
load at low revs. The one-time Napier works test driver, H.C.
Tryon, who had raced for the firm at Brooklands, suspected this
noise came from the rear main bearing and was due to lack of
rigidity in the crankcase. It was uneconomic to scrap the crankcases and redesign them, and Tryon overcame the problem in an
ingenious way by fitting a concave piston with a lower compression than its fellows to the rearmost cylinder, thus taking
some of the loading off the rear main bearing. The normal compression ratio was only just over 4 to 1, so the rear piston must
have been a bit of a passenger, but this solution worked like a
charm.

One of the best features of the Napier was its clutch, which was
light and sensitive and particularly sweet in operation. It was a
dry single-plate design, connected to the separate gearbox via
two flexible couplings. In his 'Profile' on the 40/50 Napier,
Ronald Barker remarked on the lattice girder casting uniting
these leather-and-steel laminated couplings which was light and
rigid and which replaced the conventional shaft. The shafts in

the gearbox, which was notably silent, were carried on roller bearings, and the musically inclined Cecil Clutton, in a road test of a 40/50 Napier he wrote for *Motor Sport* in March, 1947, noticed that the three intermediate gears produced exactly the same note. The movement of the gear lever was short, and it was reminiscent of a Bugatti in that one pushed the lever into top gear, the opposite of normal.

Transmission was via a torque tube to the rear axle, and at the front of the torque tube there was a unique anti-rolling device incorporating two helical springs which combated any tendency of the torque tube to twist. The rear axle was carried on cantilever springs, in the best luxury-car tradition, whilst the front springs were semi-elliptic. Other notable features of the car were that it was one of the first to fit a bellows-type thermostat which was situated in the water pump housing and ensured that the water by-passed the radiator until it was warm, also the silent electric starter which was pre-engaged with the flywheel by pressure of the driver's foot, a further pressure turning the engine. There was a further refinement, in that if the coil ignition was inadvertently left on, the expansion of a hot wire worked an automatic switch to turn it off.

Sports cars can be judged and compared on their performance, handling and looks, but with a luxury car it is probably comfort, silence and an impressive appearance which are most important. Certainly in the Napier the performance was sacrificed for silence, the power curve peaked at about 2000 rpm when 82 bhp was produced. At these revs the makers quoted the maximum speed in top as being 60 mph with the 3.33 to 1 final drive, and 54 mph with the alternative 3.75 to 1 ratio. Nevertheless an open tourer which did a tour of the Alps under official RAC observation in 1921, returned a speed of 72.38 mph over the half mile at Brooklands after coming back from the Continent, and it was fitted with the lower 3.75 ratio. There was little acceleration after 40 mph in top, and on this essentially top-gear car the quite sporting three upper ratios of 3.75, 4.48 and 6.75 to 1 were rather wasted, bottom gear having an emergency ratio of 13.3 to 1. Equivalents on the higher axle ratio were 3.33, 4.48, 6.00 and 11.80 to 1. This gearbox has been compared by Cecil Clutton to the Bentley C-type box, but he says a wide-spaced 3-speed box (reminiscent, presumably, of that on the Hispano-Suiza) would have served just as well.

The Napier rear-wheel brakes just did not compare with the Hispano-Suiza operation on all four wheels; the foot transmission brake was liable to fade if heavy use was made of it, and the handbrake on the rear wheels only was not effective for stopping purposes, only for parking. The four-wheel brake system on the later models came in for praise from Cecil Clutton, however.

The worm-and-quadrant steering was definitely heavy, having a high ratio of $1\frac{3}{4}$ turns from lock to lock, and the heaviness must have increased with the massive braked front axle and low-pressure tyres of the later models, early cars having 895×135 beaded-edge tyres. Rudge Whitworth centre-lock wire wheels featured on all models. The back seats were very comfortable, although the suspension was fairly hard, and a fuel consumption of 13–16 mpg was normal.

Napiers owned the Cunard coachwork company, consequently a large proportion of the chassis produced up to the final year of 1924, when car manufacture ceased, were made by this company. The Cunard bodies tended to be heavy. In all under 200 40/50 Napiers were made before the firm concentrated entirely on aero engine manufacture. The cost of the chassis in 1919 was £2100.

Although the alloy engine was beautiful to look at, the fact that it was compact meant a relatively short bonnet, so the 40/50 Napiers, although superbly made, did not have the grace of their Rolls-Royce and Hispano-Suiza rivals. S.F. Edge summed the Napier up in a letter to *The Autocar* in which he observed that the engine design was a long way ahead of the general arrangement of the chassis.

It has been said that practically every car was at some time or other raced at Brooklands, and the 40/50 Napier was no exception. In 1929 Captain Alistair Miller ran one with a smart two-seater racing body and cowled radiator. Painted navy blue, the car was called the Auto-Speed Special, but little if any tuning can have been carried out on the engine to take advantage of its potential, for the fastest lap recorded was at only 78.18 mph, whereas tuned versions of the 40/50 Rolls-Royce and 40-hp Lanchester had achieved 100 mph and more on the track.

Chapter 13
ROLLS-ROYCE

What a pity that the Hon Charles died so young. If only he had lived into the Vintage period, and kept a critical eye on the motor cars made by the admirable Henry, what magnificent cars they would have been.

For all his faults, and he had as many as most of us, the Hon Charles Rolls was a man of excellent taste and great business talent. The 40/50 Rolls-Royces made in his lifetime were without question the best cars available at the time; he died in 1910 in an aeroplane crash and the Rolls-Royce Company, and the world of motoring, suffered a grievous loss.

Henry Royce was a perfectionist and a truly admirable engineer, but there was an element missing from his character which is difficult to define. He certainly knew what his aristo-cratic public wanted; but perhaps this was his trouble. Rolls would have given them what they ought to want. Royce gave them what they expected to get.

It will be said that this hypothesis does not bear close examina-tion, partly because Rolls might well have drifted away from the motor car industry, and partly because Royce was certainly not allowed by circumstances to do what he would have liked to do, but it may serve to illustrate a point. It can, indeed, be said that Rolls had already drifted away from the motor car industry before his death, but his interest in aviation, not yet a practical means of transport, would have involved him in a great deal of long-distance motoring. During the years immediately preced-ing the First World War there was a great deal of progress in automobile design throughout Europe, and it is unlikely that Rolls would have allowed the car that bore his name to be over-taken by events. Equally, it is quite logical to suggest that Royce could never have made the early, light Silver Ghost such a splendidly all-round car, a delight alike to the sportsman and the dowager, without the influence of Rolls.

118

To drive an early Ghost at speed on a twisty road is a revelation to any critical motorist. Its manners are impeccable, the silence is uncanny and the performance is deceptively good. The same drive in a Phantom II, the last of the six-cylinder 40/50s, is a disappointment. The manners are not in the same class, the noise level, though low by most standards, is not by any means absent, and the performance, though better than the Ghost's, should be better than it is. As an effortless touring car the Phantom II is indeed all it sets out to be, and the top-gear performance in hilly country is exhilarating. The standard of workmanship is above reproach (though not as far above as the workmanship on the Ghost). But it feels the heavy car it is, which the Ghost does not, and there is no escaping the fact that it wallows.

Scott-Moncrieff has written of the Silver Ghost: 'Anyone who is lucky enough to drive one counts it as a really great and unforgettable experience, like tasting a noble Burgundy or seeing St Peter's lit up with a myriad of candles for Easter'. Here, indeed, is the Vintage car to be compared with the great Vintage wine. The secret lies not so much in the ingredients as in the method, for to be frank there is nothing exceptional about the design. The engine is a side-valve six, the cylinders cast in two blocks of three with non-detachable cylinder heads. The crankshaft was of very advanced design when it was first introduced in 1906. Pressure-fed, with very large diameter journals, it is a remarkably light component for such a large engine, and indeed all Rolls-Royce crankshafts are surprisingly flimsy when they are not held in their seven main bearings. The crankpins and journals are drilled through to such a size that they are little more than thick-walled tubes, the ends blocked off with tapered plugs held in position with a through-bolt.

Every part of the car is of exquisite workmanship. One of the most beautifully constructed parts is the carburettor and governor, the latter designed not to limit the speed, but to maintain the same speed regardless of the road conditions. There are three hand levers and the ignition switch in the centre of the steering wheel (except on the American models which never managed to achieve this complication, and made do with a horn button; also it should be stated, for historical accuracy, that until 1910 the mixture lever and the ignition switches were mounted on the bulkhead). One lever is for ignition control ('early' and 'late'), one for speed ('fast' and 'slow') which is effectively a governed hand throttle, and one for mixture ('strong' and 'weak'). This last lever controls the two mixture jets whose movement over the range is so small that it is difficult to believe they move at all. The linkage for this control has to be perfect, and one of the nicest things about the Ghost, or indeed any Rolls-Royce, is the beautifully light, positive feel of the hand controls.

The Silver Ghost was in production from 1906 until 1925 in England, the American-built Springfield Silver Ghost continuing in production for a further year. During this long production span a number of detail changes were made in the design. Power output was gradually increased from the original 48 bhp at 1250 rpm, first to 55 bhp by increasing the stroke, which increased the capacity from 7036 cc to 7428 cc, then to 64 bhp with the 1911 'London–Edinburgh' model, which had the compression raised from 3.2 to 1 to 3.5 to 1, and a larger carburettor. After the war there were a number of changes, notably electric starting introduced in 1919, and four-wheel brakes in 1924. To cope with the extra weight the power was further increased, with some loss of smoothness, and the steering became heavier. The final drive ratio was reduced from 2.7 to 1 to 3.25 to 1, and finally to 3.7 to 1. This was the insidious beginning of the downward path for Rolls-Royce. By failing to see the wood for the trees the car was gradually allowed to become more complicated, more 'modernized' and heavier without any fundamental re-think of the motor car as a whole.

The chassis remained unchanged from 1911. The front suspension was always by semi-elliptic springs, but the rear-suspension layout was changed twice. Originally of the platform type with a transverse spring holding the rear shackles of two semi-elliptic springs, threequarter-elliptic springs were fitted from 1908 to 1911, and cantilever thereafter, underslung for the 1911 'London–Edinburgh' and overslung from 1912. The writer is of the opinion that it was a mistake to abandon the three-quarter-elliptic springs, because the only example of this type of Ghost that he has driven – a particularly good one owned by John Bolster – seemed to him to handle better than later examples he has tried.

The other important change made to the car was in the gearbox. Originally the car had four speeds, third direct and fourth an overdrive. This was the gearbox from the unsuccessful 'Thirty' which preceded the 40/50. The car was meant to have a 3-speed gearbox, which was not ready until 1909. In 1912 a Ghost failed to re-start on a 1 in 4 incline during the Alpine Trial with its 7.8 to 1 first gear, and from 1913 a conventional 4-speed gearbox was fitted. In fairness it should be explained that it could do such a re-start at normal altitude, but at 2000 feet the effort was too much for a fully-laden car.

Mention has been made of the fact that four-wheel brakes were fitted in 1924. It is perhaps a symptom of the gulf that existed between Claude Johnson (the policy-maker) and the directors on the one hand, and Henry Royce (in exile for health reasons since before the war) and his engineers on the other, that it was decided by the board in 1923 that the time was ripe for the introduction of four-wheel brakes, and an announcement was made to the world in that year, without proper consultation with Royce, who was not ready to produce them. His design, when it came a year later, was superb. The Ghost's rear-wheel brakes were as good, and as light to operate, as they could be, but this light control over four-wheel brakes could not be achieved without servo-assistance. The servo designed by Royce may have been developed from the Hispano-Suiza system of a friction disc alongside the gearbox, but it was very largely original thinking, and was certainly very effective. The servo worked only on the front wheels, the rear-wheel braking mechanism remaining as before.

The Vintage period, then, had seven years of the Silver Ghost, and during this time the car had four speeds, cantilever rear springs and a power output of some 68 bhp from the 7½-litre engine, which was ultimately pushed up to the dizzy compression ratio of 3.8 to 1. But it was still a 1906 side-valve engine with exposed valve gear. Superlatively well made, beautifully engineered down to its last square-headed bolt, it was still a 20-year-old design.

Claude Johnson decreed soon after the war that it was time for a change, and indeed it was fully time. But what did they do? First, they spent seven years experimenting with many different ideas – V12, straight-eight, ohc six, supercharging – and then what? They put a pushrod cylinder head onto the two three-cylinder blocks of the Ghost engine, covered in the valve gear, and called it the New Phantom. The bore and stroke were altered from the $4\frac{1}{2}$ in × $4\frac{3}{4}$ in of the Ghost to $4\frac{1}{4}$ in × $5\frac{1}{2}$ in, but this was more because of the iniquitous RAC horsepower rating, which was based solely on cylinder bore, than for reasons of efficiency. The chassis was virtually the same as the late Ghosts', and indeed some late Ghosts were made into Phantoms before delivery by putting in the later engine and fitting a radiator with shutters. The Phantom I retained one particular failing of the Ghosts – it required an immense labour to keep it properly lubricated. Of course the car was sold to people with chauffeurs, and they had to be kept occupied when the car was not on the road, but by the mid-'twenties the enormous number of lubrication points could surely have been reduced.

The result of this compromise, which it must be agreed at once was largely dictated by economic circumstances and an intransigent board of directors, was a car with all the archaic faults of the Ghost, but with much of its charm missing. The charm of exquisite workmanship was, of course, still there in abundance, but the steering was dead by comparison, the engine was noisier, and the car felt heavier. Surely Rolls would have found a way round the problems that beset Johnson and Royce? In two respects the Phantom I may be said to have been a better car than the Ghost. The clutch was smoother and the gear change nicer. The increase in power from the overhead valves did little to enhance the performance on a normal road since the advantages of power were more than outweighed by the disadvantages of weight and consequent sluggish handling: this by comparison with the Ghost as originally designed and perfected before the First World War.

During the seven years from 1918 to 1925, when Rolls-Royce were deciding what to do about the 40/50, they did design and make a completely new car, the Twenty. This was a car for a different market and we are indebted to John Fasal for discussing its merits with us. Introduced in 1922, it was aimed at a less-opulent purchaser. By no means cheap at £1100 for the chassis only, it was still little more than half the price of a Ghost. The Twenty was developed from the Ghost, but it had two features in particular which were not introduced for the 40/50 model until the Phantom II of 1929 – semi-elliptic rear springs and a monobloc engine.

By Rolls-Royce standards the Twenty was way ahead of its time, and is still a thoroughly underrated car. Certainly it was an underpowered car for the heavy coachwork with which it was usually fitted, but by scaling down without sacrificing the quality for which Rolls-Royce were justly famous, a very pleasant, unassuming jewel of a car was born. Not a grand car, unpretentious, but with a special charm. The Twenty, 3.1 litres with pushrod valve gear, started out with two-wheel brakes and a three-speed gearbox with central change. In 1925 the servo-assisted front brakes were fitted and, against Royce's wishes, four speeds and right-hand change. Anyone who has driven a Twenty and done the 'trouser-leg trick', as he is bound to do, will agree with Royce about the right-hand change. It is, perhaps, the best place for the levers once you are in the car, but there is not the space in the Twenty to get your leg past the levers without getting one of them up your trousers. Royce was probably right about three speeds, too. The engine is very flexible, and there is really no need for four.

In 1929 the Twenty was bored-out from 3 in to $3\frac{1}{4}$ in and called the 20/25, and in the same year the Phantom I was replaced by the first new 40/50 design, the Phantom II. This was a scaled-up Twenty, boasting some 120 bhp from a 7.6-litre engine. Nonetheless, as George Oliver has pointed out in his excellent 'Profile', the Phantom II had a lower output per litre than the Twenty. The Phantom II inspired some of the most elegant coachwork ever fitted to a motor car; it was a car with effortless torque in top gear, and an inspiring car to drive in a straight line, particularly uphill. But we have already discussed the shortcomings of this car at the beginning of the chapter.

Even by the end of the Vintage period, Rolls-Royce still had good claim to the title of 'Best Car in the World'. If this chapter seems unduly critical, it is because such a claim should be regarded critically. In 1906 the title was earned on every count. By 1930, their hold on it was very much less secure.

Chapter 14
SALMSON

'Salmson – The Car that Wins!', ran the slogan in the mid-'twenties. Indeed, for much of the Vintage decade the Salmson was the most successful competition car in the 1100-cc class, and often beat its 1½-litre opponents. The other Salmson claim to fame is that the firm built the world's first production touring car to be fitted with a twin overhead camshaft engine, and put it on the market in 1922.

As Chris Draper has revealed in his entertaining book *The Salmson Story* (David & Charles, 1974), the expansion of the Salmson factory at Billancourt, Paris, during the First World War was due to the interest of the firm's founder, Emile Salmson, in flying machines. Born in 1859 (he was to die in 1917), he was a manufacturer of general-purpose machinery who, in 1909, financed two Swiss engineers, Canton and Unné, in developing a seven-cylinder water cooled radial engine in which the inherent imbalance of this type of engine was overcome by a rather complicated system of epicyclic gearing, known as the 'Système Canton Unné'. A Breguêt biplane fitted with one of these engines became, in 1912, the first aeroplane to cross the English Channel carrying two passengers, the pilot being W.B. Rhodes-Moorhouse.

During the war Salmson built up an enormous business in the manufacture of magnetos, and continued making aero engines in bigger and bigger numbers. Over twenty-five different types of engine were made during the war of the water cooled radial type, and between 1916–18 nine different types of reconnaissance, fighter and trainer aeroplanes were built, all Salmson-powered, except for one trainer which was fitted with a Clerget engine.

After the war, Salmson continued to manufacture aircraft engines, but other activities were necessary in times of peace, and at first car bodies were made, and also tools for producing woodwork. The big breakthrough came when they obtained a licence to build the British G.N. cyclecar for France and the Latin countries. An initial batch of 3000 was planned.

Certainly in some respects the Salmson version of the two-cylinder chain-drive G.N. was superior to its English counterpart, and some competition successes were gained with the cars, one of the drivers being André Lombard, who also doubled as team manager. Lombard had much to do with getting the production of the French G.N. going, but cyclecar production was only a phase and by 1922, when only half of the projected first batch had been built, the market demanded that it was replaced by a light car or 'voiturette'.

Emile Petit, then aged 38, now comes on the scene, a man who had worked for Clement and Ballot before the war, and who at the age of 19 had patented a peculiar form of valve operation, whereby both inlet and exhaust overhead valves, which were at $60°$ to each other, could be operated by a single pushrod. Just after the war he had designed a four-cylinder 1087-cc air-cooled engine incorporating this arrangement, and it was a thermo-siphon fanless water-cooled development of this 62×90-mm engine which powered the bulk of the Salmsons produced during the Vintage period. This is an interesting point brought out by Chris Draper in his book, and goes against the accepted theory that most Vintage Salmsons had twin overhead camshaft engines.

The four-pushrod arrangement was quite simple, there being a single rocker for both the inlet and the exhaust valve. The exhaust was opened by the normal rocker action when the pushrod was raised by the cam, but there was a T-bar fitted to the inlet end of the rocker operated by two springs which could overcome the inlet valve spring, and there was a recess in the cam lobe into which the pushrod and tappet was forced down by the action of the T-piece springs, thus causing the inlet valve to be opened by the rocker. Each cam lobe therefore incorporated a cam for the exhaust valve and a recess cam for the inlet. Clearances were .008 in for the exhaust and .020 in for the inlet.

The Salmson valve gear was described in a 1922 road test as being 'by no means quiet' due to the use of 'rather rapid acting cams . . . since great pains had been taken to obtain considerable power from the engine'. The advantages of the system were

quoted as being simplicity and a reduction in the number of
moving parts, thus less inertia at high speeds. From the factory
point of view there was probably a saving in manufacturing costs
when 100 cars a week were being made, but it has been said that
the valve gear tended to become a little confused at high revs.
The pushrods were exposed, but there was a cover over the valve
gear.

It has also been said that Petit's valve arrangement had been
used in wartime aircraft engines, but certainly his little air-
cooled engine was strictly for land travel as it had a fan, and if the
fan belt got out of adjustment, or broke, the magneto immediately cut out – an arrangement that would hardly have endeared
itself to an aviator, even had he been in need of a fan.

The water-cooled version of this engine was put in a G.N.-like
chassis with quarter-elliptic springs all round, and the car was
known as the Type AL (André Lombard). Also in recognition of
Lombard the cars carried a St Andrew's cross made out of metal
strips across the radiator block. There was a two-bearing crankshaft, with lubrication by a combination of a plunger pump,
which pumped oil into a cavity from which the main bearings
were lubricated under slight pressure, and splash. Crankcase and
sump were cast aluminium, and the 3-speed gearbox was bolted
to the engine, with the drive via a cone clutch. There was a
torque tube, and no differential was incorporated within the
alloy back axle. The footbrake worked on the offside rear wheel
and the handbrake on the nearside.

If these cars weighed under 350 kg, or just under 7 cwt, which
they could be made to do if one or two fairly vital parts were not
incorporated, they were called cyclecars and qualified for a
special tax concession in France, but if they had a number of
creature comforts and mechanical necessities and weighed over
350 kg, then they became more heavily taxed and were known as
voiturettes.

Being light in weight, the sports versions with two-seater skiff
bodies had a reputation for liveliness in 1922, 10 mph to 30 mph
in 9 seconds being recorded, using the gears.

The writer's first car was a 1925 four-pushrod Salmson, which
the previous owner had bought dismantled, and consequently
he took a long time looking for what he assumed to be the four
missing pushrods. Another memory of this previous owner was

that he had a large hole in the palm of his left-hand driving glove, but this was simply because no effort was ever made to replace the knob missing from the gear lever. In order to get the car's performance to match its screenless and racy bodywork, this 18-year-old driver used to get the car wound up on its 4 to 1 top gear regardless of road hazards, which could be somewhat terrifying to a passenger in the London suburbs of 1939. The valve clearances needed frequent adjustment if power was not to fall off, and the valve gear lubrication was by hand.

At this time the radiator badge of the Société des Moteurs Salmson recognized the work of the Swiss engineers Canton and Unné by bearing the legend 'Syste. Canton Unie', although why Unné's name was amended to 'Unie' is not immediately obvious.

Maximum speed of a Type Sport pushrod car was between 50 and 60 mph, and their works competition record was fairly brief. After Lombard had won a gold medal with the prototype in the 1921 Swiss Six Days' trial, a team of three works cars filled the first three places in the French Light Car Trial held near Paris in February, 1922. In the 1922 Bol d'Or 24-hour race for 1100-cc cars, two Salmson cars came second and third to a side-valve Amilcar, with a Bignan fourth, the latter car being a Salmson with a different radiator.

In their last competition the following year, the inaugural Le Mans 24-Hour race, the two four-pushrod Salmsons beat the Amilcars, and were the first 1100-cc cars to finish, Desvaux and Casse being 12th at 43.8 mph, tieing with a 2.1-litre side-valve DE Delage, and Maurice Benoist and Bueno coming 15th at 41.6 mph. These cars had what was known as the VAL 3 chassis, with half-elliptic front springs, the only departure from standard being the adoption of Rudge hubs and wheels instead of the normal single key drive with one central locking nut, a G.N. legacy. As the result of a disagreement with S.M.S. over the Le Mans entries, Lombard departed from the firm after this race.

Chris Draper's researches have shown us that the four-pushrod cars were the mainstay of Salmson production, over 12 500 having been built between 1921 and 1929. With the introduction of the VAL 5 chassis and larger and more comfortable bodywork, the weight went up and the performance and steering gear ratio went down. Four-wheel brakes were standard (the Perrot system of operation being used at the front), as were shock absorbers. The next chassis, the VAL 3 Series 6, introduced in 1926, had larger brakes and a pressed-steel back axle incorporating a differential, with more weight and a final drive ratio of 5 to 1. Nevertheless, the cars were reliable and comfortable and they found buyers, who in England had to pay around £250. The Type Sport, with the light VAL 3 chassis, continued until 1926.

The design of the four-pushrod cylinder head, with its inclined valves, cried out for the use of twin overhead camshafts to increase its efficiency, and Emile Petit converted the Swiss Six Days car to dohc in about four weeks. This car had the same head and block as the four-pushrod, but a three-bearing crankshaft running on ball races. It won the 1921 Cyclecar GP at Le Mans with ease, Lombard at the wheel. Later in 1921 Lombard drove it in the first 200-Mile Race at Brooklands, averaging 67.39 mph after losing 15 minutes through hitting a kerb, having covered the first hundred miles at 72.8 mph. The delay caused Lombard to lose the lead in the 1100-cc class to Frazer-Nash's G.N.

In 1922 the D type twin ohc touring car was produced with the same 90-mm stroke as the four-pushrod, but the bore increased to 65 mm, giving a capacity of 1193 cc. The camshafts were driven from the front of the engine by a vertical shaft, which in turn drove a cross-shaft for the magneto on one side and the dynamo on the other. The crankcase was cunningly contrived by Petit so that a three-bearing crankshaft could be fitted to it when necessary, and although the D type had a two-bearing shaft, the same crankcase was utilized for the three-bearing racing Salmsons. Early D types had the original 3-speed gearbox, but the second series had a 4-speed box, and a plate clutch to replace the original cone type.

The D type was better finished in detail than its four-pushrod counterpart, and had the distinction of a V radiator. Its successor, the D2, made from 1926 to 1929, continued to have the front-wheel brakes of the later D types, but had a different crankcase to incorporate a Paris-Rhone dynastart at the front and it was the only Vintage Salmson with a full pressure-fed crank.

The D types had heavy, comfortable bodywork and consequently had an adequate rather than a scintillating performance from their small, if advanced, engines, and for this and a better finish the buyer had to pay about £100 more than he would have had to lay out for a similar four-pushrod-engined car. Thus production figures were not large, just over 900 D types built between 1922 and 1926 and nearly 200 D2 types from 1926 to 1929, although the total D and D2 sales of 1111 compare interestingly with the total sales of 1561 of the twin-cam sports models and 12 622 four-pushrod cars.

The first of the twin ohc sports cars appeared in 1923, known as the Grand Sport (Grand Prix in England), and this had the D type engine, with 62-mm bore to keep it in the 1100-cc class, in the VAL 3 chassis, with the same flat radiator as the pushrod cars. This gave way in 1926 to the well-known cowl as seen on the works racing cars. With a compression ratio of 5.8 to 1, 27 bhp at 5300 rpm was produced. In 1926 the four-pushrod sports Salmson cost £165 in England and was supposed to be capable of 60 mph, whereas the twin-cam version cost £285, was guaranteed 70 mph and could do 50 mph in second gear, ratios being 4 to 1, $6\frac{1}{2}$ to 1 and 16 to 1. Weight was 11 cwt, and fuel consumption approximately 35 mpg.

From January, 1927, it was possible to buy a three- or four-seater Grand Sport which utilized the VAL 5 chassis, the car being known as the Grand Sport AL 6. In May of the same year this was replaced after a production run of only 38 by the AL7, which simply had larger brake drums and a pressed-steel back axle (but still with no differential) of which 454 examples were built up until June, 1929.

The last Grand Sport chassis was the GS8, of which 130 were built between 1927 and 1930. This was underslung, with a wider front axle, and the engine set lower in the frame to lower the centre of gravity, with a consequent improvement in handling.

The Grand Sport Special, or GSS, was the fastest Salmson on general sale, of which 138 were made from 1924 to 1927, including a mere 5 Weymann saloons. The main point about the GSS was that it had a three-bearing crankshaft, an increased compression ratio, modified camshafts and a 4-speed gearbox. The sports two-seater cost £350 and the saloon £425 in 1927. The engine would rev happily to over 4500 rpm, giving over 80 mph on the $3\frac{3}{4}$ to 1 top gear. 65 mph was possible in 3rd ($4\frac{1}{2}$ to 1), 40 mph in 2nd ($7\frac{1}{2}$ to 1) and 30 mph in bottom ($13\frac{1}{2}$ to 1). Externally the GS and GSS cars were similar, both as regards the bodywork and engines.

The third type of engine was the fabled San Sebastian, which had a finned sump holding twice as much oil as the GS or GSS, with the same three-bearing crankshaft as the latter engine. The block and head were the same as on the works racing cars, the block having a square-ended sheet-steel water jacket, sealed by rubber rings, and the head was much wider than normal with two vertical sparking plugs per cylinder, the second magneto taking the place of the dynamo on the sports engines. Although originally unblown, the San Sebastian engine could be fitted with a Cozette supercharger driven by a train of gears at the rear of the engine.

A rather special racing chassis and body was produced between 1926 and 1928 of which only 20 examples were built. This was known as the GSC or Grand Sport Course, and it was intended for what became known as 'Service de Course' cars, which were cars used for racing by agents in various countries. The body was narrow and fabric-covered with a very staggered passenger's seat, the front axle was forged H-section with self-wrapping brakes, and the rear axle was the AL cast-aluminium type suitably strengthened. Rudge hubs and wheels were fitted and, of course, the 4-speed gearbox.

Eleven San Sebastian-type engines were fitted into these chassis, and in Chris Draper's opinion are the only cars entitled to be called 'full San Sebastians'. To complicate the issue, some single-plug GSS engines were put into this GSC chassis, and, conversely, some twin-plug San Sebastian engines were put into GSS chassis, without the staggered passenger's seat. Fabric bodywork with a pointed tail was the usual wear for most of the two-seater bodies on the GS and GSS chassis.

The last development of the Service de Course cars was known in France as the Grand Prix, and the total production was 18 between 1927 and 1930. All the Grand Prix cars were supercharged with a No. 8 Cozette and the twin-plug San Sebastian-type engine, and had the underslung GS8 type chassis, often with the narrow GSC type bodywork.

Mention has been made of the works racing cars. These constituted a team of only four twin-plug head cars which, developed over the years by Emile Petit, were highly successful between 1922 and 1926. In the latter year Goutte lapped Brooklands in a blown example at 114.29 mph. A notable feature of

these cars was their desmodromic tappets, and they gave over
100 bhp in blown form.

A one-off 750-cc Salmson raced in 1923, winning the 750-cc
GP des Voiturettes at Le Mans driven by Lombard from a
Senechal and an Austin. It had an 1100-cc engine suitably
reduced in capacity, but its *raison d'être* is difficult to fathom, no
other 750-cc Salmson ever being produced.

The most remarkable Salmson racing engine of the Vintage
decade was Petit's 49.9 × 70-mm straight-eight, 1085-cc design,
which would rev up to 8000 rpm and gave 100 bhp at 5800 rpm.
For short periods it could produce 170 bhp at 7200 rpm. With
central drive to the camshafts and twin Cozette superchargers,
the overall design was similar to that of the straight-eight Alfa
Romeo which appeared three years later, in 1931. The 4-4 type
crankshaft had five ball and roller main bearings and roller
big-ends, in contrast to the 2-4-2 crankshaft of the Alfa Romeo,
which had ten main bearings, all plain, as were the big-ends. The
Salmson had two plugs per cylinder and desmodromic tappets
as on the four-cylinder racing engines.

Casse drove a Salmson with one of these straight-eight engines
in the 1928 200-Mile Race at Brooklands, and found the exhaust
burning his feet as on the straight-eight 1½-litre GP Delages,
whilst a broken oil pipe caused his car to fall further and further
back in the race. Some hill-climb successes were obtained at
Limonest and Gaillon, with Yves Giraud-Cabantous at the
wheel.

From 1927, Salmson tended to concentrate on sports car
racing and were very successful at Le Mans, winning the Rudge
Cup in 1927 and 1928, and in the former year Salmsons were
second and third overall in the race, remarkable for 1100-cc cars.
The average of the Rudge Cup winners in 1927 was 52.28 mph
and in 1928 the average rose to 57.1 mph when the successful car
driven by Casse and Rousseau had a twin-plug head. By 1929
factory interest in racing had virtually ceased, though private
owners continued to do quite well. In this year Emile Petit left
the firm.

To return to the touring cars, between 1927 and 1929 a rather
interesting four-cylinder car was made which had quite an
eccentric engine for a Salmson, as it boasted no less than eight
pushrods. Anyone thinking this engine was built on the lines of

other conventional pushrod four-cylinder engines, however, was doomed to disappointment, for although there was a separate cam lobe for the exhaust and inlet valve, the inlet still operated on four-pushrod lines, the inlet lobe having an inverse cam in place of a normal one. Block and head were almost identical to their four-pushrod counterparts, and with a row of inlet valves on one side of the head and exhaust valves on the other, this was a suitable way of getting around the problem of opening and closing them. The alternative, other than the four-pushrod method, would have been to have two camshafts in the crankcase like a Riley, or else resort to methods used by B.M.W. in the 'thirties and Peugeot later on at considerable extra cost. With several thousand four-pushrod engines in use by 1927, the inverse cam method of inlet valve opening was not exactly unproven, and, of course, with a separate cam for both inlet and exhaust valves there was more scope for optimum valve timing. The chassis was the same as the VAL 3 Series 6 except that the front crossmember was swept down to make room for a Paris-Rhone dynastart, and for this it was renamed the VAL 3 Series 7. The car was a good workhorse, and over 750 examples were built and sold. Prices ranged from £225 for the four-seater tourer to £285 for the saloon.

Two other Salmson products at the end of the Vintage period were a six-cylinder model and the S4. The '15/30' six of 1928 had a pointed radiator and the traditional 62 × 90-mm dimensions gave it a capacity of 1630 cc. It had a V radiator and the twin overhead camshaft drive was at the rear of the engine. It was priced at £450 with saloon bodywork, £75 more than the D2 saloon. Very few examples were made.

The S4, or (12/24), also had a twin ohc engine, but cylinder dimensions of 65 × 90 mm, giving a capacity of 1193 cc the same as the D type. However, the engine design was different as like the 15/30 six-cylinder it had its camshaft drive at the rear and it was not a Petit design, thus owing little to the Vintage racing and sports cars. It was quite a successful touring car, and its manufacture was carried on in the 'thirties, when it was to form the basis of the excellent British Salmson sports cars.

Clutton and Stanford, writing in 1954, described the small French Vintage sports cars like Salmson and Amilcar as the ephemerals of the Vintage period and said it was too much to expect consistent performances from them after nearly thirty years of hard use.

Chris Draper has told of how the cost accountant-minded S.M.S. managing director, Heinrich, saw that the production cars were built down to a price in spite of Emile Petit's protestations, and thus guided the firm successfully through years of financial recession. Yet, thanks to the genius of Emile Petit, Salmsons carved a unique niche for themselves in the 1100-cc class by way of their commercial success, competition achievements and originality in design. They were only equalled by Amilcar with the advent of the latter's C6 design.

Amicale Salmson in France and the Salmson Register in England still keep enthusiasm for the cars alive, although a tiny percentage survive to support the Clutton and Stanford viewpoint. The four-pushrod and even the GS cars are slow by modern standards, and more often than not the smaller the engine capacity the greater the unreliability factor of surviving Vintage sports cars. Like their Alfa Romeo and Bentley counterparts with overhead camshafts, Salmsons of late have been known to suffer from stripped cross shaft gears. Nevertheless, the few surviving San Sebastian-engined cars still have a remarkable turn of speed, and must be looked upon as being classics, along with the Amilcar Sixes.

Chapter 15
SUNBEAM

Sunbeam were not unique in building fine touring cars during the Vintage decade, but they were certainly unique in also building during that period successful Land Speed Record cars, successful Grand Prix cars, and a sports model with a remarkable engine based on Grand Prix practice.

The founder of the Sunbeam company was John Marston (1836–1918), who was educated at Ludlow Grammar School and Christ's Hospital, and who was the son of a Mayor of Ludlow. By 1859, at the early age of 23, he was already a manufacturer of tinplate and japanned goods, having taken over a business at Bilston, Staffordshire. In 1871 he moved his business to a works in Wolverhampton, where in 1887 he founded the Sunbeamland Cycle Factory. The Sunbeam bicycle achieved a fine reputation and was famous for its enclosed oil-bath chaincase. A certain Thomas Cureton, who had joined the company as an apprentice from Rugby school, eventually became Marston's right-hand man, and it was Cureton who built an experimentar car in 1899 and persuaded Marston into an interest in motor car manufacture. However, the first Sunbeam car to be put on the market in 1901 was a curious cyclecar powered by a 2¾-hp De Dion engine known as the Sunbeam-Mabley, which had single staggered undriven wheels front and rear and an axle in the middle supporting two driven wheels. Its designer was not Cureton but a Mr Mabberley-Smith, who was used to strange shapes through being connected with ornamental ironwork, and he drew a royalty on each Sunbeam-Mabley sold.

In 1902 Thomas Charles Pullinger joined the firm, an engineer with experience of light car design in France, having gone to Darracq as designer and personal assistant in 1892. Pullinger suggested buying chassis from Berliet of Lyons, and selling them in England under the name of 'Sunbeam'. He envisaged eventually using Berliet engines and gearboxes and mounting these in chassis built by Sunbeam, and this is what happened. A Sunbeam carburettor was fitted in 1904, which was the last year of Sunbeam-Mabley manufacture. A six-cylinder Sunbeam was built in 1904 and was offered to the public at about the same time as the more celebrated Napier 'six', but little came of it and the four-cylinder T-head 12-hp was the staple Sunbeam diet. From 1903 it had its final drive chains enclosed in oil-bath cases like the Sunbeam bicycles.

By 1906 Pullinger had left Sunbeam to join Humber, and the Berliet connection was dropped and complete Sunbeam cars, still with enclosed chain final drive, were built to the excellent designs of Angus Shaw, who had worked under Pullinger in the drawing office. Meanwhile Sunbeam's famous Moorfield Works had been expanded in the Moore St and Cross St area of Wolverhampton. These works actually grew from a disused coachhouse beside the Villiers Works, where pedals and other parts for Sunbeam bicycles were made by the Villiers Company. This was the same coachhouse where the first experimental single-cylinder Sunbeam cars had been made by Cureton.

In 1909 a catalyst was introduced into the Sunbeam Company, destined to have a profound effect on their activities during the Vintage years. This was Cureton's engagement on the design side of Louis Hervé Coatalen, then 30 years old, a native of Britanny. Coatalen had worked in the drawing offices of Panhard, Clément and De Dion Bouton in France before he was 21 and had then come to England where he became chief engineer at Humber's for nine years. For a year after this he was in partnership with William Hillman, who made the Hillman-Coatalen car, and then he made his move to Sunbeam.

In the words of Anthony Heal, the Sunbeam historian, Coatalen 'revitalized the whole concern', inspiring the design, supervizing the manufacture and himself testing the completed cars. The notable Angus Shaw designs had been the 16/20 with a 95 × 120, 3402-cc L-head engine, and a 5103-cc six-cylinder version of the same car called the 25/30. Coatalen revised these models, and introduced a new smaller model called the 12/16 hp, with a four-cylinder 80 × 120-mm, 2412-cc, T-head engine, with a live axle.

Most significant from the point of view of future developments in the company was Coatalen's interest in racing-car design. In

the winter of 1909 he had built a chain-drive single-seater car for
Brooklands racing called *Nautilus* with an experimental four-
cylinder 92 × 160 (4257-cc) engine, having a 16-valve head, the
valves being operated via pushrods by two camshafts in the
crankcase. More successful was the shaft-drive single-seater
which followed, called *Toodles II*, another four-cylinder of
80 × 160 mm (3217-cc), but with 8 overhead valves at a 100°
angle operated by a single chain-driven overhead camshaft.
Coatalen raced these cars himself, and also had successes with
competition versions of the 12/16 hp, whilst the 16/20 hp also
won competition awards.

By 1912 all three Sunbeam models marketed had long-stroke
L-head side-valve engines, this head design being adopted the
year after the first Sunbeam had been entered in a race abroad.
This car had a prototype long stroke L-head engine and was
basically a standard 12/16-hp model. It ran in the Coupe de
l'Auto race at Boulogne, but retired with a broken steering
connection after 8 laps of the 12-lap race.

In 1912 Coatalen was given a seat on the Sunbeam board, and
his cars achieved a great success in the French GP at Dieppe,
where they won the team prize and came 1st, 2nd and 3rd in the
Coupe de l'Auto run in conjunction with the GP as well as
gaining 3rd, 4th and 5th places in the GP itself behind a Peugeot
and a Fiat with engines respectively 3 and 5 times the size of
those of the Sunbeams. The Sunbeams were improved versions
of the 1911 Coupe de l'Auto car, with 80 × 149-mm (2996-cc)
engines, whereas the engine of the standard 12/16 hp was now
80 × 150 mm (3016-cc) and just over the 3-litre Coupe de l'Auto
engine capacity limit.

A six-cylinder version of the Coupe de l'Auto side-valve engine
made up of two blocks of three cylinders was used in the 1913
Grand Prix Sunbeams, giving them a 4524-cc capacity, whilst a
9043-cc V12-cylinder car was built for record breaking known
as *Toodles V* using four blocks of three cylinders. Third in the
French GP, 3rd in the Coupe de l'Auto and 4th at Indianapolis
were notable 1913 Sunbeam successes, *Toodles IV* with a six-
cylinder 90 × 160-mm (6107-cc) side-valve engine scoring at
Indianapolis. This 1911 car was fitted with Coatalen's first six-
cylinder racing engine, based on the production 25/30 engine.

A big advance in Sunbeam racing-engine design was made in

1914 when the Swiss Ernest Henry's ideas were adopted and cars with four-cylinder 16-valve twin overhead camshaft engines were entered for the French GP and cars with similar, but slightly smaller bore engines, were entered for the Isle of Man Tourist Trophy race, the latter effort ending in victory, although in the French GP at Lyons Sunbeam finished no higher than 5th.

During the First World War the 12/16-hp Sunbeam was built under licence by the Rover Company, who fitted a taller, narrower, radiator, and this model and the four-cylinder 16/20-hp (90 × 160-mm, 4070-cc) was supplied to the War Office for use in France. Coatalen had been developing aircraft engines since 1913, and production of these was greatly increased during the war, their design showing the influence of Ernest Henry.

Amazingly enough, Sunbeam also produced racing cars during the hostilities, the Belgian Jean Christiaens, who acted as Sunbeam's test pilot, driving a new six-cylinder twin overhead camshaft 4.9-litre Sunbeam (8.15 × 157 mm) to 4th place in the 1916 Indianapolis 500-mile race. These cars, which were the first Sunbeams with aluminium pistons, as well as 1913 and 1914 GP Sunbeams were campaigned in races in the USA in 1915 and 1916 by drivers such as Louis Chevrolet, Galvin, the Englishman van Raalte, and Grant, whilst the 1913 V12 9048-cc racer *Toodles V* was driven to a win in a 6-mile race at Sheepshead Bay in 1915 by Ralph de Palma and to a 3rd place at Los Angeles Dirt Track in 1916 by Hughie Hughes. It was not until 1922, however, that a Sunbeam agency was established at 25 West 57th Street, New York, managed by racing driver Dario Resta.

In their book *Motoring Entente*, Ian Nichols and Kent Karslake tell us that John Marston never retired, and in 1916, at the age of eighty, he still used to ride a bicycle from his home in Tettenhall to the tram terminus, and continued the journey into Wolverhampton by public transport. He died in March, 1918, and Thomas Cureton took over the chairmanship, but he was in poor health and died in 1921, shortly after his retirement.

In 1919 Sunbeam offered two models to the public, the four-cylinder 16-hp, which was the highly successful pre-war 12/16 model with slight modifications, and a similarly modified version of the pre-war six-cylinder 25/30, now known as the 24 hp. Both had a bore and stroke of 80 × 150 mm, giving capacities of 3016 cc and 4524 cc respectively. Main differences from the pre-war models were semi-elliptic instead of threequarter-elliptic rear springs, re-designed rear axles and brake operation, and the taller, narrower, radiator. Both had L heads, non-detachable, with the slightly inclined side valves on the nearside of the block which had been a Sunbeam feature ever since Angus Shaw's old T-head design gave way to Coatalen's L-head.

The 16-hp had a single monobloc iron casting, whilst the 24-hp had two blocks of three, the cylinders being offset by 20 mm. The crankcase was aluminium and the plain bearing crankshaft ran in five bearings on the four-cylinder engine and seven bearings on the six-cylinder. Pistons were cast iron and the camshaft on both models was chain-driven, with the valve springs retained by cotter pins through the valves, a popular method at that time which became Riley Nine practice. On the 16-hp the magneto and water pump were driven by a cross-shaft, but the drive was by inverted tooth chain on the 24 hp.

As the Sunbeam directors were also directors of the Claudel-Hobson carburettor company, it is surprising to find SU carburettors were originally specified on these Sunbeam models, although these were later replaced by Claudel-Hobsons, which were on the offside of the engine feeding into a water-heated manifold, with a ribbed exhaust manifold on the near side. The sparking plugs were screwed into the inlet valve caps.

Leather-faced cone clutches took the drive to a separate 4-speed gearbox with a right-hand lever. The gearbox had a foot-operated transmission brake behind it, the cast-iron-faced shoes on the brakes on the rear wheels being operated by a hand lever. Top gear ratio for both models was 3.59 to 1, although for some strange reason the 24-hp long-wheelbase limousine had a higher 3.4 to 1 axle ratio with larger tyres (880 × 120 instead of 820 × 120). An open propellor shaft was fitted, and the 1919 rear axle was curiously offset, but a heavier axle more like the pre-war one was introduced for 1920 and 1921.

Jean Christiaens, who was head of the experimental department in 1919, was tragically killed and his mechanic, Frank Bills, injured, in March of that year when driving an Indianapolis car in the street outside the works. In this year two 4.9-litre Sunbeams were entered for Indianapolis, but were withdrawn. However, they were successful at Brooklands and in sprints in 1920 and 1921.

It was in August, 1920, that the Sunbeam Motor Car Co amalgamated with A. Darracq and Co (1905) Ltd. A year before the Anglo–French Darracq Company, with works at Suresnes, Paris, had absorbed the Clement Talbot Motor Co of Anglo–French derivations, and had also taken over the spring makers Jonas Woodhead & Co, the engineering firm of Heenan and Froude and W. & G. Du Cros Ltd, coachbuilders and commercial vehicle makers. The new group combined the names of Sunbeam, Talbot and Darracq, and became known as S.T.D. Ltd, whilst James Todd, the Darracq chairman, became chairman of S.T.D. and also of Sunbeam.

On October 10th, 1920, a huge new Sunbeam racing car driven by René Thomas averaged 108.6 mph over the flying kilometre to take the record for the Gaillon Hill Climb between Mantes and Rouen, in France. This was the famous 350-hp, destined to break the World's Land Speed Record in 1922 at Brooklands driven by Kenelm Lee Guinness with a speed of 133.75 mph, and at Pendine in 1924 and 1925 at 146.16 mph and 150.87 mph respectively, driven on both these occasions by Malcolm Campbell. It was thus the first car officially to exceed 150 mph. Although often described as an aeroplane-engined car, in fact the 120 × 135-mm, 18 322-cc, V12-cylinder engine was specially built for the car, the Sunbeam aero engine to which it bore the closest resemblance in design being the V8 Arab. The engine was a 60-degree V made up of four cast-aluminium blocks of three cylinders, with an overhead camshaft to each bank operating one inlet and two exhaust valves per cylinder. Two twelve-cylinder B.T.H. Magnetos fired two plugs per cylinder, and two Claudel HC7 twin-coke carburettors were fitted. There was a seven plain main bearing crankshaft with each crankpin taking two connecting rods, and there was dry-sump lubrication. 355 bhp at 2300 rpm was developed.

The engine, mounted in a sub-frame, was put into a channel-steel chassis with a 10 ft 7-in wheelbase and a 4 ft 6-in track, which may be compared with the 10 ft 4-in wheelbase and 4 ft 6-in track of the contemporary 16-hp Sunbeam touring car. The chassis of the 350-hp car was fitted with Rudge-Whitworth wheels with 880 × 120-mm tyres, and a multi-plate clutch took the drive from the 22-in diameter flywheel to a separate four-speed gearbox. Traditionally the aero-engined monsters were chain-driven, but the 350-hp Sunbeam showed its superiority by having Hotchkiss drive to a 1.5 to 1 ratio bevel back axle. Like the 1913 Coupe de l'Auto and Grand Prix cars, with their Goodyear artillery wheels, the 350-hp car had no differential gear in the back axle.

There were semi-elliptic springs all round, and damping by both hydraulic and Hartford friction shock absorbers. The brakes on the rear wheels were operated by a pedal, whilst the handbrake worked on the transmission. A single-seater body was fitted and, including the lumps of lead in the chassis side members over the rear axle to give extra stability, the weight worked out at just over 31 cwt.

Lee Guinness had some successes with the car in Brooklands races, after which in Campbell's ownership, and with altered bodywork, it appeared on the sands at Skegness as well as Pendine. It was last used competitively by Billy Cotton, who covered the flying kilometre on Southport sands at 121.57 mph in 1936, and today it is kept in the National Motor Museum at Beaulieu, having done some demonstration runs in more recent years.

Whilst the side-valve 16-hp and 24-hp models were still the only production Sunbeam offerings, a new Grand Prix car was on the stocks for 1921. This was a straight-eight 3-litre of Ernest Henry design, which bore a relationship to his 3-litre Ballot.

On both cars the valve gear of the twin overhead camshaft design with 4 valves per cylinder at a 60° angle was the same, as were the bore and stroke of 65 × 112 mm, 2973 cc, the 'four-four' offset crankshaft and the 1-8-3-6-4-5-2-7 firing order. Both engines had dry sump lubrication, but the Sunbeam's five-bearing crankshaft had plain main and big-end bearings and the bottom end design allowed higher revs than the roller mains and plain big-ends found on the Ballot. For this reason the Sunbeam had a longer engine than the Ballot, but its weight was not excessive in comparison due to its having two blocks of four cylinders with integral heads made of aluminium, whereas the Ballot blocks were cast iron. The Sunbeam engine produced 108 bhp at 4000 rpm, and was more flexible than the Ballot unit, which gave 107 bhp at 3800 rpm. For 1921 the Sunbeam had coil ignition and four Zenith carburettors, whilst the Ballot had two Marelli magnetos and two Claudels. Both cars had 4-speed gearboxes, and whilst it is known one Sunbeam was geared at

3.6 to 1 for the hilly Isle of Man circuit in 1922, the Ballot top gear ratio has been quoted at 3.0 to 1. The Ballot engine was fitted with a flywheel and a cone clutch, but the Sunbeam was unusual in having no flywheel, whilst the clutch was a Hele-Shaw multi-plate. The Sunbeam had front-wheel brakes, and these were operated by the handbrake, whilst the pedal worked the rear brakes. With an all-up weight of 24 cwt, the Sunbeam was 1 cwt heavier than the Ballot, and the fact that its maximum speed of 108 mph was 4 mph slower than the Ballot's 112 mph was probably due to the fact that its frontal area was 14 ft² to the 12 ft² of the Ballot.

The complexities of the S.T.D. organization were shown by the fact that three of the 3-litre straight-eight cars were entered for Indianapolis in 1921, two with Sunbeam radiators and one with a Talbot radiator. Streamlined tails were fitted to the cars, and the American Ora Haibe, taking the place of Dario Resta, finished 5th in one of the Sunbeams at 83.86 mph, whilst the other two cars retired. In the 1921 French GP at Le Mans, the two Sunbeam entries were scratched and four straight-eight 3-litre cars were entered, two as Talbots and two as Talbot-Darracqs, although to add to the confusion the two Talbot-Darracqs appeared to have Sunbeam radiators. The cars were plagued by tyre troubles, and Boillot's blue Talbot-Darracq was 5th and the green Talbots of Kenelm Lee Guinness and Henry Segrave were 8th and 9th respectively, Thomas's Talbot-Darracq retiring. It is significant that a 3-litre Ballot was second to the winning Duesenberg.

1922 was the first year of the 2-litre GP formula, but the 3-litre Sunbeams were eligible for the Isle of Man TT in June for which cars were entered to be driven by Segrave, Lee Guinness and Jean Chassagne. For this race two vertical Claudel C2C, 42-choke carburettors replaced the four horizontal Zeniths, and two four-cylinder B.T.H. magnetos replaced the Delco coil and distributor, the compression ratio was raised from 5.7 to 1 to 6.3 to 1 and camshafts with a lower lift but longer overlap were substituted. Lee Guinness non-started, Segrave retired with ignition trouble after putting up fastest lap, but Chassagne won easily from Vauxhall and Bentley opposition. This must have helped to justify the £50 000 which S.T.D. spent on the cars.

Chassagne's car survives today in New Zealand, and Segrave's car in England, where it is still raced. Its present owner, Guy Shoosmith, is of the opinion that the engine was probably made at Suresnes, and the chassis at Wolverhampton. These Sunbeams are renowned for their excellent handling, and the 'invincible' four-cylinder Talbot-Darracq voiturette racing cars of 1921/22 had engines which were virtually half the 3-litre Sunbeam engine.

At the 1921 Motor Show, where the 1922 models were on view, it was seen that Sunbeam had phased out their side-valve models, the 16-hp and 24-hp. They were replaced by the '16/40' four-cylinder and '24/60' six-cylinder, and these had pushrod overhead valve engines in the existing chassis. Both the four- and six-cylinder blocks were monobloc castings, with detachable heads, and aluminium pistons were now used. The new engines were still of 80 × 150 mm, and John R. Coombes and John Wyer in an informative article in *Motor Sport* of December, 1949, stated that the bottom half was identical with that of the side-valve units, and, indeed, it is believed that several sv cars were converted to the new specifications. The valve gear was enclosed in an aluminium cover, with the Claudel carburettors still on the opposite side of the block to the exhaust. The main chassis change was the lowering of the final drive ratio from 3.59 to 1 to 4 to 1. Prices had been reduced from £1225 for the 16-hp to £960 for the 16/40 and from £1510 for the 24-hp to £1295 for the 24/60.

However, an entirely new model was also introduced at the end of 1921 which set the pattern for future Vintage Sunbeam models. It was called the 14-hp, although its RAC rating was only 12.8 hp, and it was listed at £725. It was a four-cylinder and its bore and stroke of 72 × 120 mm, 1954 cc, was destined to be adopted by Lagonda with their famous 14/60 and 2-litre cars from 1926 onwards. The 14-hp Sunbeam engine did not have the complications of the Lagonda design, however, having a single camshaft driven by a silent chain from the three-bearing crankshaft, and pushrod overhead valves, two per cylinder. The block was aluminium with shrunk-in steel liners, and the integral crankcase top half was aluminium. Aluminium pistons were, of course, employed on this design. This was the first Sunbeam engine to have the inlet and exhaust hot-spotted together on the offside of the cast-iron head. A single vertical Claudel carburettor was fitted and ignition was by coil and distributor with automatic advance. Cooling was by water pump and fan, with the dynamo driven by whittle belt from the crankshaft. Whilst all the other models had cone clutches, the 14 had a single-plate clutch, and the aluminium gearbox, which was in unit with the engine, had 3 speeds, with ratios of 4.5, 7.92 and 13.19 to 1. On this model torque tube transmission was adopted with a spherical joint behind the gearbox, and the semi-floating rear axle had spiral bevel drive and a two-star bevel differential enclosed in a casing made up of two steel pressings welded together. Although the front springs were semi-elliptics, a new Sunbeam feature was introduced with the idea of giving a more comfortable ride – cantilever rear springs, which had been a Darracq feature.

The time had not yet arrived to fit front-wheel brakes to a production car, and separate sets of fabric-faced shoes for the hand and foot brakes were fitted in the aluminium rear drums with shrunk-in steel liners. Like all the other models, the 14 had steel artillery wheels, but the size was 815 × 120 mm instead of 820 × 120 mm. Wheelbase was 9 ft 10¾ in and track 4 ft 6 in.

Also listed for 1922 were the extremely interesting 'O.V.' sports versions of the four-cylinder 16/40 and six-cylinder 24/60, which were an adaptation of the Henry racing designs for general sale. These had alloy crankcases, 80 × 150-mm cast-iron blocks, and detachable heads with a single overhead camshaft driven by bevels and a vertical shaft from the front of the crankshaft and operating four inclined valves per cylinder through rockers. There was a single Claudel carburettor and two coils and distributors fired two plugs per cylinder. Unfortunately hardly any cars with these engines seem to have been sold, it being rumoured that only one engine was actually manufactured. Instead a light sports 24/60 which retained the old higher 3.59 to 1 back axle ratio was sold with a slightly tuned version of the pushrod engine. This was an extremely handsome car, though still with artillery wheels, in fact in the words of William Boddy in his *Sports Car Pocketbook* it was 'one of the most beautiful open cars of this era ever made'.

The last Henry-type Grand Prix Sunbeam was built for the 1922 season, but only appeared in the French GP at Strasbourg and at Brooklands. The 1914 four-cylinder GP Sunbeam engine had been a copy of Henry's contemporary Peugeot design, and the 4.9-litre 1916 Indianapolis Sunbeam engine was a six-cylinder version of the same thing, whilst the 1921 GP Sunbeam engine had copied Henry's Ballot design. The 1922 Sunbeam car was a design by Henry for Sunbeam alone, and was his last complete racing car design. It was a 68 × 126-mm, 1975-cc, cast-iron monobloc four-cylinder, with a fixed head and twin ohc, each camshaft running in three ball bearings, the aluminium pistons having a 6.5 to 1 compression ratio, and the engine giving 88 bhp at 4200 rpm. Maximum speed was 100 mph. There were four valves per cylinder with the inlets larger than the exhausts, the former being at 20° from the vertical and the latter at 40°, with the inlets higher in the head. The big-ends were plain, but the crankshaft ran in three ball bearing mains. Two Scintilla magnetos fed two plugs per cylinder, one between the two inlet valves and the other central, and two Zenith or Claudel carburettors were fitted. Lubrication was by dry sump. The engine was mounted direct on the chassis frame, Henry having deserted his usual sub-frame arrangement, and a cone fabric clutch transmitted the drive to a 4-speed gearbox in unit with the engine. There was an open propellor shaft Hotchkiss drive, semi-elliptic springs all round and cable-operated four-wheel brakes with a friction drum servo driven off the gearbox. 835 × 135 tyres were fitted to the wire wheels, and the weight was under 14 cwt. The spare wheel was carried longitudinally in the tail, and the front axle was built up with a forged H-section centre and tapered tubular outer ends. Wheelbase was 8 ft 2 in with a 3 ft 11-in track.

These cars handled, braked and accelerated well, and in trials had proved faster over the Isle of Man TT circuit than the 3-litre cars. They were firm favourites for the French GP until the red six-cylinder Fiats appeared, which proceeded to lap 30 seconds faster than the Sunbeams. To counter this lower axle ratios were fitted to the Sunbeams and the oil pressure increased. Due to consequent high revving, the cars of Chassagne and Lee Guinness were out with valve trouble after five laps, but Segrave was battling with the leading four-cylinder Ballot and eight-cylinder Type 30 Bugatti behind the Fiats, only to retire with a broken piston, after 29 laps of the 60-lap 498.85-mile race. These Sunbeams were far from being a successful Henry design, but certainly seem to have been as good as any of their contemporaries, barring the invincible Fiats, and examples have continued to race up to the present day, where three of the four cars built are in running order in England today and a fourth car is in Australia fitted with a Talbot-Darracq engine. The writer once had great difficulty in changing down into third gear in one of these cars at Silverstone, until he realized third was very much closer to top than it was on the 22/90 Alfa Romeo he was using as his road car, and less revs when changing down produced better gear changes.

Two hybrid Sunbeams, which had already performed extremely well at Brooklands, took part in the 1922 Coppa Florio race over four laps (268½ miles) of the Medium Madonie circuit in Sicily against two sleeve-valve Peugeots, three Diattos and two O.M.s. The Sunbeams had 1916 4.9-litre Indianapolis engines in the chassis of 1921 3-litre cars such as had won the 1922 Tourist Trophy the previous June – the Sicilian race taking place in November. Segrave finished a poor second, one hour and seven minutes behind Boillot's Peugeot after averaging 32.5 mph for just over 8¼ hours. Chassagne, after breaking an oil pipe, finished fourth behind Becquet's Peugeot, but was outside the time limit for the race. Segrave's hybrid car later had a long and successful career at Brooklands, whilst Chassagne's passed into the hands of an Argentinian racing driver, Martin de Alzaga. A third single-seater car was built with record attempts in view.

For 1923 both the 16/40 and the 24/60 had front-wheel brakes, and a mechanical servo was optional for those who liked to pay extra for it. Apart from this the specification was unchanged, but there were extensive changes to the 14-hp model, which was reduced in price from £725 to £685, at the same time as the 16/40 was reduced from £960 to £895 and the 24/60 from £1295 to £1220.

The changes to the 14-hp were mainly in the engine department, wherein the block became a separate iron casting, and the coil ignition was replaced by a magneto incorporating manual advance and retard. The dynamo was now incorporated in the magneto drive on the nearside of the engine, a fan was optional and the valve cover became deeper and squarer. The brake drums became steel pressings with cast-iron facings on the foot brake shoes (braking was still only on the rear wheels), and the track was increased by 3 in to 4 ft 6 in.

From the competition aspect, 1923 was an *annus mirabilis*.

Malcolm Campbell took the 350 hp Sunbeam to speed trials at
Fanöe Island, Denmark, in June, where, unfortunately, the
146.4 mph he achieved over the mile was not recognized as a
world's record as the timing apparatus was not approved by the
F.I.A. However, he won the over 6-litre class. After having had
a loan of the car from Coatalen for the Saltburn Speed Trials in
June of the previous year, Campbell kept worrying Coatalen to
sell it to him, and he had bought it for a high but undisclosed
sum just before the Fanöe trials were due to be held. The car had
been lying at Brooklands for a year, and it was delivered by rail
to Horley station in Surrey, from where Campbell elected to
drive the car to his home at Povey Cross, a few miles away. The
car ran very badly, with clouds of smoke pouring from the
bonnet and exhaust, and inspection at Povey Cross revealed that
the oil scavenge pump had ceased working. Extensive last-
minute repairs to the gearbox also had to be made. Campbell had
previously acquired the ex-Segrave 4.9-litre Coppa Florio car,
with which he won his class at Fanöe, and at Shelsley Walsh the
following September, and made ftd at Porthcawl Speed Trials
on the weekend following the Fanöe meeting.

The highlight of 1923 from the Sunbeam point of view was the
French Grand Prix held at Tours on July 2nd. It was obvious
that the Fiat racing design team was made up of the most formid-
able talents, and with typical astuteness Coatalen lured one of
the team away to work for Sunbeam in the same way as Ferrari
was destined to lure away another Fiat designer, Vittorio Jano,
to work for Alfa Romeo. Coatalen's choice was Vincenzo Bertarione, and for the 1923 Grand Prix Bertarione came up with
a six-cylinder engine on the lines of the 1922 Fiat GP engine, but
an improvement on it. The six cylinders were of 67×94 mm,
1988 cc, to the Fiat's 65×100 mm, 1991 cc, and the Sunbeam
engine produced 108 bhp at 5000 rpm, with a 7.4 to 1 compression ratio, to the 96 bhp at 5500 rpm of the Fiat on a 7.1 to 1
compression ratio. Twin ohc and two valves per cylinder were
employed, and although the Fiat's valves were large, the
diameter of Bertarione's exhaust valves was larger, and they were
set at the same angle of 96°. Cylinder-block construction was the
same, two blocks of three with welded-on water jackets. The Fiat
had a Scintilla magneto and Fiat carburettor, the Sunbeam had
a Bosch magneto and Solex carburettor. On both engines split-

cage roller races were used for mains and big-ends, the Sunbeam
having 8 main bearings to the Fiat's 7. Both engines had dry-
sump lubrication.

The Fiat had a wheelbase of 8 ft 2½ in, and by a curious
coincidence the wheelbase of Henry's 1922 Strasbourg GP
Sunbeam had been only half an inch shorter, with the same track
of 3 ft 11 in. It is said that the Henry chassis was used for the 1923
cars, which certainly had the same wheelbase and track, with the
same front axle construction, but the engines could not have been
dropped into the old chassis as the Strasbourg cars still continued
to survive. It would seem that new chassis were constructed, and
in *The Racing Car* (Batsford, 1956), Cyril Posthumus has said that,
externally at least, the new Sunbeam chassis appeared to follow
Fiat layout quite closely. The body was also Fiat-like.

Not much has been made of the fact that the Sunbeam gearbox
only had 3 speeds, most unusual on a GP contender between the
wars, the only other makes actually to win Continental Grands
Prix in that period with 3-speed boxes being Duesenberg in 1921
and Alfa Romeo in 1935. Admittedly the Tours course was
practically flat, and one side of the triangular 14.78-mile circuit
was virtually straight for some five miles, although there were
corners on the other legs. The road itself was steeply cambered,
narrow, poorly surfaced with many potholes, and dusty.

The 3-speed gearbox on the 1923 GP Sunbeam was in unit
with the engine, and the clutch was multi-plate. Not only did the
Sunbeam have one less gear than the Fiat, but it also differed in
having Hotchkiss drive instead of the Fiat's torque tube. Both
cars had semi-elliptic springs all round and servo-assisted brakes,
and their weights were similar.

The story of the 1923 French GP is well known; the surprise
appearance in practice of new eight-cylinder supercharged Fiats,
which quickly supplanted the Sunbeams as favourites for the
race, thus bringing a repetition of the practice at Strasbourg in
1922: the race itself, run in hot sunshine and dust, with the
Sunbeams challenging the Fiats, which suffered troubles through
grit entering their supercharger intakes: the exciting appear-
ances of the Sunbeams of Lee Guinness and Divo at the head of
the field at different times, until they experienced troubles: and,
finally, the defection of Salamano's Fiat with two laps to go,
allowing Segrave to win after his car's clutch slip had cured itself,

with Divo coming second, Friedrich (Bugatti) third, and Lee Guinness fourth. And the realization that this was the first-ever win by a British car in the French Grand Prix, a feat not to be repeated until 1960.

The following October Divo won the Gran Premio de Automoviles in a Tours Sunbeam by 50 secs from Zborowski's Miller, after averaging 97 mph over 248½ miles, or 200 laps, of the banked track at Sitges in Spain.

Unlike all the other racing Sunbeams, which had competitive careers of some length in amateur hands after the works were done with them, the Tours cars never appeared again, as they were evidently dismantled and their parts used in the 1924 GP Sunbeams.

The year 1924 saw a proliferation of Sunbeam models which, fortunately for the reader's patience and powers of assimilation, was not to last for long.

The one model that was unchanged was the traditional old 24/60 with the 80 × 150-mm cylinder dimensions going back to the 12/16-hp and Coupe de l'Auto cars of pre-war days. For 1924 only, the model name was changed from 24/60 to 24/70, for no apparent reason except, perhaps, seemingly to give better value for money due to an increase in the price from £1220 in 1923 to £1295 in 1924. It was, however, hail and farewell to the 24/70, which did not appear again after 1924.

The new models were really all variations on the newest design, the 14-hp, which itself underwent some changes for 1924, and was renamed the 14/40. The main change was an increase in the bore size from 72 mm to 75 mm, so that the 75 × 120-mm engine had a capacity of 2121 cc instead of the old 1954 cc, the RAC rating now being 13.9 hp. The price remained the same at £685. A new inlet manifold of greater efficiency was fitted, and front-wheel brakes were optional. These were rod-operated, without servo assistance, and cost £35 extra. On the 14-hp the right-hand gearchange had had no visible gate, but a gate was now visible and a reverse catch was fitted. A sports four-seater version was made available, said to give 50 bhp at 3000 rpm, to the 41 bhp at 2800 rpm of the standard model.

A smaller model, the 12/30, was introduced in 1924, but few were made, and none after 1925. The car cost £570, and had rear-wheel brakes only. The bore and stroke were 68 × 110 mm

(1598 cc and 11.4 hp) and the block and crankcase were a monobloc iron casting, whereas the 14/40 had a cast-iron block and aluminium crankcase. Otherwise design followed that of the 14/40, clutch, gearbox and back axle being the same, except the latter had a lower ratio of 4.9 to 1, and the wheelbase was 9 ft 7 in instead of 9 ft 10½ in.

Another short-lived new model which only lasted a year was the 16/50, which cost £850, and might be described as a six-cylinder version of the 12/30, although it had a bigger bore, its dimensions of 70 × 110 mm giving a capacity of 2540 cc, 18.2 hp. The crankshaft ran in seven bearings, and like on the 12/30, the block and crankcase were cast in one. The 14/40 clutch, gearbox and back axle were used, but Rudge-Whitworth wire wheels with 820 × 120-mm tyres were fitted, and the wheelbase was 10 ft 9¾ in. As befitted their 14/40 relationship, the 12/30 and 16/50 had 3-speed gearboxes and cantilever rear springs.

The final new model, the 20/60, could be described as a seven-bearing crankshaft six-cylinder version of the 14/40, as it had the same cylinder dimensions of 75 × 120, giving a capacity of 3181 cc and 20.9 hp, and like the 14/40 it had an aluminium crankcase and cast-iron block. It cost £950. It had the usual single dry-plate clutch and a unit gearbox, but the latter had the advantage over the other new models of containing four speeds. Axle ratio was 4.5 to 1 on the standard 10 ft 11¾-in chassis, but a long chassis version of 11 ft 5⅜ in, produced in 1924 only, had a lower axle ratio of 4.77 to 1. Rear springs were cantilever.

All these pushrod engines had a camshaft driven by a silent chain, with the water pump at the front and the dynamo and magneto driven from it through vernier couplings on the near-side of the engine, giving the whole a very neat appearance, typically Sunbeam.

For the 1924 racing season Bertarione produced his finest Grand Prix design, basically the 1923 engines with the addition of a supercharger fitted into new, longer, chassis, but the result was a completely new car. In view of the fact that the 1923 GP cars were dismantled, it is fair to assume that their engines formed the basis of the engines for the 1924 cars, as the design, dimensions etc were the same. The new Roots-type supercharger was mounted horizontally at the front of the crankcase and blew at 6–7 lb pressure. It was of great interest at the time as it drew from the carburettor and compressed the mixture, whereas previously on European racing cars (though not American), superchargers had compressed air and blown it through the carburettor. Eventually the Sunbeam method was adopted universally, as, combined with the use of alcohol, it meant manifold temperatures were reduced. The fuel mixture used consisted of about equal quantities of petrol, benzole and methyl alcohol. Much of the credit for the development of the supercharger must go to the chief engineer of the Sunbeam racing department, Captain J.S. Irving, whose brother Harold was at this time an engineer with the Alvis racing team. The Sunbeam's carburettor was a barrel throttle 48-choke horizontal Solex. Compression ratio was 6 to 1, the same as that of the rival straight-eight P2 Alfa Romeo, which had a higher blower pressure of 10 to 1. It will be recalled that the 1923 six-cylinder GP Sunbeam engine gave 108 bhp at 5000 rpm, whereas the new supercharged version now gave an impressive 146 bhp at 5000 rpm. The P2 Alfa Romeos, which ran against the Sunbeams in the 1924 French GP, which was also the Grand Prix of Europe, at Lyon in 1924 gave 134 bhp with a single Memini carburettor. The Sunbeam was slightly heavier than the Alfa Romeo, but it is extraordinary how once again Sunbeam came up with nearly the same chassis dimensions as its main Italian rival, the Sunbeam wheelbase was 8 ft 6½ in to the 8 ft 7 in of the Alfa Romeo, whilst the tracks of the two cars were identical, both being crab-tracked, and measuring 4 ft 3 in at the front, and 3 ft 11 in at the rar.

The new longer chassis on the Sunbeam was partly the result of the engine being longer due to the presence of the supercharger, but a completely different transmission was employed compared with that on the 1923 cars, a torque tube being used as on the latest Sunbeam touring cars. The rear of the chassis followed the contour of the tail as on the Fiat and subsequently the Alfa Romeo Grand Prix cars. The construction of the front axle remained the same as on the 1922 and 1923 Sunbeam GP cars, except that the track was increased, and the servo-brake actuation was also the same.

A 4-speed gearbox was now fitted, in unit with the engine, and taking the drive via a Hele-Shaw multiplate clutch, the position of the gear lever being central where it had been right-hand on the 1922 and 1923 cars. Springs were semi-elliptic.

The first public appearance of one of these cars was at Aston Clinton Hill Climb in May, 1924, when its driver, Dario Resta, made fastest time of day and set up a new record for the hill. A fortnight later he repeated his success by putting up fastest time at South Harting Hill Climb.

For the 35-lap, 503-mile, GP de l'Europe at Lyon in August, the Sunbeams were the fastest cars entered in one of the greatest Grand Prix races ever held. Here Segrave led at the start and Guinness also led the race for a time, but the Sunbeams, apart from Guinness's car, were bedevilled through faulty magnetos having been fitted, so that Segrave only finished 5th, in spite of making fastest lap of the race, which was won by Alfa Romeo, whilst Resta was 9th and Lee Guinness retired on his 21st lap whilst lying second. Things went better in the Spanish GP at San Sebastian in September when Segrave won, although Lee Guinness had a bad crash in which his mechanic, Barrett, was killed. In the same month Dario Resta was killed at the wheel of a 1924 Grand Prix car during a record attempt at Brooklands when a tyre left the rim after four laps.

For 1925 just three models were listed in the Sunbeam catalogue, the 12/30, the 14/40 and the 20/60, the last surviving Edwardian, the 24/70, being dropped from the range. Four-wheel brakes were now standard on the 14/40, but the 12/30 continued to have a brakeless front axle. The 14/40 and 20/60 now had worm-and-nut steering boxes, a feature borrowed from their new Talbot cousin, the 16/50-hp, which had appeared in July, 1924. One inch was added to the wheelbase of the 14/40 and a more comprehensive range of bodywork was now available on the two larger models. The 14/40 engine gave its 41 bhp at 2800 rpm using a 4.6 to 1 compression ratio.

In May, 1924, a new super-sports 3-litre Sunbeam had been announced, but it was not offered for sale until the 1925 Motor Show at a price of £1125. Two of these cars had been entered for Le Mans in 1924, only to be withdrawn as they were not ready in time, but two pre-production models did run at Le Mans on June 20th/21st, 1925. The 3-litre Sunbeam was something of a landmark in sports car design as its six-cylinder engine had twin overhead camshafts and was closely allied to Sunbeam's racing car designs. The chassis, however, was just as closely allied to

Sunbeam's touring designs, having quite a long wheelbase and, surprisingly for a sports car, it retained the cantilever rear springs of the touring cars.

The two four-seater tourers for Le Mans, looking very smart in their fresh coats of green paint, were driven to the circuit from the ferry at Dieppe by their drivers Segrave and George Duller and Jean Chassagne and Sammy Davis, the latter driving in his first road race. The French road surfaces were atrocious, and when the bonnet of the Chassagne/Davis car slid back over the scuttle, something appeared to be wrong. It was – a side member was cracked right through. After crawling into Le Mans, the car was put on a huge lorry and taken to the Talbot-Darracq works at Suresnes for the chassis to be repaired and strengthened, and Segrave also took the second team car to Paris for chassis modifications.

In the race itself Segrave led at the start from Kensington Moir's 3-litre Bentley, the pace causing the latter car to run out of petrol before its allotted mileage for refuelling, so it retired. Before midnight, the Segrave/Duller Sunbeam had retired as well with clutch trouble. Both the Bentleys entered retired, but the second Sunbeam carried on and finished the race in second place behind the $3\frac{1}{2}$-litre pushrod Lorraine-Dietrich of de Courcelles and Rossignol. In the final stages of the race, over hideous potholes due to the road surface breaking up, Davis was steadying the instrument panel with his hand in case it fell off, the tops of the tyres were nearly touching the body due to the rear axle being bent when Chassagne hit a hidden gulley after being forced on to the grass and, finally, the dust was causing the barrel throttles to stick open, so that on at least one occasion Davis had to get his foot under the throttle pedal to free it. The Sunbeam averaged just under 56 mph to the 57.83 mph of the winning Lorraine, and it won a 500-franc prize for having the most comfortable body. Segrave's car won the Gustave Baehr special premium for the greatest distance covered in the first hour.

Apart from Campbell's feat in reaching over 150 mph to gain the land speed record in the 350-hp car, already described, the main Sunbeam competition successes in 1925 were achieved by the 1924 GP cars on sprint courses, although Segrave and Parry Thomas took some records of up to three hours duration with a GP car at Montlhèry. In sprint events, Segrave made fastest time at Kop, Shelsley Walsh and Blackpool Speed Trials, and Count Masetti put up fastest time and broke the 1924 record by 1 min 20.6 secs at the 13.35-mile Klausen Hill Climb in Switzerland, taking it from Merz's 2-litre s/c Mercedes, despite the collapse of a piston as he neared the finish. Masetti was third behind two Delages in the French GP at Montlhèry after his team mates Segrave and Conelli had retired and, later in the year, Masetti, driving the sole Sunbeam entry, retired at half distance in the Spanish GP at San Sebastian whilst lying second to a Delage. This was the last Grande Epreuve to be contested by a works Sunbeam.

For 1926 two new models were added to the range, the twin-cam sports 3-litre, and a big straight-eight, mainly intended for closed bodywork and known as the 30/90. These Sunbeams were the first models to have slightly pointed radiators. The 20/60 six-cylinder remained virtually unchanged, but the 14/40 had a £60 price reduction to £625. Because of an increase in body weights, the axle ratio of the 14/40 was reduced to 4.72 to 1 for the open cars and 5 to 1 for the saloons, and the 3-speed gearbox was still retained.

The 30/90 straight-eight engine was a pushrod ohv which followed the design of the 14/40 and 20/60 in having an aluminium crankcase and separate cast-iron block, but with cylinder dimensions of 80 × 120 mm, 4826 cc. For long-chassis models the bore was before long increased to 85 mm, giving a capacity of 5448 cc. The cylinder head was in two parts, each covering four bores, with two tulip valves per cylinder, and the camshaft was gear driven from the front of the engine. The substantial nine-bearing crankshaft had a large vibration damper at the front. The layout of the engine ancillaries, dynamo, magneto etc, followed normal Sunbeam practice and there was the usual single Claudel carburettor, but an unusual feature for a formal carriage was the adoption of dry-sump lubrication. This engine was put into a chassis with the normal Sunbeam cantilever rear springs with either an 11 ft 5⅜-in wheelbase carrying a chassis price of £1050, or else a 12 ft 3-in wheelbase, which cost £1250, with the standard limousine coming out at £1850. The shorter chassis had a 4 to 1 axle ratio, and the longer a 4.77 to 1. The 4-speed gearbox had a right-hand lever, but we are told that due to the inertia of the heavy plate clutch this model did not have the usual pleasant Sunbeam gear change. The four-wheel brakes were servo-assisted. Few straight-eight Sunbeams were made, and survivors are practically unknown today.

The sports 3-litre also had an aluminium crankcase and a cast-iron block, but the cylinder head was integral with the block, which had a bore and stroke of 75 × 110 mm, 2916 cc. The valves were at a 90° angle instead of the 96° of the racing cars, and were operated through rocking fingers. The camshafts were driven by a gear train at the front of the engine, another separate gear train driving the B.T.H. CE6 magneto. Altogether there were eleven helical gears in the gear train. Three double-lobed idler cams were fitted at the rear of each camshaft acting against spring dampers with the idea of reducing torsional vibration and a snatch in the gear train. However, in a worn engine a pheno-menon known as the 'spring-drive period' took place when the backlash in the helical gears set up a terrible clatter. The valve gear was enclosed in two cast-aluminium covers, ribbed on the later cars, but the early 'E' series had unribbed covers. To balance this, the 'E' cars had finned exhaust manifolds, which were plain on the later cars. Also on the 'E' cars, water was transferred across the block by a circular section pipe which was cast in between numbers 2 and 3 cylinders. This left insufficient metal between the bores and caused the block to crack, so on later engines a pipe of flattened cross-section was used.

The early cars had a reputation for breaking their crankshafts if 4000 rpm was exceeded. These cranks were of straight carbon steel, and they were replaced by nickel-chrome cranks by the time of the early 'F' sanction cars of 1926, the original 'E' sanction of 1925 having been for only 25 cars. The crankshaft ran in eight bearings, one bearing being in front of the timing gears.

Dry-sump lubrication was used, the oil tank being located on the nearside alongside the engine. At Le Mans in 1925 the drivers, when topping up this tank, had to fill it to a set level by eye, as if it was filled to the brim there was no room for the oil which had collected in the engine to be forced back in to the tank when the engine was restarted, with the danger that the whole thing might burst. As Sammy Davis remarked, finding the set level was no easy matter when in a hurry. Castrol 'R' oil was recommended for this engine.

The standard compression ratio was 6.4 to 1 and two Claudel-Hobson AZP carburettors were fitted, the output being 90 bhp at 3800 rpm. The car itself was good for 90 mph.

The single-plate clutch and 4-speed gearbox with right-hand lever were integral with the engine, ratios being 4.5, 6.0, 7.43 and 14.32 to 1. A beautiful gear change was one of the notable features of the car. There was a torque tube and a ¾ floating rear axle. The wheelbase of 10 ft 10½ in and track of 4 ft 7 in gave chassis dimensions close to that of the short-lived six-cylinder 16/50 Sunbeam of 1924, and there is no doubt that this basically touring chassis, with its cantilever springs at the rear, was not quite up to the design standards of the engine with which it was fitted. Although it was very long for a sports car, handsome open bodywork with cycle type mudguards gave the 3-litre Sunbeam a delightfully slim and lithe appearance, and the price of the open model was £1125. A Weymann four-foor six-light saloon version was also available. Early 'E' chassis tended to fracture at the front spring shackle bracket, and later ones were reinforced.

From 1926 control of S.T.D. participation in Grand Prix racing was transferred to Suresnes with 1½-litre Talbot-Darracq cars, but a remarkable new Sunbeam racing car appeared in March at Southport to make a successful attempt on the Land Speed Record. It was then known as *Ladybird*, but this car, and a second similar one that was built early in 1927, became famous as *Tiger* and *Tigress*. These had Roots supercharged 4-litre V12 engines constructed by mounting two Grand Prix 2-litre blocks at 75° on a special crankcase. Capacity was actually 3976 cc, and the output was 306 bhp at 5300 rpm with a 5.9 to 1 compression ratio. The chassis and body owed much to those of the 1924/5 Grand Prix cars, the front and rear track measurements being identical, although the wheelbase was increased from 8 ft 6½ in to 8 ft 10 in. At Southport Segrave raised the record to 152.33 mph, using a single supercharger, and in August he put up the fastest time achieved by a racing car on the road by winning the 6-kilometre Boulogne Speed Trials at 140.6 mph, covering the 3rd kilometre at 148.1 mph. He was less successful in the Spanish Free Formula race at San Sebastian when the front axle broke after six laps, although the Sunbeam had led for the first four laps of the 40-lap race. In the Milan Grand Prix track race at

Monza the Sunbeam retired with gearbox trouble at half distance, 20 laps. However, at Gaillon in France in October, where
a V12 Sunbeam was entered as a Talbot, Albert Divo put up
fastest time and established a new record.

Most of the Sunbeam successes in 1926 were achieved by one
of the old 4.9-litre cars at Brooklands in the hands of A.G. Miller
and Kaye Don, with G.J. Jackson successfully campaigning his
old 1921 3-litre straight-eight GP car at Southport, as he was to
continue to do well into the 'thirties.

Coatalen's influence at Sunbeams declined after 1926 as he
devoted most of his time to the Talbot-Darracq works at
Suresnes, and it is generally considered that from this time
Sunbeam no longer maintained the technical leadership they
had previously displayed, and no more racing cars were built
after the V12 4-litre except for two land speed record contenders.

Three new models were introduced for 1927, when the Sunbeam range consisted of six- and eight-cylinder models only,
with the dropping of the four-cylinder 14/40.

For the two least-expensive new models the integral cast-iron
block and crankcase was re-introduced after appearing first on
the short-lived 12/30 and 16/50 of 1924/5.

The 14/40 replacement was known as the Sixteen, and it had
a 67.5 × 95-mm, 2040-cc, six-cylinder pushrod engine, Delco-
Remy coil ignition and peculiar gear ratios of 5.3, 8.72, 12.12
and 20.94 to 1, with a 15.6 to 1 reverse. This meant that third
gear was too low to be useful, and bottom gear was quite
ridiculously low. The car cost £550, and became best selling
Vintage model.

There was a four-bearing crankshaft with a vibration damper
and the timing was by helical gears. The carburettor was a
Claudel-Hobson V.36 and the engine gave 44 bhp at 4000 rpm
with a 5.7 to 1 compression ratio. Despite this low output for its
capacity, the car was capable of 70 mph with 55 mph cruising,
and a consumption of 25 mpg or better. The engine had the
usual neat Sunbeam appearance with the manifolds on the offside and ancillaries along the nearside. The drive was taken
through a unit-mounted gearbox which had a right-hand lever,
and thence by torque tube. The clutch was single-plate. Chassis
followed normal Sunbeam practice with cantilever rear springs,
a wheelbase of 10 ft 3⅜ in and a track of 4 ft 7 in. Beaded-edge

tyres were now no longer fitted to Sunbeams, the Sixteen having 30 × 4.75-in tyres and artillery wheels.

The new Twenty engine was a four-bearing six-cylinder of similar design to that of the Sixteen but with the same dimensions as the 3-litre sports, 75 × 110 mm, although, of course, it had pushrod ohv. This engine had magneto ignition and gave 55 bhp at 3600 rpm with a compression ratio of 5.5 to 1. It also had more reasonable gear ratios than the Sixteen of 4.7, 7.9, 12.9 and 18.8 to 1. The wheelbase was 10 ft 4½ in, and with the increase in the wheelbase of the Sixteen for 1928, it actually came to have a shorter wheelbase than its smaller-capacity sister. The track of the two cars was the same. The Twenty was priced at £750.

The new Twenty-Five, with its 80 × 120-mm, 3619-cc, six-cylinder pushrod engine was really not so new as the Sixteen and the Twenty, being a development of the previous 20/60, with its aluminium crankcase and cast-iron block and a seven-bearing crankshaft driving the camshaft by silent chain. The output was 72 bhp at 2900 rpm, and the chassis was larger than that of the Sixteen and Twenty, having a 4 ft 9-in track and a wheelbase of 10 ft 11⅜ in or 11 ft 5⅜ in, with axle ratios of 4.5 or 4.73 to 1.

The 3-litre sports and the Thirty straight-eight continued, although the long-wheelbase straight-eight with the bigger bore was now called the Thirty-Five, and cost £1975 to the £1395 of the Thirty. All the range, apart from the Sixteen, had magneto ignition.

Sunbeam came into the news with a bang on Tuesday, 29th March, 1927, when Segrave became the first man on earth to exceed 200 mph on Daytona Beach, Florida, the actual speed being a mean 203.79 mph over the measured mile. Known as the 1000-hp Sunbeam, his car was fairly economically constructed around two V12 Sunbeam Matabele aero engines of 1914–18 design, having a total capacity of 44 888 cc and a power output estimated at around 870 bhp. The driver sat between the two engines, the one in front of him driving back to the 3-speed gearbox, whilst the one behind him between the two rear wheels drove forward, the final drive being through a counter-shaft with chain sprockets on each side. Statistics worked out by Cyril Posthumus show that the two engines had between them 24 cylinders, 48 sparking plugs, 96 valves, 8 magnetos, 3 clutches and 3 radiators. The instrument panel contained 28 instruments, including 6 oil-pressure gauges, 4 rev counters, 8 magneto switches, 3 radiator thermometers and one master ignition switch. Somebody looking inside the cockpit in recent years remarked that its appearance was an apt portrayal of Blake's 'dark Satanic mills'. The car had all enveloping bodywork with a rounded nose and long tail, being over 23 ft long and 6 ft wide and weighing 3 tons 16 cwt.

The chains were well lubricated and placed in armour-plated boxes, and it seems only fitting that the last successful competition machine built at the Moorfield works should have been fitted with what might be termed giant versions of the old Sunbeam oil-bath chain case.

On 7th May a works 3-litre Sunbeam sports car driven by George Duller won the Essex Motor Club's Six-Hour Race over a 386-mile artificial road circuit at Brooklands at a speed of 64.3 mph, beating the 3-litre Bentleys, which all had trouble with their Duralumin valve rockers. The fastest Bentley finished in third behind Sammy Davis's 12/50 Alvis, the best performer on handicap. A bored Segrave ran out of petrol and was disqualified for an illegal refill on his 3-litre Sunbeam after two hours when in third place, and his last motor race ended on a low note, when he left the track soon afterwards, and did not even bother to wait to see the outcome of the race.

In short Brooklands races during 1927, Kaye Don had successes with a 4.9-litre and a 2-litre blown GP Sunbeam, but the two V12 4-litre Sunbeams *Tiger* and *Tigress* driven by the distinguished French and Anglo–French drivers Wagner (who wore a 'brilliant red helmet') and Williams, of Bugatti fame, retired in a wet and windy short race at Montlhèry. At Shelsley Walsh in September the works mechanic Bill Perkins won his class and made third fastest time of the day on a V12 4-litre car, and came second to Raymond Mays's 2-litre supercharged Mercedes in the 2-litre class on one of the Grand Prix Sunbeams. In July of 1927, Captain Irving, who had been responsible for the design of the 100-hp car, left Sunbeams.

1928 was celebrated by the lowering of the axle ratio of the Sixteen from 5.3 to 1 to 5.5 to 1, whilst on the Twenty it was lowered from 4.7 to 1 to 5 to 1. The Twenty-Five and 3-litre models were fitted with Dewandre vacuum-servo assistance to their brakes at no extra increase in price, but the straight-eight models continued with their gearbox driven mechanical servos.

The compression ratio of the 3-litre was reduced slightly from 6.4 to 1 to 6 to 1, but a supercharged version was introduced. However, only six cars of this type were built, including the prototype, which was a saloon. In spite of all their pioneering work on superchargers, Sunbeam were content to fit proprietary vane-type Cozette blowers, no doubt for reasons of economy. Fitted with a No. 10 Cozette running at about 1.3 times engine speed and giving about 10 lb boost, the engine developed 138 bhp at 3800 rpm. The blower was driven off an idler gear from the timing gear, the face width of these two components being increased to two inches. The blower and its drive shaft were on the offside of the engine, the drive shaft incorporating two Simms couplings. The fuel feed was taken care of by two Amal mechanical pumps, one on each cambox, in place of the Autovac of the unblown cars.

At any rate on this supercharged model there was a raising instead of a lowering of the back axle ratio, which went up from 4.5 to 1 to 3.9 to 1, and larger brakes were fitted.

At Brooklands in 1928, Kaye Don took International Class C records with the V12 4-litre *Tiger*, as well as having successes with it in short races, during one of which he broke the Brooklands lap record, setting it at 131.76 mph. He also raced the 2-litre car which Lee Guinness had driven at Lyon, which was now named *The Cub*, with which he broke International Class E records. Just as the Grand Prix Sunbeams used to be driven by road to and from the French Grands Prix, so William Boddy tells us the 2-litre and 4-litre cars were driven from the Sunbeam works at Wolverhampton to Brooklands on pump petrol in 1928, although a 60/40 petrol-benzole mixture was used for racing. He also says in his *The Story of Brooklands*, that on E2 racing fuel the 2-litre engine produced 171 bhp at 5500 rpm. Mrs W.B. Scott also drove a 2-litre at Brooklands, whilst Miss May Cunliffe did well with another example at Southport and Shelsley Walsh.

The Sunbeam range was almost unchanged for 1929, except that one model was dropped, the smaller straight-eight. The Sixteen was now the only model without servo brakes, the Dewandre system being adopted on the Twenty. Prices generally remained the same as in 1928, although all models were fitted with pedal-operated centralized chassis lubrication, the oil tank for which was mounted on the bulkhead.

At Brooklands in 1929 Kaye Don put up a new lap record of 134.24 mph on the *Tiger*, and took more records with this car, including the first standing-start mile at over 100 mph, but retired the *Tigress* in the 500-Mile Race, in which Cyril Paul and John Cobb finished third in the *Tiger*. Jack Dunfee also broke 2-litre short-distance records in a 2-litre, and E.L. Bouts continued to campaign his old two-seater 4.9-litre-engined car. Don also made ftd at Southport in his 2-litre GP Sunbeam.

Malcolm Campbell entered a blown 3-litre Sunbeam for the Phoenix Park races, Dublin, in July. This car, registered UK 7415, was rather special in that it had a lower bonnet line and a shallower, wider, body than standard, with flowing instead of cycle-type wings, heavier springs, and eared instead of plain Rudge hubcaps. A practice car, HW 7813, with similar wings, was also taken over to Ireland, but it did not have the other differences. This car was later sold to Wally Hammond, the cricketer, was raced at Brooklands in the 'thirties by C.L.W. Barker, and is still in existence.

Campbell's performance at Dublin was rather ignominious, as he first of all stalled on the line, and did not get going until all the other seventeen cars were out of sight. As John Wyer and John Coombes observed in their *Motor Sport* article, the blown Sunbeams had the standard clutch fitted with stronger springs, and this unit looked somewhat askance at being asked to purvey a 50 per cent power increase. This clutch was the cause of Campbell's downfall when he retired on the 27th lap, after about 120 miles.

1930 saw a reduction in the range, with the withdrawal of the straight-eight model, and new chassis with half-elliptic rear springs to replace the cantilevers on the Sixteen and Twenty models, whilst the axie ratio of the Sixteen was lowered yet again to 5.6 to 1. Dewandre servo assistance was now given to the brakes on all models, and on the smaller cars the handbrake lever operated separate shoes in the rear drums. Although the Sixteen still preserved its coil, all the other models, including the sports 3-litre, were now given a B.T.H. CED 6 dual ignition unit.

Bore wear had been giving concern on some of the Sunbeam engines caused, it is thought, according to Coombes and Wyer, by the small ratio of connecting rod length to crank radius,

A 1925 Grand Sport Salmson driven by Ian Maxwell in a V.S.C.C. Light Car &
Edwardian Section event, with the well-known motoring writer, T.R. Nicholson,
in the passenger seat   *Neill Bruce*

A 1924 24/70 hp Sunbeam   *Neill Bruce*

The 350 hp 12-cylinder Sunbeam record breaker at the Talbot Works, Ladbroke Hall, Barlby Road, North Kensington in 1921   *Anthony Heal*

Induction side of the 3-litre supercharged Sunbeam driven by Campbell in practice for the 1929 Irish GP   *Anthony Heal*

H.O.D. Segrave in a 2-litre 6-cylinder supercharged GP Sunbeam at Princes Risborough station in May, 1925 prior to Kop Hill Climb   *Anthony Heal*

which was a feature of the Sunbeam engines, resulting in excessive side thrust between piston and cylinder wall. The cure was
the introduction on all models except the Twenty-Five (which
had an engine of older origins) of the Sunbeam patent bi-metal
piston, which in reality seems merely to have been the introduction on Sunbeams of the bi-metal piston designed by Georges
Roesch for the 14/45 Talbot of 1927. This piston, whose thin
steel skirt could be held much closer to the bore than its alloy head,
or a complete alloy piston, weighed no more than an alloy piston,
and furthermore it reduced oil consumption, piston slap and
bore wear. Incidentally, there is evidence that certain of the
straight-eight and twin-cam Sunbeam engines were assembled
at the Talbot factory in Barlby Road, North Kensington,
London, under Georges Roesch's supervision.

On the Sunbeam Twenty of 1930 an oil radiator was fitted
between the front dumb irons to assist the work of the new
pistons, but in actual fact it had the effect of slowing down the
oil circulation so much that the wear was worse rather than
better. The Twenty-Five now had a Stromberg UXZ carburettor
in place of the former Claudel-Hobson, and the 3-litre sports
(now the 'L' sanction) was given a new wide-ratio gearbox with
ratios of 4.5, 6.46, 9.2 and 14.26 to 1, with a 12.46 to 1 reverse.
Unfortunately few of these 'L' sanction cars were produced, but
they had some of the good features of the blown cars, including
mechanical fuel pumps and larger brakes. Furthermore, the
price of the open four-seater was now down to £850.

In their last Vintage racing season, Sunbeams came out with
their final Land Speed Record machine, the unsuccessful *Silver
Bullet*, built under the supervision of Hugh Rose. This car had
two centrifugally supercharged V12-cylinder engines of 140 ×
130-mm, 48 040-cc total capacity, with twin ohc to each bank
of six cylinders, alloy blocks and four valves per cylinder. The
driver sat behind the engines and between two contra-rotating
propellor shafts. There was a 3-speed gearbox, hydraulic clutch
and hydraulic brakes, plus an air brake between the two rear
fins. Kaye Don went with the car to Daytona in March, 1930,
but the sands were in bad condition, and the car did not handle
well. Troubles developed in it, and there was friction between
Don and Coatalen. The highest speed the car achieved was
151.623 mph before the attempt was abandoned.

B.O. Davis had acquired Campbell's blown 3-litre Phoenix Park car, and was third in it in a 5½-mile Brooklands handicap in May. He entered it for the Phoenix Park meeting in July, and showed promise in practice for the Irish GP by lapping at over 80 mph, faster than the blown 1750-cc Alfa Romeos and the Talbot 90s. An ancient (by the standards of the time!) unblown 3-litre Sunbeam driven by C.H. Manders could only manage 66 mph, and ran mostly on five cylinders.

In the race itself, Davis's Sunbeam was splitting the Alfa Romeos of Campari and Varzi, but after only four laps it fell victim to a design fault inherent in the blown 3-litre models. This was caused by the Cozette being poorly mounted in an aluminium cradle. It was held in by two metal straps which allowed the blower to shift under load reversal, cracking the main delivery pipe to the manifold, and Davis drew into his pit to retire amidst smoke and steam.

At Brooklands Kaye Don drove the *Tigress* to break Tim Birkin's lap record of 135.33 mph with the blower 4½ Bentley with a new speed of 137.58 mph, but most of the honours during the season were in the form of class records put up by the *Cub* and its sister 2-litre Grand Prix racers. Jack Dunfee took the 200-mile world's record at Montlhéry at 117.66 mph, and these cars, including the *Cub*, with bored-out engines took Class D (3-litre) class records. H.W. Purdy and L. Cushman were third in the 500-Mile Race with the *Cub* in its normal 2-litre form at an average of 104.74 mph, and won their class. Jack Dunfee averaged over 126 mph over five miles at Montlhery during his record attempts there.

By the end of the Vintage period, however, the great days of the Wolverhampton Sunbeams were over. They continued to make good, but no longer outstanding, cars, until their demise in 1935, but from 1919 to 1930 they had attempted more and achieved more than any other British firm in international competitions – though with a fair amount of help from France and a lesser amount from Italy.

FOOTNOTE: *In recent years Ernest Henry's son has claimed that his father had no connections with Sunbeam, who merely copied his engine designs, but other evidence still inclines us to the belief that the 1922 Strasbourg C.P. Sunbeam was Henry's work.*

Chapter 16
TROJAN

The phenomenon which was the Trojan could hardly have happened anywhere in the world but in England. To anyone but an Englishman this extraordinary car would have seemed too ridiculous, but the English bought them in thousands, encouraged by a very effective publicity campaign.

'Can you afford to walk?' was the headline on one pamphlet, which went on:

At one time, when bare feet were the fashion, this was undeniable, but the invention of sandals introduced into the contemplation of a journey a financial aspect, still further emphasized by the later developments of boots, shoes, socks and stockings. Even so, there was no serious rival to challenge the economy of walking until the TROJAN CAR entered the lists.

Then followed a detailed sheet of accounting to prove that the Trojan, with normal and comfortable complement of passengers (four), effected a saving over walking of nearly sevenpence a mile.

That great authority, Sir Harry Ricardo, was scathing about the Trojan. Of its engine he wrote: 'If fewness of parts were a criterion, such an engine would sweep the board. In practice this type of engine has earned almost universal condemnation because of the ingenuity with which it devises different ways of going wrong.'

Sir Harry certainly had a point. Trojans are almost animal in character, and like animals they have good moods and bad ones, but to expect them to go wrong like ordinary motor cars must lead to disappointment and frustration; their design is so utterly unlike normal motor car practice. In the heyday of the Trojan, many garages carried signs saying 'No Trojans', and when in trouble the Trojan owner was enjoined to get home if it was possible to do so. The instruction book is quite clear on this point, and suggests that if a bearing goes, the passenger should pour quantities of oil into the 'Hot Foot' as the car is driven home. The engine relies on crankcase compression to fill the cylinders, so the luckless passenger is in for a messy time, since the 'Hot Foot' is the crankcase.

The most popular model, known as the 'Utility Car', was fitted with solid tyres. These are not as uncomfortable as might be imagined because the cantilever springs are enormously long and absorb nearly all the shocks which the wheels, necessarily more solid than the tyres, have to withstand. One proud owner wrote to the makers to say 'it makes one wonder what will ultimately be the fate of cars with ordinary engines and puffed-up tyres' and another wrote 'we would not have pneumatics put on even if you offered to make the change for nothing'. Solids give the car a skittishness at the back end which makes driving entertaining, to say the least. After twenty or thirty years' use, they get perished and come off, not all at once, but in chunks, and cantilever springs or no cantilever springs, there is nothing more uncomfortable than a Trojan with half a solid tyre.

The back axle is wide and is also solid, in the sense that it has no differential, the axle shaft running in a tube to which the ends of the springs are attached. It is typical of the insularity of the designer that he assumed the car would always be driven with the camber of the road inclining to the left, and provided only one grease nipple for the axle bearings at the right-hand end, assuming that gravity would feed the grease to the left-hand wheel bearing. On a tour of the Continent, driving on the right, the left-hand bearing dries out with the inevitable results, unless the hub is removed at intervals and greased by hand, or an extra nipple inserted.

Final drive is by duplex chain to a sprocket on the off-side. The near-side of the rear axle carries the one and only wheel brake. Chain tension is achieved by pulling the axle back along the springs, which also act as radius rods. The chain is driven by a smaller sprocket attached to a reduction gearbox, which in turn connects with the engine and epicyclic gearbox, both of which are under the front seats.

The driver of the Trojan has four levers to push, pull or otherwise manhandle; the mixture lever, the gear lever, the transmission brake handle and the starting lever. The mixture lever controls a variable jet in the carburettor, and when it is at 'air' it means air and nothing else. This is very useful on long hills, as it gives the driver another method of relieving the one wheel brake. The starting lever is a long handle with 90° of movement; the first six inches of pull-up retards the ignition and the remainder of the travel turns the engine over if the pawl has engaged. If it has not engaged, the driver probably dislocates his back, and certainly gets cross.

The gear lever, pushed forward to the left, engages the low gear bands; forward to the right engages high gear, and pulled back engages the reverse bands. There is a pedal known as the clutch pedal, but this is hardly ever used as all it does is disengage the gear you are in, though a neat trick can sometimes be done with it. Kick this pedal when the gear lever is in low and the lever flies out of the low-gear slot, bounces into the reverse slot and back, with luck, into high gear.

There are various methods of making the car slow down, apart from the foot brake acting on one wheel. The 'umbrella handle' by the driver's door controls a meagre externally contracting band on the transmission drum which has some retarding effect, but the most dramatic method of slowing down is to pull the gear lever firmly into reverse. The car sits down hard on its enormous cantilever 'Wondersprings' (Trojan's name for them) and stops like anything, with a great cloud of acrid smoke coming from under the driver's posterior. These springs are so long that the front and rear springs overlap, giving a strange, shiplike motion to the car.

There can be few more straightforward methods of engaging a gear than that of pushing hard on a lever; the harder you push the more violent the take-off. Once the low gear has been selected and the lever pushed firmly home until it clicks, a plangent groaning fills the ear and then as the lever is shoved nonchalantly into high there is a dying away of all noise and only a slowly accelerating *pocketa pocketa* is heard, with a gentle rustling of chains in the background. This change has brought the engine speed down from over 1200 rpm to a mere 400 at 9 mph at both of which rates of engine speed a power output of 10 bhp is developed. The maximum power of 12 bhp is reached at 22 mph and at 35 mph it develops the nearest thing a two-stroke can get to valve bounce, known to Trojan owners as piston bounce or big-end crash. Sometimes it eschews this nasty noise and then, with a fair wind and given plenty of time, it will reach forty.

There is a large bonnet in front of the very upright windscreen and clearly the designer felt he ought to put *something* in it, so he installed the little carburettor there in solitary state, with yards of pipe leading all the way back to the strange engine under the passenger's seat. This engine is the most extraordinary of all the curiosities on the car. It is a long square-four on the two-stroke principle, laid fore-and-aft, with only two combustion spaces, one exhaust cylinder and one inlet cylinder sharing each combustion space. It has but seven moving parts; one crankshaft, two connecting rods and four enormously long cast-iron pistons. The peculiar arrangement of an inlet and an exhaust piston to each combustion space allows the exhaust and transfer ports to be uncovered separately, exhaust first and then transfer. This must be the reason why the Trojan engine will slog as no other two-stroke will, and, indeed, few four-stroke engines can match it for steam-engine slogging; though other examples of this design, notably the racing Puch motor cycles, are not renowned for low-speed torque. The con rods are 'V'-shaped and very long and spindly. At every stroke they flex by nearly $2°$, yet they never break. The engine lies down in the tin box which passes for a chassis; this box is aptly named the 'punt', for it is just like a rather short river punt. The springs are attached to the sides of the punt, and the body is put on top of it.

The Trojan is full of curious design features, the most surprising, perhaps, being the total absence of any form of locking device on any of the nuts. Not even spring washers. This idea must have seemed absurd at the time, but the nuts do not come undone, and today it is acceptable practice to assemble new cars this way, even to big-end nuts.

The most remarkable thing about the Trojan is its extraordinary ability to climb up muddy hills, which makes it an excellent trials car. The weight distribution must be of the order of 60/40 in favour of the back wheels since all the machinery is amidships, and a Trojan has been known to 'do a wheelie' on a steep slope in spite of its pathetic power output. The only observed 'wheelie', it must be admitted, was by a 'hot' Trojan belonging to the remarkable Group Captain A.F. Scroggs who, alas, died some years ago after having competed annually in the Land's End and other M.C.C. Trials in his Trojan since the early 'twenties, usually achieving a 'gold'. Scroggs was a thoroughly eccentric character (he once banned saluting on the RAF station he commanded during the war as 'a waste of time' until he was over-ruled by an outraged higher authority) and a competent engineer. At one time Scroggs even fitted an exhaust-driven turbo-supercharger to his Trojan, and any tuning done by Trojan owners is known to this day as 'scrogging' the engine.

Scroggs was eccentric. The Trojan is eccentric. Mr Leslie Hounsfield who designed the Trojan and, incidentally, the Safari Camp Bed, must have been gloriously eccentric.

When in trouble, the Trojan owner was enjoined to get home if it was possible to do so

Chapter 17
VAUXHALL

*Lord Hovenden detached from his motor car was an entirely different being
from Lord Hovenden who lounged with such a deceptive air of languor
behind the steering wheel of a Vauxhall Velox. . . . The fierce wind blew
away his diffidence: the speed intoxicated him out of his self-consciousness.*
So wrote Aldous Huxley in his satirical novel *Those Barren Leaves*,
published in 1925, his choice of a 30/98 Vauxhall Velox showing
how evocative it was of the period in which his novel was set and
the society he was writing about.

In mentioning speed, Huxley hit upon the real reason for the
fame and reputation of the 30/98 Vauxhall – in its day it was
incredibly fast. In the years just after the First World War, when
it started to go into proper production, there were virtually no
other cars on the market to touch it. It had a maximum speed of
between 80 and 90 mph, or 100 mph with a little tuning, and
when the average car was then struggling to achieve even half
these speeds, it was indeed like a Ferrari of today which is
capable of travelling at 150 to 200 mph. It is little wonder that
young Lord Hovenden was a changed man when seated behind
the wheel of his 30/98.

The E-type 30/98 (then written '30-98'), which appeared in
1919, was directly evolved from a renowned pre-war competition
car, which was itself developed from touring-car components.
Its indirect ancestor was the 1913 C-type Prince Henry Vauxhall.
This had the 9 ft 9-in wheelbase chassis of the very successful
3-litre A-type Vauxhall, dating back to 1908, fitted with the
4-litre engine out of the D-type Vauxhall, both these four-
cylinder Vauxhalls being current production models at the time,
the D-type having a 10 ft 3-in wheelbase chassis. The C-type
engine had high-lift cams and raised compression and developed
about 75 bhp. These cars, like the 30/98, were designed by L.H.
Pomeroy.

The first 30/98 Vauxhall was produced at short notice for

Joseph Higginson of Stockport, the inventor of the Autovac, to take part in hill climbs and sprints for the 1913 season. Higginson had previously campaigned an 80-hp La Buire, and wanted a smaller British car with a high power-to-weight ratio to compete against the works-backed Sunbeams and Talbots, by which the rather clumsy La Buire would have been outclassed.

In effect a C-type Prince Henry Vauxhall was taken, and the 95 × 140-mm D-type engine was enlarged to 98 × 150 mm, 4526 cc. On to the chassis was fitted a narrow all-aluminium lightweight four-seater body, without doors and with aluminium wings. A flat-fronted radiator replaced the V-shaped Prince Henry radiator.

On 3rd May, 1913, Higginson put up the fastest time at the Lancashire A.C.'s Waddington Fells Hill Climb, near Clitheroe, beating works entries from Sunbeam, Crossley and Humber. The following weekend, the Vauxhall works driver, A.J. Hancock, came second in a Brooklands handicap race in a single-seater Vauxhall fitted with a 30/98 engine; two weeks later he broke the record at Aston Clinton Hill Climb in a 1912 pointed-radiator Coupe de l'Auto Vauxhall road-racing car fitted with a 30/98 engine.

Higginson had made ftd at Shelsley Walsh on his first appearance there in 1912 with his La Buire with a time of 68.8 seconds, and it is probable he had set his heart on breaking the hill record there of 63.4 seconds, set up by H.C. Holder's 58-hp Daimler in 1911.

Although there was a cup for the fastest time at Shelsley Walsh, up until 1913 it was a rule that all cars of 20 hp and over (i.e. most of the cars taking part at that time) had to have four-seater bodies and a full complement of passengers. A formula was concocted in which weight in relation to horsepower was the main consideration relative to the time of the ascent, and many cars carried ballast in addition to the passengers. Sheer speed, therefore, was not the main object, and the times were not announced at the very early meetings, only results on formula. No doubt this was why Higginson specified a four-seater body for his 30/98.

The Shelsley rules were changed, however, for the 1913 event when stripped racing cars were allowed for the first time, so that although classes 'on formula' were still held for many years, outright speed now became the main objective. Needless to say, the old record for the hill fell almost alarmingly during the day, first C.A. Bird in a 3-litre Coupe de l'Auto Sunbeam did 60.8 seconds and then A.J. Hancock in the stripped 30/98 engined Coupe de l'Auto Vauxhall did 59.0 seconds. There was no practice in those days and this was Hancock's only ascent. Higginson, however, had entered for three classes, and on his second ascent achieved 57.2 seconds, to equal the new record already set up by Leslie Hands in a 25-hp single-seater Talbot. On his last run, in the 'Closed' event confined to members of the organizing club, Higginson finally pulverized the record with an astonishing time of 55.2 seconds. The 'Formula' competition in this class was won by a 20-hp Vauxhall.

It has been said that Higginson put up this time with three, or even four, passengers, but this seems rather open to doubt as it was not mandatory for him to have them, and it took some time for a 30/98, even a stripped one, to beat his time after the war. Hancock had lost time through the rear end of his Coupe de l'Auto car hopping around, consequently some extra weight at the back of his four-seater 30/98 might conceivably have helped Higginson's time. Nevertheless, his time was remarkable whether he carried passengers or not.

It is thought about half a dozen 30/98s similar to Higginson's were produced before the war, all characterized by 9-in brake drums at the rear, what was probably the last going to P.C. Kidner, Vauxhall's managing director, early in 1915. This was a particularly handsome car, characterized by having cantilever springs at the back, and it was later sold to T.W. Mays, father of Raymond Mays.

When the 30/98 was put on the market after the war it was given the logical name of E-type, and the open Velox four-seater bodywork followed similar lines to that on Higginson's car, except a few more creature comforts were provided such as doors, and there was, of course, electrical equipment. It does explain, however, why the back seats were so uncomfortable, as they were originally only designed for a ride of a minute or less up Shelsley Walsh. Thus E-type rear passengers found they had little leg room and were much buffeted by the wind, due to sitting on the car rather than in it. Aldous Huxley brought this out very well in *Those Barren Leaves*. Whilst driving his car in Italy, the setting

of the novel, Lord Hovenden touched eighty-eight on a straight
stretch, with a Mr Falx sitting in the tonneau, and it was
recorded that 'Mr Falx's beard writhed and fluttered with the
agonized motions of some captive animal'. Later Mr Falx
thankfully gave up his seat to a Miss Elver, who enjoyed waving
her handkerchief at the passing dogs and children. 'The only
trouble about going so fast,' Aldous Huxley wrote, 'was that the
mighty wind was always tearing the handkerchiefs from between
her fingers and whirling them irretrievably into receding space.'
After four of her handkerchiefs had blown away, Lord Hovenden
had to stop and lend her his coloured silk bandana, and one
corner of it was tied round Miss Elver's wrist to prevent its loss.

The E-type Vauxhall engine was placed in a sub-frame. This
engine had a fixed head, exposed valve springs and two large
valves per cylinder operated by roller cam-followers. The valve
clearances were extremely wide, varying from 0.048 in to 0.060
in, and as the clearances were different from engine to engine,
the correct individual figure was stamped on a plate attached to
each engine. If the clearance was set to less than 0.048 in, the
engine would not run as the valve timing was upset.

An aircraft-type Zenith carburettor was fitted, and as this had
no choke, for cold-weather starting it had to be stuffed with a
handkerchief – preferably a silk one, it was said. Undoubtedly it
was for this purpose that Lord Hovenden carried his coloured
silk bandana. Pre-war 30/98s had White & Poppe carburettors,
and it was said that Vauxhall Motors bought the Zeniths as war
surplus at a very advantageous price.

The unbalanced crankshaft ran in five large plain bearings,
and the three-bearing camshaft was driven from the front by a
silent inverted-tooth chain, which also drove the Watford
magneto and was adjustable for tension. The carburettor was
pressure-fed, and after the initial air pressure had been pumped
up in the rear tank by hand by a pump on the dash, a mechanical
pump on the camshaft took over once the engine was running.
Lubrication was by plunger pump, driven off the rear end of the
camshaft by the same cam that worked the air pump. I section
2-bolt steel connecting rods were fitted, water circulation was by
pump, and there was a fan to assist cooling.

The multi-plate clutch, which was fitted with a clutch stop,
was of the Hele-Shaw type, made up of about fourteen steel and

thirteen copper plates. After considerable use this clutch could become impossible to free once the whole unit had become hot, and declutching could sometimes only be carried out after it had cooled, or else with considerable pressure on the clutch pedal whilst it was still hot. This was due to the warping of the plates and their becoming lodged in ridges worn into the clutch shaft splines. The clutch could be restored to its former efficiency by filing away the grooves or, better still, building up the splines, and also by truing up the plates. Although a trifle heavy in operation, this was an excellent clutch, giving long trouble-free running provided it was regularly kept lubricated with flaked graphite, and the thrust race and withdrawal mechanism kept well oiled.

The 30/98 Vauxhall was the product of an era in which the use of the gearbox as an aid to performance was virtually unknown. The gearbox was used for starting, and also for ascending hills, but even in the latter case a change down was only made at the last possible moment, and was avoided if it was conceivably possible. Thus the E-type 30/98 had the fairly wide gear ratios of 3.08, 4.71, 7.21 and 11.18 to 1. The gearbox itself had a right-hand gear lever (outside the body on pre-war cars) and, like the engine, was mounted on the sub-frame. Though, like the clutch, a little heavy in operation, the gearbox was extremely robust and reliable.

Behind the gearbox was the transmission brake drum, and the drive was taken to the rear axle by a short open propellor shaft with a metallic universal joint at either end, a cast-iron pulley for the speedometer drive belt being an integral part of the front joint. The bronze trunnions in the rear sliding block universal joint were prone to wear, when they gave transmission snatch at low speeds.

The housing for the differential was made up of two steel castings bolted together round the periphery, Bugatti fashion, with the 3 to 1 crownwheel and pinion having the pre-war legacy of straight-cut bevel gears. The casing was supported by a tie-bar underneath on the E-type, but not on its successor, the OE. The rear half-elliptic springs were outrigged from the chassis, the axle tubes being trunnion mounted on the spring seats in a manner which allowed the axle to swivel. A triangular tubular turque arm on the E-type, channel section on the OE, was fitted between the gearbox chassis member and the offside of the differential casing. The torque arm has been known to come adrift on OE 30/98s under the stresses of modern driving tests.

The steering was worm-and-wheel, and was light, partly, no doubt, thanks to there being no front-wheel brakes, and the fact that 820 × 120 beaded-edge tyres were fitted to the Rudge centre-lock wire wheels.

The brakes on the E-type were in keeping with contemporary standards, the main braking being done by means of a handbrake operating on brake drums on the rear wheels, which were rather small though larger than the drums used on the pre-war models, and by a footbrake working on the transmission. However, as the performance of the E-type was far in advance of contemporary standards, the brakes were somewhat inadequate in slowing the car down from the very high speeds of which it was capable. The footbrake was always poor, partly because the drum on the transmission was too small to dissipate heat, so that the brake faded and excessive lining wear was experienced, but also because oil from the gearbox often found its way into the brake; thus the main reliance was on the handbrake.

With an engine producing 90 bhp at 3000 rpm and a total weight of approximately 24 cwt with the standard open four-seater Velox bodywork, the competition ancestry of the E-type was obvious when it was driven on the road. The engine abounded in torque, so that the acceleration was exceptional for the time, and a comfortable cruising speed in the high top gear (31 mph per 1000 rpm) was up to 70 mph, with an 80–85 mph maximum. With a small amount of tuning and special bodywork the car was capable of 100 mph on Brooklands. Apart from the beat of the exhaust, there was the noise from the wide-clearance tappets as well as the whine from the straight-cut gears of the crownwheel and pinion.

E-type 30/98s scored numerous successes in hill climbs and sprints, and also did well at Brooklands. Probably the most successful was the black-and-red two-seater driven by Humphrey Cook, which appeared with a bolster tank in 1921 and with a streamlined tail in 1922. Known as 'Rouge et Noir', this car was fairly standard mechanically, but was capable of lapping Brooklands at 98 mph, with a maximum speed of over 100 mph. It is worth recalling that back in 1913 A.J. Hancock had lapped

Brooklands at 108.03 mph in an E-type-engined single-seater Vauxhall, yet a similar car of N.F Holder's which also ran in 1913 as well as in 1921 and 1922 generally lapped at just under 100 mph.

The Velox-bodied E-type cost £1455 complete in 1919, and £1675 in 1920/21, but was reduced to £1195 in 1922, when the chassis price was £895. This was quite good value in comparison with the price asked for the new and more advanced 3-litre Bentley, which had better brakes but a lower performance at a chassis price of £1050. In all about 274 E-type Vauxhalls were produced from 1919 to 1922, after which they were replaced by the OE. Various forms of bodywork were fitted to 30/98 chassis besides the open four-seater Velox, including saloon coachwork in some cases.

The OE design was not the work of L.H. Pomeroy, who had left Vauxhall to go to the USA, but of C.E. King. His object was to bring out a more refined version of the E-type, and the recipe turned out to be a familiar one in the development of various cars during the 'twenties – the power of the engine was increased but the car itself was made heavier.

The main alteration to the engine was the adoption of a detachable overhead valve cylinder head, fitted with extremely large valves. The capacity was slightly less than that of the E-type due to the stroke being reduced from 150 mm to 140 mm, the consequent 98 × 140-mm dimensions giving a capacity of 4224 cc. It is said the reduction in stroke was necessary to keep down the height of the engine.

In contrast to those on the E-type, valve clearances were reduced to a recommended 0.025 in, though in practice it was found that the clearance had to be varied from valve to valve on an individual engine if the valve opening and closing was to be correct. This was important on an engine which proved to be sensitive to valve timing. Clearances could vary from 0.021 in to 0.027 in on a particular engine.

Big savings in reciprocating weights were made by the use of a new alloy, Duralumin, which had been invented in 1909, and which, amongst other uses, had been employed in the metal framework of Zeppelins and other rigid airships during the war. In the OE engine both the pushrods and the four-bolt H-section connecting rods were made of Duralumin. Although other manufacturers were to use Duralumin rods during the Vintage decade, Vauxhalls seem to have been the pioneers. Pistons were die-cast aluminium.

An oscillating cylinder is familiar on model steam engines, and the plunger oil pump on the E-type was replaced on the OE by a plunger working in an oscillating cylinder, the rocking motion of which covered or uncovered suction and delivery ports, thus doing away with the need for non-return valves. The plunger was driven by a peg on the rear end of the camshaft. The oil was filtered before entering the pump, and there was another filter in the form of a full-length tray in the bottom of the engine which could easily be removed for cleaning by undoing four $\frac{1}{4}$-in bolts at the front of the sump and pulling on a small finger grip.

An aircraft-type Zenith carburettor continued to be fitted, a Type 48RA. With a 32 choke, a 155 main and 165 compensating jet was recommended, and some entertaining comments on the shortcomings of the carburettor are contained in a letter written to the Zenith Company by a doctor on 31 March, 1930.

I have recently bought a 1925 30/98 Vauxhall. This has an aluminium carburettor of your make. I believe an aviation type. I cannot give you the size of the choke unless I take down the carburettor, but both main and compensator jets are No. 160.

These do not appear to me to be correct. At slow speed on top, with full throttle, the engine hunts. Also there is no flat spot. I have always found the latter to be present with one of your carburettors when properly adjusted. The petrol consumption is on the high side – 15 miles per gallon.

No reply to the letter survives, and it has been suggested that the manufacturers were nettled by the reference to their built-in flat spot.

The inlet manifold was water-heated on the OE, whilst the exhaust manifold was made from steel tube and has frequently had to be replaced with a cast-iron substitute as it was not very long-lasting. Fuel feed was still by air pressure on the early OEs.

A thermostat was now fitted, which proved very useful in preventing spitting back in the carburettor due to the engine running too cool, as it was prone to do. The magneto was still a Watford, set in a moveable cradle to allow any slack in the timing chain to be taken up. As the magneto was on the opposite side of the engine to the plugs, the high-tension leads were fed,

two at a time, though a pair of small holes in the valve cover –
rather less drastic than the tunnelling of a larger hole through
the block to contain all four leads as resorted to on the DISS
Delage. Firing order was 1-2-4-3. A reducing valve in the rocker
cover controlled the supply of oil to the rockers. Castrol 'R' was
the oil officially recommended by the makers.

This engine, still in a sub-frame, was put into rather a heavier-
gauge chassis than that of the E-type, with a 9 ft 9-in instead of a
9 ft 8-in wheelbase. With its more robust chassis and heavier
engine, the OE, in chassis form only, at 24½ cwt, weighed
slightly more than a complete Velox-bodied E-type, the total
weight of a Velox-bodied OE being about 29 cwt.

Because of the extra weight and the higher revving capabilities
of the OE engine, a lower back axle ratio of 3.3 to 1 was fitted,
and the assembly was made quieter by spiral gears replacing the
straight-tooth crownwheel and pinion of the E-type. Electrics
were still 12 volt C.A.V., with double-pole wiring, but the electric
starter button was shifted to the dashboard, whereas on the
E-type it had been on the floor just in front of the driver's seat, so
that it was easier to stand up when starting the engine.

The OE engine produced 110 bhp at 3300 rpm, and although
it lacked the torque of the E-type, and was not so thunderous, it
delivered a similar performance with considerably more refinement. Nothing was done about improving the brakes until 1923.

*R.H. Whitworth, driving the 30/98 that Dr Beaver used to race at
Brooklands, was making dark investigations into the braking mechanism
at a very late hour on the Friday night. Large and somewhat shapeless
leather bags depended from each of the front brakes, and from these
emerged what appeared to be speedometer cables. Some doubt seemed to
exist as to whether these contained pieces of string, an hydraulic fluid or,
indeed, just speedometer cables.*

This comment in the report of the 1938 Donington Park race
meeting of the Vintage Sports-Car Club appeared in the club's
Bulletin, and is a rough description of Vauxhall's method of
improving the 30/98's brakes. They did this by the fitting of
front-wheel brakes which were initially seen on the car which
Major C.G. Coe had entered for the Georges Boillot Cup race at
Boulogne in the late summer of 1923, although Coe's 30/98 was
unusual in apparently having ribbed front drums. Unfortunately

The very rare S-type 25/70 Vauxhall sleeve-valve engine showing the tank for the hydraulic brake fluid beside the Autovac on the bulkhead

Roger McDonald A.I.I.P.

1926 S-type Vauxhall Ormond saloon   *Roger McDonald A.I.I.P.*

30/98 Vauxhalls are pre-eminant in present-day vintage trials, here is a 1924 OE with Velox bodywork and non-standard front brake actuation in a typical setting

Neill Bruce

Nigel Arnold-Forster on Beggars Roost in an M.C.C. Land's End Trial in his 1926 Trojan on pneumatic tyres, *c.* 1953

James Brymer

Coe retired in this race. Probably he had works backing, but in the few long-distance races at Boulogne or Brooklands in which 30/98s were entered by private owners, they invariably retired, although they were very successful in sprints and short-distance races. They were also successful in taking long-distance cross country records in South Africa and Australia, Paddy Adair being the South African driver and John Burton the Australian. Just before the war an original 30/98 had taken second place to a 15-litre Benz of 150 hp in the 1914 Russian GP, held near St Petersburg, over 7 laps of a 20-mile circuit, according to 'The Story of Vauxhall, 1857–1946', published by Vauxhall Motors.

To return to the front-wheel brakes, it might have been thought that provision would have been made for their operation in the design of the new OE chassis, but as this was not the case they had to be designed so that the various components could be fitted easily to existing chassis more as an appendage than as an integral part of it. As a result the compensating mechanism was attached to the cross-member in front of the radiator, out in the open, inside a casing known as a kidney box.

The human kidney has been described as bean-shaped, in which case the Vauxhall kidney box can only resemble a human kidney that has become badly misshapen in a serious accident involving a steam roller, for it is flat, more like a pancake, and vaguely like an elongated parallelogram in shape, with rounded corners. Inside this is the T-shaped compensator, attached to a vertical shaft, itself operated by a rod running forward from the brake pedal. The transmission brake was still retained, so that the brake pedal acted on this as well, with the handbrake working the brakes on the rear wheels. What the V.S.C.C. Bulletin described as speedometer cables running from the compensator to a fulcrum arrangement on the top of each king-pin on the front axle were actually the front-brake cables with their outer coverings. The inner cables pulled up wedge expanders through the hollow king-pins and expanded the brake shoes, which were pivoted at the top and operated in 12-in diameter steel drums with cast-iron liners.

'A compensating mechanism will never give equal braking' stated the maker's handbook, gloomily. What was meant, however, was that the compensator could not compensate for brakes that were grossly out of adjustment, this being taken care of by thumb-screw adjustments behind each drum. More often than not, any falling off in the effectiveness of the front brakes was due to stretching of the inner cables, and the slackness was taken up by tapping brackets attached to the cable ends along the cross-member after slackening their security bolts.

Certainly the kidney box looked a rather untidy affair, and it could not even be located in the centre of the cross-member due to the presence of the starting handle, and so it was placed slightly over to the offside of the car conveniently opposite the brake pedal. Despite having gone to all this trouble, the makers recommended that the handbrake should always be used as the normal method of braking, with the pedal reserved for use in emergencies. Initially, cars fitted with fwb cost £25 extra.

30/98s fitted with the original kidney box braking system now tend to be the exception rather than the rule as it was not satisfactory without frequent maintenance and adjustment, so that front axles and braking systems of other Vintage cars have been fitted, DMS or D8 Delage axles being a favourite as they are easy to adapt, and 3-litre Bentley. In most cases the transmission brake has been discarded. In later years many cars have been converted to a modern hydraulic system to operate the front shoes.

In 1924 the boat-tailed four-seater Wensum bodywork was made available, with no doors or hood, flared wings, outside handbrake and gear lever, V-screen, wooden decking on the tail and polished-wood interior panelling, selling for some £150 more than the Velox. Although described as being 'an ultra-sporting body for very fast touring and for racing' the bodywork was no lighter than the Velox and if anything was heavier. Major Coe took an apple-green example over to Boulogne for the 1924 Speed Week there, but although he won a prize in the Concours, he retired in the Georges Boillot Cup race with a run big-end.

From 1925 the 30/98 chassis at £950 cost £25 more than the 3-litre Speed Model Bentley chassis.

In 1925 the last modification was carried out on the OE engine in the form of a balanced crankshaft, with balance weights bolted to the webs and an increase in the main bearing diameter from 2 in to 2¼ in. The engine could be taken up to 3500 rpm when 120 bhp was claimed, and it was remarkably smooth and refined for a large four-cylinder unit. Compression ratio was normally

5.2 to 1. Also from 1925 an Autovac replaced the pressure fuel feed from the 12-gallon rear tank and the roller tappets were replaced by normal ones. The large dynamo, belt-driven from behind the clutch, was now replaced by a smaller unit driven in tandem with the magneto, and consequently more accessible. It was in 1925 that the beaded-edge rims were replaced by $32 \times 4\frac{1}{2}$ straight-sided.

The last modifications to the 30/98 appeared in late 1926, and cars thus modified were sold throughout 1927, and were the last of the species. Externally the final model was distinguished by a taller radiator and very large finned alloy front brake drums. These were the same front drums as were fitted to the then new six-cylinder S-type 25/70 sleeve valve Vauxhall, and a new front axle forging to take them was made for the 30/98. As on the S-type, pedal-operated hydraulic front and transmission brakes were now featured, and the handbrake still worked the rear brakes, which were given larger drums. The transmission brake was of the contracting shoe type. At the same time a newly designed four-speed gearbox, lighter and easier to operate, with a higher third gear than its Edwardian predecessor, was also taken from the S-type.

The hydraulic brake system was under air pressure which had to be maintained at 10 lb per square inch as indicated by the air pressure gauge on the dashboard. A fairly small pressure tank was fixed to the offside of the bulkhead and fed fluid to the master cylinder connected to smaller pistons attached to the king-pin housings and the frame of the transmission brake. As a contrast to the kidney box brakes, the hydraulic brakes were self-adjusting due to the smaller pistons being a tight fit in their cylinders and the brake pull-off springs being weak. A solid copper pipe led into each wheel cylinder through the top of the king-pins, the cylinder operating a short rod which forced the shoes apart through ball bearing expanders.

These were good brakes, but their big drawback was their unreliability, mainly due to the use of leather seals throughout, and the fact that if the driver forgot to prime the air pressure system before driving off, he had no footbrake. Brian Morgan, well-known co-author of the book *The Restoration of Vintage and Thoroughbred Cars* (Batsford) has modified his Vauxhall's hydraulic system for present-day use by fitting modern rubber cups and doing away with the air pressure system, leather seals and the transmission brake.

As a result the footbrake works with complete reliability on the front brakes only, and Brian Morgan says the result is really first-class braking, which makes one realize how comparatively superfluous rear brakes are! On the Morgan car these are, of course, still operated mechanically by the handbrake. The modification has been carried out using the minimum of replacement parts, so that externally the system is as it originally was, except there is no air pressure gauge on the dashboard with the use of a conventional master cylinder.

The total 30/98 production figure was small, its great reputation arising from only around 270 E-types and 312 OE, of which probably about 30 had the hydraulic brake system.

It is generally conceded that the fastest Brooklands lap by a 30/98 Vauxhall was at 114.23 mph by R.J. Munday's four-seater Velox in the Gold Star handicap at the 1932 Whit Monday meeting, this car being fitted with oversize rear tyres and reaching 4000 rpm with judicious slipstreaming of faster cars. Since then Clive Windsor-Richards has spoken of a 117-mph lap by his 30/98 later in the 'thirties. As the best lap mentioned for him in W. Boddy's *The Story of Brooklands* was 112.47 mph at the 1936 Whitsun meeting, his claim seems very believable when the average 30/98 like Dr Beaver's lapped at around 100 mph. Boddy tells us that Munday's engine was specially tuned by Laystalls and, later, when placed in a 1921 GP Sunbeam chassis, it propelled that car to a lap at 117.19 in 1935. This Vauxhall-engined Sunbeam was known as the Munday Special and, later, the Bainton Special. Its 30/98 engine had a compression ratio of 10 to 1, two Zenith 48 carburettors with 38 chokes and a Scintilla magneto. Boddy states that after being bored out from 98 to 99 mm, it developed 162.8 bhp at a safe maximum of 3800 rpm using racing fuel.

If circumstances had allowed, there might never have been an OE 30/98 in its known form, for L.H. Pomeroy had intended to replace the side-valve E-type unit with a single overhead cam-shaft engine known as the H-type, but his departure from Vauxhalls for the USA in late 1919 seemingly prevented this coming about. One or two of these engines were made and photographs exist of them. They had four 100 × 140-mm cylinders, giving 4.4 litres.

A well-known 30/98 enthusiast and competitor in V.S.C.C. events, Mike Quartermaine, revealed in the Winter, 1967/8, V.S.C.C. Bulletin that his own E-type 30/98 had been fitted with one of these engines in 1933, when it was also given a Voisin front axle (which it still has) and registered as the Guy North Special. The conversion was done by Guy Arengo, whose name may be remembered in connection with the Arengo 500-cc racing car just after the Second World War. Quartermaine quotes Laurence Pomeroy Junior as saying that the overhead camshaft was driven by three eccentrics from the front of the crankshaft and that the engine developed 100 bhp at 2500 rpm. From a photograph of the H-type engine, Quartermaine remarks that the crankcase and sump are definitely 30/98 type, and the fan, water pump, starter etc are quite recognizable.

Unfortunately the H-type engine that had been in the Guy North Special expired later in the 'thirties when a normal OE-type engine was substituted, but not before the H-type had powered the car for a 10 000-mile tour of the USA in 1933.

One ploy for getting more power from a 30/98 Vauxhall is to use an E-type bottom end and an OE block and head, thus getting an ohv engine with the larger E-type capacity, which goes best with the higher ratio E-type rear axle, but there seems no doubt that if a Vauxhall engine is very highly tuned, despite the exhilarating performance, some of the traditional charm of the 30/98 goes by the board.

The two main authoritative works on the 30/98 are the 'Profile' by John Stanford, which came out in 1966, and an article by George Sanders in *Motor Sport* for April, 1948, and we are grateful to both these authors for a large amount of information.

Several guesses have been made as to why Vauxhalls bestowed the model name of '30/98', the most popular being that it was because the engine gave about 30 bhp at 1000 rpm and 98 bhp maximum. Another equally tortuous theory is that as the 30/98 had an enlarged version of the 25-hp Prince Henry Vauxhall engine, given a 98-mm bore, the name could have come about in this way, remembering that the original Prince Henry engine was 20 hp. The treasury rating of the 25-hp was 22.4, and of the 30/98 23.8 for both the E and the OE, this rating only taking bore size into account, not the stroke.

As we have seen, the 30/98 launched in 1919 was a pre-war design, as was its touring counterpart, the 25-hp D-type, with a 4-litre (95 × 140-mm) L-head engine. The first completely new Vintage-designed Vauxhalls appeared in 1922, a 3-litre Grand Prix racing car and a 14-hp with a 75 × 130-mm (2297-cc) L-head side-valve engine, known as the M-type. This became the mainstay of Vauxhall production, thirty cars a week being produced by 1925.

The 14-hp engine had a detachable Ricardo aluminium head, and the tappets had a clearance of 25 thou. Pressure lubrication was by plunger pump, and the crankshaft had three bearings, whilst the induction pipe was exhaust-heated. Petrol was brought from the 9-gallon rear tank by Autovac. Ignition was by magneto.

Instead of the multi-plate clutch of the bigger cars, the 14-hp had a single-plate clutch, and the 3-speed gearbox was in unit with the engine with ratios of 4.5, 9.3 and 15.9 to 1. Transmission was via a torque tube, and the rear axle was very light, being made of aluminium alloy reinforced by steel tubes. As on the bigger Vauxhalls, the differential casing was split longitudinally, and beneath it were two tie-rods. There was no transmission brake, the wide rear drums containing shoes for both the hand-brake and the footbrake. Although the front springs were semi-elliptic, the back pair were cantilever. Several similarities in design to the overhead valve 14-hp Sunbeam will be noted, which came out at about the same time and was also Sunbeam's first postwar design. Both the Vauxhall and the Sunbeam 14-hp models later became 14/40s. The 14-hp Vauxhall was fitted with steel disc wheels and 815 × 105-mm tyres. Steering was by worm and sector.

With a wheelbase of 9 ft 6 in and a track of 4 ft 2 in, the Vauxhall was slightly smaller than the Sunbeam, and it was also less expensive at a chassis price of £420, the Sunbeam costing over £100 more. 12-volt electrics on the Vauxhall were by Lucas, and the chassis weight was 16¼ cwt, with 21 cwt for the complete four-seater open car, with full tanks. Maximum speed was about 50 mph.

By 1925 the 14-hp M-type had been developed into the 14/40-hp LM. Externally the most noticeable difference between the two models were a taller radiator on the LM, which also had wire wheels with Rudge hubs and 31 × 5.25 tyres replacing the steel disc wheels and beaded-edge tyres of the M-type. In fact, the LM had a new and more robust chassis and a 4-speed gearbox and four-wheel brakes. The new chassis gave a wheelbase longer by 3 in, a track wider by 5 in and an increased chassis weight which totalled 18½ cwt. The complete 14/40 tourer weighed 24 cwt. Chassis price was £450 in 1925, reduced to £395 in the last year of production, 1927.

There were a number of subtle changes in the engine design. The cylinder head was the same, but stud layout changes prevented a mixture of an M block and an LM crankcase, whilst the manifolding and the rods, pistons etc were all to a degree different. Any changing of the latter components, whilst possible between the two models in a case of necessity, would have to be done in sets in order not to upset the famous Vauxhall balance, by which the works put so much store.

Quite whether the works should have been so proud of this feature of their product is open to doubt, for the fact is that the designer of the engine, C.E. King, had a very curious theory about balance.

His idea was that if the centre of balance of the connecting rod was made to coincide with the centre line of the crankpin, and if this weight was counterbalanced by suitable weights on the crank webs opposite the crankpin, perfect balance would result. So he made the connecting rods of aluminium alloy and bolted lead-filled steel weights to the big-end cap, and then bolted heavy counterbalance weights to the crank webs. The crankshaft itself was of modest proportions, with nothing like enough torsional stiffness to withstand all this extra weight, with the inevitable result that it was subject to severe torsional vibration at critical speeds. The speed at which it usually had its harmonic was around 45 mph in top gear, which was about as inconvenient as it could have been.

A side effect of this vicious vibration was a tendency to shear the teeth on the fibre idler wheel which took the drive from the crankshaft drive gear to the camshaft gear. This idler wheel was on an eccentric, and adjustable for mesh, though when properly adjusted for the crankshaft and camshaft, the magneto/dynamo drive platform had then to be adjusted separately to bring their drive gear into proper mesh with the idler, which was all a bit of an unnecessary complication.

If the lead-filled steel weights on the connecting rods and the counterbalance weights are removed, the 14/40 goes a lot better, and the torsional vibration period moves up to about 60 mph in top, which is a lot better.

It is interesting that a competent designer in the 'twenties could have got his sums so drastically wrong.

The 14/40 brakes were rod-operated to the rear, still with separate shoes for the handbrake, and cable-operated to the front, with the pedal working on all four wheels. The compensators were designed into the chassis, working off the brake cross-shaft, in contrast to the kidney box of the larger Vauxhalls. The brakes had to stop a car which was not only heavier than the M-type, but also faster, as the LM was capable of 65 mph.

The 14/40 showed yet another variation on the Vauxhall theme of front-brake operation, wedge expanders either pulled up by cables or pushed down by hydraulic cylinders playing no part in the 14/40 front-brake design. Instead the shoes, which were pivoted at the bottom, were forced apart by 'shoe struts' actuated by a rocking lever. This rocker was pushed upwards at its other end by an 'actuating drum' or cylinder above the king-pin to which was attached the brake arm, so that when the brake arm turned the drum, a rising cam arrangement raised it to work the rocker.

The rising cam arrangement was most extraordinary, as a cam was not, in fact, employed, instead it was raised by three 'small toggle pins'.

Imagine a 3-legged stool with the legs (or toggle pins) socketed to the underneath of the seat and to the ground. If the seat is twisted, the legs will start to collapse, and the seat will be lowered. Twist it the other way and the seat will be raised. If the seat is twisted too far in a downward direction, the legs will collapse completely, and no amount of twisting will raise the seat. This was one peculiarity of the Vauxhall system, as if the brake arm was moved for any reason in the 'off' direction whilst the cable was 'off', the pins would collapse, and the whole assembly would have to come to pieces to re-erect them.

John Price, who runs the Vintage Vauxhall Register and to whom we are indebted for much information, says that all the components of this rather curious arrangement were beautifully made, and the worm-and-wheel adjustment, acting directly on the shoes, worked very well, making fine adjustment possible. Lubrication of the parts was not very good, though, and the rocker in particular was subject to very high pressure on its operating points.

The 14/40 brakes were reasonably effective, but not outstandingly good in operation. John Price has one criticism of them which John Stanford also applies to the 30/98 brakes, this being a lack of proper backplates, there being merely aluminium dust covers at both front and rear which do nothing to stop rainwater from entering the drums. The effect of water in the brakes on the 14/40 gives absolutely minimal stopping powers at the front.

Approximately 1850 M-types were built in 1922–25, and 3200 LM types in 1925–27.

Only three British manufacturers attempted to build formula Grand Prix cars during the Vintage years, Sunbeam, Vauxhall and Alvis. Sunbeam were successful, but Vauxhall and Alvis, although extremely enterprising in their designs, both suffered through lack of finance and, as a consequence, of inadequate preparation.

The Vintage Grand Prix Vauxhall was designed for the 3-litre formula, but due to a misunderstanding of the Grand Prix rules by Vauxhalls, it appeared in 1922, the year the formula was changed to 2 litres. Thus Vauxhall had a team of new cars which were ineligible for any Grand Prix. Fortunately, however, the Isle of Man Tourist Trophy in 1922 was run under the rules of the old formula, so a team of Vauxhalls was able to take part. They did not do very well, for although one car finished third behind a straight-eight GP Sunbeam and a 3-litre Bentley, the other two cars of the team retired. Had the cars produced their designed performance, they would undoubtedly have dominated the race, but they did not get enough preparation.

Engine design was by H.R. Ricardo and chassis design by C.E. King. The engine was a four-cylinder of 85 × 132 mm, 2996 cc, with twin overhead camshafts, four valves per cylinder and two bronze detachable heads, one for each pair of cylinders. The block was aluminium with wet cast-iron liners, the carburettor was a double-choke Zenith and ignition was by Delco coil and battery, with twin distributors. There was provision for two sparking plugs per cylinder, although in practise only a single central plug was used. There were roller big-ends and six ball main bearings, and the counterbalanced crankshaft had a central flywheel. Lubrication was by two oscillating valveless plunger pumps, one for the bottom end of the engine and the other for the valve gear. This very efficient, if somewhat complicated, engine produced 129 bhp at 4500 rpm on a compression ratio of 5.8 to 1 running on petrol.

As on its contemporary, the M-type 14-hp Vauxhall, the gearbox was integral with the engine, but the clutch was the familiar Hele-Shaw multi-plate, and the gearbox internals were similar to those on the 30/98 and D-type, but giving closer ratios of 3.75, 4.63, 6.5 and 9.4 to 1. Such things as the steering wheel, pedals and levers were also the same as on the production cars. There was Hotchkiss drive to a straight-tooth 3.75 to 1 differential-less back axle, a road speed of 25 mph per 1000 rpm contrasting with the 31 mph per 1000 rpm of the E-type and 28 mph per 1000 rpm of the OE.

The front brakes had 12-in drums and the rear 16-in, and the front brakes had conventional Perrot-type actuation, like many other Vintage cars, but not the production Vauxhalls. The pedal was connected to the front brakes only (there was no transmission brake) and the handbrake operated on the rear wheels. However, a lever at the top of the steering column also operated on all four brakes simultaneously by means of compressed air working a system of pistons, cylinders and rods. Thus the driver could set this lever on approaching a corner and the pneumatic servo would look after the braking whilst he used his hands and feet to steer and change down. Unfortunately it was found that the brakes then had a tendency to stay on, so the compressed air system was not a success and was not used. A large-capacity air pump driven from the front of the engine supplied the compressed air for the brakes, and a smaller pump driven from the same source maintained pressure in the fuel tank.

Wheelbase was 8 ft 11 in, and springs were semi-elliptic front and rear, whilst shock absorbers were Hartford friction, as on the OE.

An unstreamlined body with two seats and two spare wheels at the back was fitted, and the all-up starting line weight was 27 cwt, but 22½ cwt unladen. Maximum speed was 112 mph at

4400 rpm, but over 116 mph was later reached at Brooklands with a long-tailed body.

The team cars were afterwards run at Brooklands and in sprints by the works, and then had more successes in the hands of private owners. Most famous was the car which became the supercharged Vauxhall Villiers, driven by Raymond Mays, which is still successfully raced by Anthony Brooke.

In 1922 the 95 × 140-mm, 3969-cc D-type side-valve Vauxhall (which, incidentally had a rear axle of internally different design to that of the 30/98), was, like its E-type counterpart, fitted with a pushrod ohv head, and renamed the OD 23/60. Its engine was also given a Lanchester harmonic balancer, driven off the crankshaft at twice crankshaft speed and situated below the centre main bearing. It consisted of a pair of bob weights mounted on two shafts geared together to turn at the same speed, but in opposite directions. This helped to make the engine unusually smooth-running. It had the same gearbox as the 30/98, but a lower final drive ratio of 3.6 to 1 instead of 3.3 to 1, and the wheelbase was a foot longer than the OE's and the track wider in order to take formal coachwork. In 1923 the OD was given the kidney box front brakes. It had also been destined to take the H-type engine, had the latter ever gone into production. Chassis price was over £200 less than that asked for the OE, but the engine only produced 60 bhp in ohv form, compared with 50 bhp as a side-valve, so that although as an open tourer it somewhat resembled a 30/98 (as did the 14/40 LM, although it was smaller), it was a good deal slower, yet very pleasant to drive.

The Vauxhall company fell into the hands of General Motors of USA in 1925, but the designs of the original company continued to be made for the next two or three years, including one announced in September, 1926, known as the S-type 25/70, an expensive replacement for the 23/60. This had a remarkable 81.5 × 124-mm, 3882-cc, single-sleeve-valve six-cylinder engine produced under Burt McCullum and Ricardo patents, which had a central flywheel like the 1922 TT cars. Wheelbase was 11 ft 4 in, there was a tubular front axle as on the LM 14/40, and, as has already been mentioned, the 25/70 shared its gearbox and hydraulic brake system with the later OE 30/98s. The familiar multi-plate clutch was fitted and chassis price was £1050. Although the engine was quite lively, it had to cope with a heavy chassis and bodywork, and the car was given a 4.7 to 1 axle ratio. Not many of the sleeve-valve cars were produced, and only one is known to survive in England.

At the 1927 Motor Show there appeared the first Vauxhall to show the General Motors influence on the firm, known as the R-type 20/60. By this time the first figure of a Vauxhall 'maker's horsepower', as it was known, referred to the approximate treasury rating, and the second figure referred to the approximate brake horsepower.

The company were at some pains to point out that this was a British design originating from Luton and produced with the help of General Motors capital, and that it was not a design imported from the USA. This was probably true, but the R-type catered for a different market from the traditional Vauxhall one, as evidenced by a chassis price of only £375 for a fairly large capacity six-cylinder car powered by a 73 × 110-mm, 2762-cc, pushrod engine having a seven-bearing crankshaft. Early models apparently had cast-iron pistons.

The 20/60 did not have the look of traditional Vauxhall quality, artillery wheels were fitted instead of wire wheels on Rudge hubs, painted pressed steel replaced alloy castings in the engine, and although early examples had radiators seemingly stolen off LM 14/40s, the later radiators were rather depressing chromium-plated affairs.

Plunger-type oil pumps were now out, and the 20/60 had a submerged gear pump driven from the centre of the camshaft, whilst in memory of the 1922 TT Vauxhalls, Delco coil ignition replaced the traditional Watford magneto. The 20/60 tappet clearance was a modest 0.0075 in, and the camshaft was chain-driven.

As on the 14/40, the gearbox was in unit with the engine (ratios were 4.73, 7.25, 10.93 and 16.75 to 1) and also there was a single-plate clutch. Unlike the 14/40, the 20/60 had an open propellor shaft to a one-piece banjo-type rear axle. The wheel-base at 10 ft 3 in was 5 in longer than that of the 30/98, and a complete car was 2 cwt heavier than an OE. Proprietary Marles steering was fitted to the 20/60, and the gearchange was central, although the cranked lever worked in a gate. An Autovac brought fuel from the 14-gallon rear tank to a Claudel-Hobson carburettor.

There were effective cable brakes to all four wheels operated by the footbrake, whilst the handbrake was connected to an external contracting transmission brake and was 'only intended for parking use'.

'The cables are very lightly loaded and it is very unlikely that any stretching will be encountered,' the makers stated, which might have encouraged former 23/60 and 30/98 owners. According to tradition, the rear brakes were cam-operated, and the front brakes were also traditional to the big Vauxhalls in that wedge expanders were used, though running through the king-pins to divide shoes pivoted at the top. In this case the wedge expander was forced down by the operating arm working a screw arrangement. There were adjusting knobs on the top of the king-pins.

For 1929, when the 20/60 was the only Vauxhall model listed, the bore was enlarged from 73 to 75 mm, bringing the capacity up to 2916 cc, and an American-type ball change operated by a straight lever was introduced. Alloy pistons were fitted and improved Hartford shock absorbers, whilst the styling of the radiator and front wings was altered, the radiator being taller with deeper flutes. A limousine with a 10 ft 10-in wheelbase and a 5.1 to 1 axle ratio was introduced during the year.

For 1930 the R-type evolved into the T-type with a stiffer chassis, a mechanical pump in place of the Autovac, and hydraulic shock absorbers, and it was on this chassis that the last Vintage Vauxhall of sporting appearance was marketed, known as the Hurlingham. This was a two-seater with a V-screen, a single seat in the streamlined tail and bolt-on wire wheels. Nothing was done to raise the axle ratio or the low-geared steering of the touring models, so that although the Hurlingham would do over 70 mph (with 55 mph in third gear), it was more sporting in looks than in manner.

It would certainly not have intoxicated Lord Hovenden.

INDEX